Measure Twice

Measure Twice

TIPS AND TRICKS FROM THE PROS TO HELP YOU AVOID THE MOST COMMON DIY DISASTERS

BRYAN BAEUMLER

Photography by Shannon J. Ross

Published by Collins, an imprint of HarperCollins Publishers Ltd

First edition

HarperCollins books may be purchased for educational, business, or sales promotional use through our Special Markets Department.

HarperCollins Publishers Ltd
2 Bloor Street East, 20th Floor
Toronto, Ontario, Canada
M4W 1A8

www.harpercollins.ca

Library and Archives Canada Cataloguing in Publication information is available upon request

ISBN 978-1-44341-432-6

Printed and bound in China
PP 9 8 7 6 5 4 3 2 1

CONTENTS

To Sarah, Quintyn, Charlotte, Lincoln and Josephine

INTRODUCTION

The seeds of this book were planted more than a decade ago, a few years before we started shooting my first show for HGTV. My construction company was getting a lot of calls from homeowners who needed professionals to come in and repair work that had been done by the resident "handymen" who had no idea what they were doing. In one home, they'd taken out a wall to make a new sewing room, and it turned out to be a load-bearing wall. There was a kitchen on the floor above, and most of the house was being supported by a single 2 × 4. Another guy had renovated his basement using metal studs, and he ran the electrical through the framing without the right insulators and then glued drywall directly to the concrete foundation—the interior walls were all electrified, and the exterior walls were full of mould!

Botched jobs like these were the inspiration for *Disaster DIY*, which debuted in 2007. Before the show aired, I contacted the producers and offered our construction services in exchange for some advertising. As it turned out, they were looking for a little more than just labour. We shot 91 episodes of that show over five seasons, and then followed it up with *Leave It to Bryan*, which is now in its fourth season. I've also filmed three seasons of *House of Bryan* and *Canada's Handyman Challenge*. I think it's fair to say I've seen just about every mistake a homeowner can make—and I've collected 191 in this book to help you avoid them.

These days almost all homeowners think they can do their own renos. Many of them can—it's not all that hard to replace a faucet or lay a few flagstones. I've even met a lot of handy folks who have done a respectable job of tiling a backsplash or laying a hardwood floor. But doing these projects properly takes experience, and most homeowners just don't have the opportunity to gain that experience. I mean, if you're not a professional, how many times are you going to build a deck or install a countertop? Do it many times, and eventually you might learn all the tricks, but your early mistakes will all be on display in your home—and those mistakes can be costly. Have you ever tried to take out a granite countertop? They don't always come out in one piece. It's a lot cheaper to have someone do it right the first time.

I have to accept part of the blame here. When you watch shows like mine, it's easy to get the impression you can quickly turn any rundown home into a show-piece. The truth is those episodes are filmed over several weeks, and many hours of footage are edited down to the 22 minutes you see on TV. Viewers don't always appreciate how many people were involved in turning that ugly bathroom into a spa or that dungeon into a man cave. But they see the show and think, "I should do that in my house, it looks easy." Well, I promise you it's harder and more time-consuming than it looks.

The other danger with TV renos is that when we uncover a major problem, it's always fixed by the time we come back from break—which can leave you thinking that even if you do make a mistake, fixing it won't be a big deal. But the reality may have been that more than a week (and thousands of dollars) elapsed in those three minutes of detergent commercials.

There's another idea I want to stress in this book. You'll notice I don't spend any time talking about how to pick the prettiest tiles or the most stylish lighting. That's because people often have a difficult time getting their priorities right when they're renovating: they tend to dwell on superficial improvements while ignoring larger problems. That was the idea behind *Leave It to Bryan*: I wanted to help homeowners under-stand that renos should add long-term value. Everyone understands that goal on some level, but it's like we have an angel on one shoulder and the devil on the other. The angel is saying, "There's water coming into your basement, and you need to fix that now." But the devil is saying, "You need a big flat-screen TV." Almost everybody listens to the devil.

We're a consumer society, and we all want the pretty finishes. That's fine, but it can't come at the expense of dealing with the larger issues. You probably won't get a lot of enjoyment from a properly spray-foamed basement or a well-insulated attic. You're not likely to invite friends and family over to see your well-installed eavestrough or the proper grading the landscapers did in your backyard. But these sorts of projects can save you thousands of dollars by lowering your energy bills and preventing serious water damage to your home. I know this stuff isn't as fun as a new kitchen island, but you should always remember that your home is an investment and you need to preserve its value.

Speaking of which, bad DIY renovations are one of the surest ways to lower the value of your home. One of the worst mistakes—and it's one that comes up several times in this book—is not getting permits for major projects like running new wires, building a raised deck or removing a structural wall. I know it can be expen-sive and time-consuming to do surveys, get drawings and pull permits, but building codes were created for a reason. If you do this work wrong, you can put your home and family in danger.

Measure Twice is not meant to be a compre-hensive, step-by-step guide to every job you'll ever encounter around your home. My main goal is to help you as a homeowner to anticipate common problems and to use that knowledge to determine which jobs you can tackle on your own and which ones require a professional. You'll notice I haven't included chapters on electrical or plumbing, and there are no instructions for how to cut rafters or underpin your basement: that's because I don't think any homeowner who is not prop-erly trained and very experienced should be doing that kind of work. But after reading these pages, you might just be ready to frame a small partition wall or replace an undermount sink or build a fence to keep your dog in the yard. Or at least you'll be able to discuss the job intelligently with the contractor you eventually hire.

Sometimes I think homeowners—and maybe this is just a guy thing—feel calling a pro is an admission of failure. That's crazy—no matter how handy you are, no one can do everything on their own. Although I've been around construction sites since I was a kid, I'm the first to admit there are lots of pros better than me at stonework, putting down shingles and many other specific jobs because I'm not using the tools every day and they are. You have to know your limits. And to help with that, I've given you difficulty ratings at the beginning of each chapter. The lower the number, the greater the chance you'll be able to successfully tackle a project on your own.

Be honest and ask yourself, Do I really have the skills for this job? Do I have the time? Remember, renovations always seem to take twice as long as you expected. And in my experience, I'd say about 80% of renos go at least 50% over budget, at least in part because professionals are ultimately called in to fix mistakes or to complete work that was started by homeowners who turned out to be less handy than they'd thought. Perhaps most important, ask, Am I going to enjoy it? Because if you don't enjoy the project, you're not going to finish it.

We've all made mistakes on jobs around the house. But I hope after you read this book, your mistakes will be smaller and less frequent. Now grab your tool box and get to work!

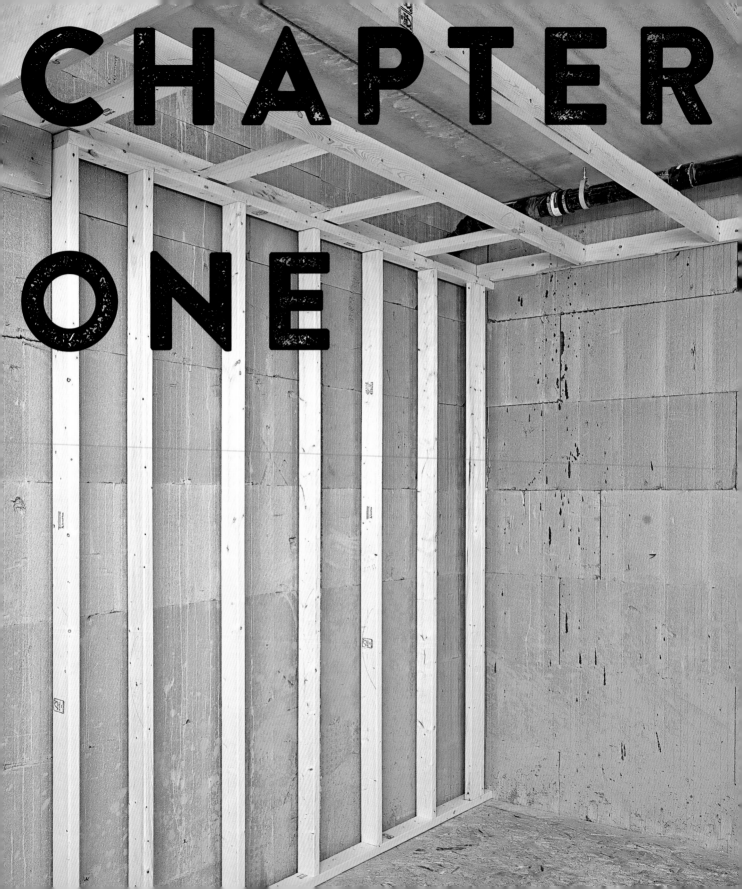

CHAPTER ONE

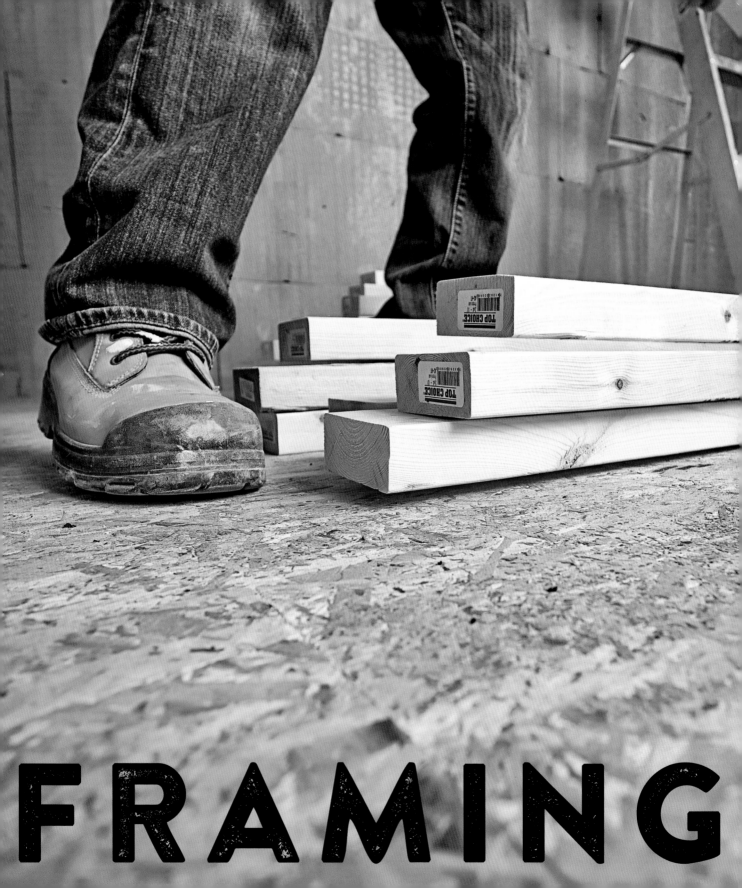

FRAMING

FRAMING IS THE SKELETON OF YOUR HOME. IT'S NOT ONLY WHAT HOLDS UP THE ROOF OVER YOUR HEAD; IT'S ALSO WHAT SEPARATES THE INDIVIDUAL ROOMS AND PROVIDES BACKING FOR THE DRYWALL.

These days most houses use what's called Western platform framing: a floor section supports a wall, which supports the floor section above it, and so on. A much older technique is balloon framing, where the walls go up first, from the foundation right up to the roof, and then the floors are attached to those walls. One reason that method is seldom used anymore is that it's hard to find 20-foot-plus lumber now. But if you are renovating an old home, there's a good chance you'll encounter balloon framing, so it's helpful to at least know what it is.

There's a lot of lumber in a typical home, but homeowners rarely see it unless they have an unfinished basement or they poke their head into the attic. So it's not surprising that most people understand very little about how walls, floors, ceilings, windows and doors are framed. That's generally okay, since advanced framing projects are beyond the scope of most DIYers. But if you have some basic carpentry skills, you can learn to frame your basement or maybe even build a partition wall on an upper level. Let's look at some common challenges you'll face.

FRAMING BASICS

DIFFICULTY: 7 OUT OF 10

The individual pieces of lumber holding up your home are called framing members. The most common are *studs*, the vertical members that make up the walls, and *joists*, the horizontal members that make up the floors and ceilings. Framing is traditionally done with natural lumber, but other materials are also commonly used.

CHOOSING FRAMING MATERIALS

- **Dimensional lumber** is sold according to its width and thickness (e.g., 2 × 4s, 2 × 6s). Interior walls are typically framed with 2 × 4s, but exterior walls now use 2 × 6s to allow room for more insulation as well as to provide additional strength. Floor joists are typically 2 × 10 or 2 × 12. Note that a 2 × 4 is not 2 inches thick and 4 inches wide anymore—it's actually 1½ inches by 3½ inches. The same is true of all dimensional lumber: you can subtract ½ inch from each dimension.

- **Engineered lumber** is popular in new construction, in part because it is available in very long lengths. Laminated veneer lumber (LVL) is made from strips of wood glued together, similar to a thick plywood except that the strips are made into long beams that are incredibly strong. Parallel strand lumber (PSL) is made from little pieces of wood chopped up and glued together in the same direction. Its strength is vertical: we use PSLs as posts to replace steel. Oriented strand board (OSB) is a kind of particleboard often used in engineered joists that replace traditional 2 × 12s.

- **Steel studs** are lightweight and have one big advantage: they're dead straight and they'll never warp or twist. They're useful for framing ceiling boxes or bulkheads, and some DIYers will even frame a whole basement with steel studs. They may be fine for partition walls, but they have a tinny, hollow quality, and I'm not a big fan of them for residential framing.

TOOLS AND MATERIALS YOU'LL NEED

- measuring tape
- pencil
- chalk line
- speed square
- 6-foot level
- framing hammer (heavier than the one you use to hang pictures)
- framing saw (a small circular saw)
- framing nails or screws (typically 2½ or 3½ inches)
- safety glasses

BASIC PARTS OF FRAMING

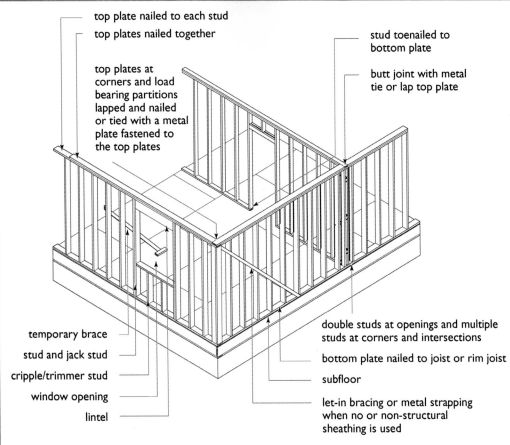

top plate nailed to each stud

top plates nailed together

stud toenailed to bottom plate

top plates at corners and load bearing partitions lapped and nailed or tied with a metal plate fastened to the top plates

butt joint with metal tie or lap top plate

temporary brace

stud and jack stud

cripple/trimmer stud

window opening

lintel

double studs at openings and multiple studs at corners and intersections

bottom plate nailed to joist or rim joist

subfloor

let-in bracing or metal strapping when no or non-structural sheathing is used

Note: Where the lintel exceeds 3 m (10 ft.), the jack stud needs to be doubled on both sides of the opening.

MISTAKE #1:
IMPROPERLY REMOVING A LOAD-BEARING WALL

Removing a wall isn't particularly hard—I've met a lot of people with no experience in home construction who have done it. With the right amount of cutting, hammering and elbow grease, any wall will come down eventually. Of course, doing it safely and properly—well, that's a little trickier.

Before you pick up that sledgehammer, you need to determine whether you're dealing with a partition wall or a structural wall. A partition wall is just a frame of 2 × 4s dividing a room, and removing one won't cause any major issues—assuming it's not full of plumbing, electrical or HVAC (heating, ventilation and air conditioning). But a structural (or load-bearing) wall is an integral part of your home: it's holding some of the weight above it, so you can't take it out without

Put down that sledgehammer! Before you do any demolition, use blueprints and an on-site evaluation to determine structural walls and columns.

putting in some other support to compensate. Let me be clear: removing load-bearing walls is not a DIY project—it's a job for professionals.

Think of your home's framing as a skeleton: you can remove a rib and stay standing; even if you take out a few, you'll just lean a little to one side. But if you pull out a femur, you're on the ground. If you take weight off one leg, the other has to carry double the load. The lower you go on your body, the more weight the skeleton has to carry. And if your bones are no longer able to provide support, you have to use a cane or crutches. You get the idea. These same principles apply to the structure of your home.

The absence of a structural wall can present that same sort of risk. I've seen many homes that have had a bearing wall removed. Sometimes, especially in older homes, you'll notice the hardwood flooring has been repaired because a wall has been removed, and directly above, there's a significant bow in the ceiling. That's a telltale sign. You may also notice the doors and windows on the upper floors don't close properly because the frames are out of square. That's a good indication the whole house is sagging. Sometimes the floor above will have a lot of deflection, meaning it gives a bit when you walk across it.

By now, I know you're asking, How can I tell whether a wall is a partition or load-bearing? That's one of the most common questions I get, but there are few hard and fast rules. Someone with experience needs to do a little investigating behind the scenes. Even if you have the original blueprints, an on-site evaluation is critical to determine if everything is where it's supposed to be and there were no changes or omissions made during construction. So if you have no idea—or even if you have a shadow of doubt—call a structural engineer or architect to inspect it. Unfortunately, you can't always

This yellow support beam was installed to replace a load-bearing wall.

tell by looking at the exterior of the wall: you may have to open it up and take a look inside.

That said, I can offer a few suggestions about what to look for. Load-bearing walls in modern homes usually have another wall—or a horizontal beam supported by posts—below them. So if you're sizing up the wall in your main-floor living room, have a look in the basement. If you have a beam and steel posts under that wall, it's almost certainly structural. Another clue is that load-bearing walls often have a double top plate (a pair of horizontal 2 × 4s across the top, instead of only one) or double studs (vertical 2 × 4s secured together for additional strength). Walls that run the entire width or length of your home are also likely to be structural, even if they have door openings. Same thing with basement walls that are resting on a concrete footing. Keep in mind many of these features will not be visible unless you open up the drywall.

With older homes it can be more difficult to determine whether a wall is load-bearing. I once found myself in a 100-year-old house, opening up a wall to build a simple pass-through between rooms. We found that the wall was actually carrying the weight of the roof and was unsupported on the two floors below, so that had to be addressed in a big hurry with new footings, posts and beams in the basement.

I've been in many older homes that have problems with the framing around the stair openings. Today you need to have a doubled-up joist or beam on both sides of the stair opening, with another doubled-up beam or joist carrying the weight of the floor where the stair opening is, both secured with joist hangers. But in older homes, there is often a wall beside and under the stairs to hold that floor section up. People rip out that wall to open up the stairs, and then you have these homes where three levels of floor are all sagging and at risk of collapse.

If you want to remove a structural wall, there are ways to do it safely. The fundamental idea is that weight needs to be supported from the roof all the way down to the foundation. So if you remove something that's bearing a load, you have to replace it with something else that will take the weight—just like using a crutch to support a broken leg. One technique is to install what's called a drop beam, which sits underneath the floor/ceiling joists and holds them up. Another option is to install a flush beam: in this case, the builder cuts all the floor joists back, slides a beam into that new opening and then hangs all the floor joists on that beam. A flush beam is much more difficult to install, but unlike with a drop beam, you won't bang your head on it.

Either way, you have to support that beam on both ends with a post going down to the floor and then down to what we call a point load, so you've got solid, continuous lumber going right down to a concrete footing. (The post can't just sit in the middle of a concrete floor in the basement; it has to bear either on a beam or on the foundation wall, or you have to dig a hole and pour a new footing for that post so that it has the support it needs.) The floor or ceiling must also be temporarily supported on both sides while the wall is removed and the beam is installed. The sizes of the beams and posts are determined by the load that the wall is carrying, which is determined by the building code in your area. If you don't have access to span tables (or you don't understand them), you should definitely consult an architect or structural engineer.

MISTAKE #2:
COMPROMISING YOUR HOME'S FRAMING

How often does something like this happen? You think you've got a simple job of replacing the tiles in the bathroom or installing some pot lights, and all of a sudden you're in a lot deeper. You rip up the subfloor and discover the previous owner has cut through four or five floor joists to make room for some new plumbing or removed a piece of a beam to install some ductwork.

It's really important you don't compromise the structure of your home when you're doing a renovation. If you want to install a central vacuum or run new wires or pipes, there are specific rules about the modifications you can make. Making changes in partition walls is pretty much fair game, but when it comes to floor or ceiling joists, or structural walls or beams—parts designed to hold up the house—there

No one wants to live in a house with a weakened structure. Floor and ceiling joists, structural walls and support beams like this metal beam in a basement (*top right*) and the LVL (laminated veneer lumber) beam (*bottom right*) are designed to hold up your house. Cutting (bottom right) or drilling (*far right*) can compromise the strength of the framing. In both of these cases you'd be okay, but it's best to leave these cuts to a pro.

are specific drilling and cutting patterns you need to follow. (For more about the differences between structural and partition walls, see Mistake #1, on page 6.)

For example, the code might say any hole drilled through a 2 × 10 joist must be no larger than 3 inches in diameter and no less than 2 inches from the edge. That's challenging for plumbers, especially, because they need to make sure the drainpipes have enough slope to carry the water away. It's also one of the reasons a framing inspection doesn't happen until after the mechanicals have been installed—otherwise, the inspector could say the framing looks good, but then the HVAC installer, plumber or electrician could come in and hack it apart. This is also why permits are required for any structural or mechanical modifications.

These problems can remain hidden in the floors and walls for a long time, and it's tempting to ignore them. But if you open up the drywall and find an issue with the framing, you're required by law to bring it up to current code.

The usual rule applies here: if you're doing a reno that involves cutting through any structural framing members and you're not experienced, call a professional.

MISTAKE #3:
ALLOWING YOUR LUMBER TO WARP

I remember one big job where the homeowner ran out of money just after we'd finished framing the whole house. The project sat like that for two years while the homeowner pulled the rest of the money together. When we finally got back to work, all the framing was twisted and warped. Even though the exterior walls were in place, the house had been unheated during that whole time, and the changes in temperature and moisture had caused the lumber to expand and con-

tract. We spent a lot of time straightening things out.

That's an extreme example, but if you're the type who drags out DIY projects over weeks or months, you can run into similar problems. For example, if you're planning to buy your lumber one weekend, do the framing over the next couple of weeks and then have the drywall installed the next season, that's a bad idea, because the wood is likely to warp over that time.

Lumber is a natural product, so your studs will twist and bend a little. That's why you get nails popping out of drywall—it's not because your contractor didn't know what he was doing; it's because the wood expands and contracts according to the environment. But there are some things you can do to keep warping to a minimum.

Most importantly, don't expose the lumber to big changes in moisture or temperature. If you leave your wood in the back of your truck in the rain and then bring it into the basement, it's going to look like a pile of hockey sticks when it dries out. If you're storing lumber outside, keep it covered!

It's also a good idea to try to get your framing done reasonably quickly and then have the drywall installed as soon as possible. Not only will the screws hold the wood in place somewhat, the drywall will also control the moisture inside the wall and reduce the likelihood of warping.

Mistake #4:
STICK-FRAMING WHEN YOU DON'T NEED TO

Stick-framing means assembling a wall in place, one piece at a time. You can get good results doing that, and it's really your only option when you're working around a lot of obstructions. But stick-framing is awfully time-consuming.

A much easier way to frame a non-bearing wall is to build it on the floor and then raise it into place. In a basement you can likely use this technique for most of the walls, including those around the perimeter. Here's how you do it.

Measure the wall height: The first step is to measure from floor to ceiling at several points where you plan to build the wall. Basement slabs are never perfectly level, but if you have only ¼ inch in height difference along that span, it won't be a problem to lift the whole frame into position. If the variation in height is more than that, then you'll probably have to resort to stick-framing (see page 14).

Mark the location of your top and bottom plates: The plates are the horizontal 2 × 4s along the top and bottom of a stud wall. The top plate attaches to the ceiling joists, and the bottom plate is secured to the floor. In a basement, if you're framing along an external wall, leave at least 1 inch between your plates and

the foundation: your concrete foundation walls won't be perfectly straight, so you'll need a little wiggle room. You also don't want untreated lumber touching the concrete, where it can absorb moisture. So measure about an inch from the wall at each bottom corner and then snap a chalk line across the floor. Do the same at the ceiling. This will help you see whether the foundation wall is bowed in or out. If it isn't straight, your 1-inch clearance may disappear at some point along the wall, and you'll need to adjust. The idea is to maximize the amount of space you have inside your basement while leaving enough space behind the framing to avoid contact with the concrete, and have a perfectly straight wall.

Measure the length of your top and bottom plate: You always want to use the longest top and bottom plates you can. If you're framing a large wall, you don't want to build a series of 8-foot sections if you don't have to—that's a lot of unnecessary work, and it won't be as sturdy. You can usually find 16-foot 2 × 4s, which are definitely preferable for your top and bottom plates. (Note that if you have to attach two pieces of lumber together to create a longer top plate, you can't leave that joint unsecured: you need to make sure there's a stud underneath.)

Mark the location of the studs: Once you've cut the top and bottom plates to the right size, hold them together and make pencil marks to indicate where the studs will go. You want to mark the first edge of each stud location and make the second mark ¾ inch short (to account for the 1½-inch thickness of the first stud) and then make the rest of the marks every 16 inches, the standard spacing for studs. Mark an X on the long side of the lines where the stud will sit.

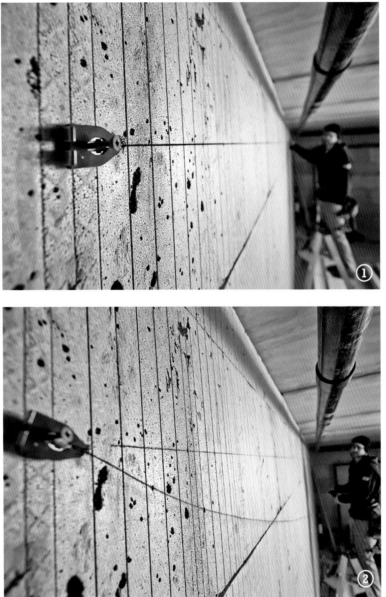

It's usually easier to build basement perimeter walls on the floor and raise them into place. Start by measuring the wall height in several places where you plan to build the wall. Then mark your top and bottom plates. Measure about an inch from the wall at each bottom corner and then snap a chalk line (*photo 1, 2*).

(Your last mark will be ¾ inch from the far edge, even though this may be less than 16 inches from the previous stud.) Use a speed square to make lines on both plates at the same time. That way when you separate the top and bottom plates to build the wall, both are already marked out for stud locations.

Measure, cut and attach the studs: Determine the length of each stud by measuring the distance from floor to ceiling and subtracting 3 inches for the thickness of the two plates. Make sure you don't cut the studs too long, or you won't be able to raise the wall into place: better to be ⅛ inch too short than too long.

Once you've cut the top and bottom plates, hold them together. Make the first mark ³/₄ inch from the edge (to account for the 1¹/₂ inch thickness of the first stud), then mark every 16 inches, which is the standard spacing for studs (*photo 1*). Use a speed square to make lines on both plates at the same time (*photo 2*). Determine the length of each stud by measuring from floor to ceiling, and subtract 3 inches for the thickness of the two plates (*photo 3*). Once the studs are cut, look down the long edge of each one to see which way it's "crowned" (*photo 4*). Most dimensional lumber has a slight bow, and you should install studs with the crowns facing the same way. Attach the studs by screwing through the top and bottom plates and into the end of each stud.

When all your studs are cut, look down the long edge of each one so you can see which way it's "crowned." Pretty much all dimensional lumber has a natural crown, or a slight but obvious bow along the narrow edge. When you're framing a wall, it's important to make sure the crowns of all the studs face the same way. Contractors disagree about which direction is correct, but I prefer to attach the drywall to the convex side, so there is a slight bulge rather than a hollow in the middle of the wall. No matter which way you crown your studs, changes in humidity will cause

Above you can see the crown on the left side of the stud. Mark your crowned sides to make installing them all in the same direction idiot-proof.

movement at some point—I've even seen crowns reverse!—so don't beat yourself up too much. The idea is to keep them all the same so you end up with a straight wall.

Attach the studs by nailing or screwing through the top and bottom plates and into the end of each stud, using two nails or screws at each end. For most DIY renos, you're going to use 3-inch framing screws and a drill. The pros use nail guns, but these can be dangerous in inexperienced hands. In our first season of *Disaster DIY*, we used nail guns, but every time I handed one to a homeowner, they would point it at me. In the second season, we started using a hammer and nails, but we soon found out most homeowners can't drive a nail properly either. Now I usually hand them a few screws and an impact driver—much safer for me! Bottom line: use a nail gun if you know what you're doing. Otherwise, use screws.

The studs may move while you're nailing, so check frequently to make sure the centre of each stud is

Attach your studs to your top and bottom plates by screwing through the plates. Make sure you always attach the stud on the same side of your mark, or your studs won't be evenly placed.

aligned with your pencil lines. When all the studs are attached, measure diagonally from corner to corner to make sure the section is square: you should get the same measurement along each diagonal. If you're out of square, move the top plate toward the shorter of the two measurements until they're both equal. (This method is more often used for exterior walls that will be sheathed before being lifted into place.) For basement walls, you can lift them first and use your level and a hammer to knock them into the correct square (or plumb) position.

Raise the wall into place and attach it: You may need a helper for this part. Lift your newly built frame off the floor and align it with the chalk lines you made on the floor and the ceiling and tack it in place with a couple of nails. You don't need to get fancy at this point: the idea for now is just to hold the frame loosely while you make your adjustments. For example, if there are any gaps between the top plate and the ceiling joists, slide in some shims—which are just tapered pieces of wood—to compensate.

If you're working with a wood subfloor, you can secure the bottom plate using one screw between each pair of studs, and then attach the top plate to each ceiling joist. If your wall is parallel to the joists (but not directly under a joist), you'll need to install blocking between the joists every 24 inches to attach your wall and provide backing for the drywall on the ceiling. Blocking every 24 inches will provide a solid surface in between parallel joists to attach the top plate to.

If you're attaching the bottom plate to a concrete slab in the basement, use Tapcon concrete screws. You will need a hammer drill and a masonry bit. Keep in mind you can't put untreated lumber right on top of concrete, so you need to separate them with a sill

gasket, which is a moisture-resistant foam that comes in a roll. The best method is to first install a DRIcore subfloor in your basement and then build the walls directly on top of the subfloor.

But sometimes you do need to stick-frame: As I've said, sometimes stick-framing is your only option— such as when your floor is not level, when there are a lot of obstructions on the ceiling (HVAC ducts, electrical or plumbing) or when you don't have a helper to raise a frame into place. If that's the case, the steps are a little different:

Install the bottom plate: Begin by marking the location of the wall by snapping a chalk line along the floor. (Remember to leave at least 1 inch of clearance from the foundation wall.) Then measure, cut and install the bottom plate along that line.

Align and install the top plate: This step is tricky, and it's important you get it right. You need to make sure your top plate is directly above the bottom plate so the wall will be perfectly straight.

If you don't have a plate level, take the straightest 2 × 4 you can find and cut it to about the height of your ceiling. Then place a long level vertically along the edge. The longer the level, the more accurate it is—a 6-foot level is ideal, but a shorter one should also do the trick. (No, you can't use your iPhone.) Position the 2 × 4 at one end of your bottom plate, make sure it is perfectly plumb—that's the vertical equivalent of level—and then mark the spot on the ceiling joist directly above. Do the same thing again at the other end of the bottom plate. Then snap a chalk line across those two points and attach your top plate by screwing or nailing into the joists along that line.

You may need a helper for this next part. It's time to lift your newly built frame off the floor and tack it in with a couple of nails. You don't need to get fancy at this point: the idea is to hold the frame loosely while you make adjustments to get rid of gaps between the top plate and ceiling joists. Use a level to make sure each of the studs is plumb (that's the vertical equivalent of level), then screw the wall firmly in place.

If you're dealing with ceiling obstructions or an uneven floor or if you don't have a helper, you'll need to use stick-framing. Start by installing the bottom plate along the floor, leaving an inch of clearance from the foundation wall.

Installing the top plate is tricky. You have to make sure it's directly above your bottom plate so your walls will be perfectly straight. Take your straightest 2 × 4 and cut it about the same height as your ceiling. Place a long level (ideally, a 6-footer) vertically along the edge. Position the 2 × 4 at one end of your bottom plate, make sure it's perfectly plumb, and mark the spot on the ceiling joist directly above (*photo 1*). Do the same at the other end of the bottom plate. Then snap a chalk line across those two points (*photo 2*) and attach your top plate by screwing or nailing into the joists along that line (*photo 3*).

Once your two plates are fastened, install the studs using a technique called toenailing. About 1½ inches from the plate, firmly poke the screw into the stud at just less than a right angle, using the weight of the gun to force the first thread into the wood. Tilt the screw at a 45-degree angle and finish installing it.

Cut the studs: If there is a fair bit of variance in height along the wall, you'll have to measure and cut each stud individually. Make them about ⅛ inch too long: that way you can tap them snugly into place with a hammer, and they will stay put before you screw them in.

Install the studs: Once your two plates are fastened, attach the first stud at one end. Once it is plumb and nailed or screwed in place, hook your measuring tape onto that stud and measure your 16-inch centres all along the top and bottom plates. Remember, you're measuring from the face of the first stud, so you're marking the left-hand side of the rest of the studs, not

the centre. Continue marking every 16 inches thereafter. Putting a small X on the right side of the line avoids confusion when it comes time to install the studs.

When you build a wall on the floor, you can drive the screws through the top and bottom plates into the end of each stud. But obviously you can't do this when you're stick-framing, so you need to use a technique called toenailing. Start about 1½ inches from the plate and firmly poke the screw into the edge (the short side facing you) of the stud at a right angle, using the weight of the gun to force the first thread or two into the wood. Then tilt the screw at a 45-degree angle and install it the rest of the way. Don't worry if you mess this up a few times—it takes a while to get the hang of it.

Put in one screw using the toenailing technique, making sure it goes all the way in and doesn't protrude, or it will poke the back of the drywall. Then put a second screw in through the side using the same method to stop the stud from turning. Make sure the screws don't run into each other. If you're nailing your studs into place, you have to account for the movement that will occur with each swing of the hammer. If you knock the stud slightly past the line, don't panic—just tap it back a little from the other side!

Most of the time when you're framing a wall, especially in a basement, you'll have to work around beams, ductwork or other nuisances. Sometimes you will need to divide the wall into sections. Look for places where you can run studs from floor to ceiling: you can build those sections on the floor and lift them into place, and then stick-frame the areas underneath the obstructions. (Experienced framers can often build the whole wall, including the notches, and then lift it all into place, but I wouldn't recommend that for a DIY project.) It's still important to keep your wall straight, even if you are building different sections, so snap a chalk line along the floor and use the longest possible board for the bottom plate. You will then have to use your 2 × 4 and level (see the process described on page 14) to attach the top plates directly above the bottom plate, making sure they are plumb all the way along. A double top plate provides more support for load-bearing walls.

MISTAKE #5:
NOT SQUARING CORNERS WHEN FRAMING WALLS

I use a simple trick when framing walls to get the corners perfectly square. Well, maybe not 100%, but as close as possible. If the wall corners are off square, the flooring will look off, too. To prevent that, use the 3-4-5 rule.

Think back to geometry class, where you learned about right-angle triangles. The square of the longest side (the hypotenuse) equals the sum of the square of the other two sides ($A^2 + B^2 = C^2$). You might also remember the famous 3-4-5 triangle: if the two sides of the right angle equal three and four units, the hypotenuse is exactly five units. You probably thought you would never need to apply that math lesson in real life—well, now you can! It's called the Pythagorean theorem—one of my favourites.

Say you've already framed one wall in your basement and you want to build a second wall perpendicular to it. Start in the corner, measure 3 feet along the bottom plate of the existing wall, and make a mark. Then grab the 2 × 4 you'll be using for your new bottom plate and lay it on the floor perpendicular to the existing wall. Measure 4 feet along that new bottom plate and make a mark there, too. Now measure the distance across the floor between those two marks. If it's 5 feet, your corner is square: you can go ahead and run a chalk line along the edge of your new bottom plate and follow that along the whole length of the new wall. If the distance is less than 5 feet, your corner measures less than 90 degrees; more than 5 feet, and your corner is greater than 90. Adjust until you hit 90 degrees.

This trick works better than using a framing square because that tool is often too small to get accuracy over greater lengths. You can also adjust the math as long as you use multiples of 3-4-5—such as 6-8-10, 9-12-15 and so on.

MISTAKE #6:
NOT PROVIDING ADEQUATE SUPPORT AROUND DOORS AND WINDOWS

If your wall will include a door or window, the framing is not much more difficult, but you do need to make sure you provide the proper support around the open-

I use the 3-4-5 rule—your math teacher called it the Pythagorean theorem—to square the corners when I'm framing. Starting in the corner, mark 3 feet along the bottom plate of an existing wall (*photo 1*). Grab the 2 × 4 you'll be using for the bottom plate of the wall you're about to build and lay it perpendicular to the existing wall; mark 4 feet along that 2 × 4 (*photo 2*). Measure the distance between those two marks (*photo 3*). If it's 5 feet, your corner is square.

ing. For this you'll learn the names and functions of a few other framing members.

When you're framing an opening for a door or a window, both vertical edges need to be adjacent to studs that the span the entire height of the wall. Your frame will have studs on 16-inch centres already, and in many cases one of these will form the left or right edge of your opening. But you will likely have to install a new stud on the other side. These two studs, which run all the way from the top plate to the bottom plate, are called **king studs**.

In a partition wall, the top and bottom edges of a window opening are called **sills**. The bottom sill carries the weight of the window, so it needs to be supported. Simply toenailing it to the king studs isn't enough: you need to install **cripple studs** underneath. The first and last cripples are "sistered" to the king studs—which just means they are nailed to the king studs to provide extra support. The others are placed on 16-inch centres all the way under the window to provide backing for the drywall. Cripple studs are also installed between the upper sill and the top plate.

As I've said, you probably shouldn't be framing too many structural walls unless you're a pro, but it's useful to understand the technique. In a structural wall, the horizontal piece at the top of a door or window opening is called the **header**. Unlike with a partition wall, you can't just use a single 2 × 4 here, because the header is taking a load from above. Headers are often doubled 2 × 6s or 2 × 8s; they may even be as large as 2 × 12. Because the header is supporting a load, it needs to be supported by a couple of **jack studs** (also called trimmers). These are 2 × 4s that are sistered to the king studs directly underneath the header.

There are different ways of framing door and window openings in a structural wall. Many people put the header directly above the door or window opening and place the cripple studs above it. However, experienced framers often place all the headers right under the top plate and frame down to the top of the door or window with a sill and cripple studs. That way if you make a mistake on the height calculations, you can easily adjust without any structural work. Plus, if you ever want to raise a window or replace a window with a door, it's much simpler to remove a sill and some cripple studs than it is to remove and replace a header. Placing all the headers at the top of the wall also standardizes the length of your jack studs for every opening—only the lower sill measurements will vary from opening to opening—so it simplifies some of the math.

As always, check your local building code to make sure you're using the right size and number of framing members and that you've spaced them appropriately.

MISTAKE #7: MAKING LOUSY CUTS

A successful framing project begins with your ability to make straight, consistent cuts. You'd think that would be simple, but I've watched DIYers mangle plenty of good lumber. Here are some tricks I use to measure and cut accurately.

First, when you're marking your measurement on the board, don't try to draw a line freehand: it's not going to be accurate. Instead, use an inverted V-shape to mark a point at the exact measurement and then use a speed square to draw the cutline at a right angle, intersecting the point of the V.

If you're making only one cut on a board, you can probably get away with cutting right on top of the line. But remember the saw blade is about 1/8 inch wide, so you will lose 1/16 inch on either side. If you're planning to make a series of cuts along the same board, then you definitely need to account for that 1/8 inch, or some of the pieces are going to come up short. If you're confused, it may be best to measure and cut each piece individually.

When you make the measurement, mark an X on the offcut (the piece you won't need). That way you won't accidentally cut the wrong part of the board when you get to the saw.

Framing around a window or door isn't any harder than framing a wall, but you do have to provide proper support. Both vertical edges of the door or window need to be adjacent to studs that span the entire height of the wall (these are called king studs). Your frame will have studs on 16-inch centres already, and in many cases, one of these will form the left or right edge of your opening. But you will likely have to install a new stud on the other side. For the jack studs, cut two 2 × 4s to the appropriate length—typically 2 inches longer than your door—and attach them to your bottom plate and your king studs. Then cut a header for the rough opening—this will sit on top of the jacks, running from one king stud to the other (*photo 1*). You'll need to install a second header to sit on top of the first, connecting it to your king studs (*photo 2*), and then run a cripple stud between that header and the top plate—this is for you to attach your drywall securely later (*photo 3*). Finally, cut out the bottom plate in the door opening (*photo 4*). That's it—you've got a finished rough opening for an interior non-bearing door.

Always make sure to double-check your measurements (*above*) before making a cut.

Everyone has accidentally cut the wrong part of the board. To avoid this mistake, simply mark an X on the offcut, and you'll know which piece to keep.

It's also a good idea to rest the lumber on a sawhorse or other surface that makes cutting easier. Make sure your work is at a comfortable height so you're not stooped over. You'll want to position the wood with the offcut end hanging over your cutting surface so it will fall away and won't pinch the saw blade.

MISTAKE #8:
FAILING TO PROVIDE PROPER BACKING FOR DRYWALL

Framing the middle section of a wall is pretty straightforward. But what happens when you need to frame a corner or work around obstructions? This can be tricky because you need to make sure your framing provides enough backing to properly attach your drywall.

One important framing technique is called a three-stud corner. The easiest way to describe this technique is with a diagram (see below):

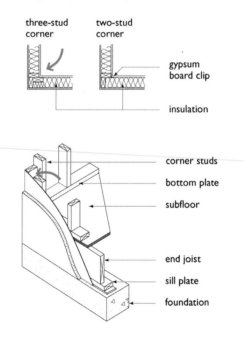

As you can see, a three-stud corner includes an extra 2 × 4 that protrudes 1½ inches to provide backing for your drywall (see blue arrows in the diagram). If you're stick-framing (see Mistake #4, page 10), you can add this extra corner stud after you've framed both walls. If you're building the frame on the floor, you should attach the extra stud before you lift the wall into place. Just make sure you put it on the correct side—

that is, at the front of the frame, not at the back. If the frame is lying down, you also need to make sure you don't accidentally nail that extra stud to the floor. Hey, we've seen it done.

In a basement you'll often need to build a box or a bulkhead to hide ductwork or pipes and create the backing for your drywall. It's hard to offer specific advice here because every situation is different. But, in general, you'll probably find it easier to use 2 × 2s or even steel studs, which are simpler to work with and still provide good backing. If you have a number of obstructions at the ceiling, you don't want to build a lot of small individual boxes to hide them. Instead, consider hiding everything with a single bulkhead. Not only will it look better, it will make the drywall much easier to install. The key here is to build it strong—you don't want anything above your head that isn't well attached.

You may need to build a box or a bulkhead to hide ductwork or pipes and create the backing for drywall. One large bulkhead is easier to work around—and looks better—than many small ones.

One important framing technique I use is called a three-stud corner: it adds an extra 2 × 4 that protrudes 1½ inches to provide backing for your drywall. If you're stick-framing, you can add this extra stud after you've framed both walls. If you're building the frame on the floor, you should attach the extra stud before you lift the wall into place. A simple technique for attaching walls at the corners and still providing backing for drywall is called the three-stud corner. At the end of the long wall (the first wall you build that the others will attach to), attach two 2 × 4s together (*bottom left*) to provide an extra 1.5 inches of backing. This allows you to connect the next wall to the corner and leaves 1.5 inches protruding from the corner as backing for the drywall. Without this extra 2 × 4 attached to the last king stud, you'll have nothing to attach to in the corner.

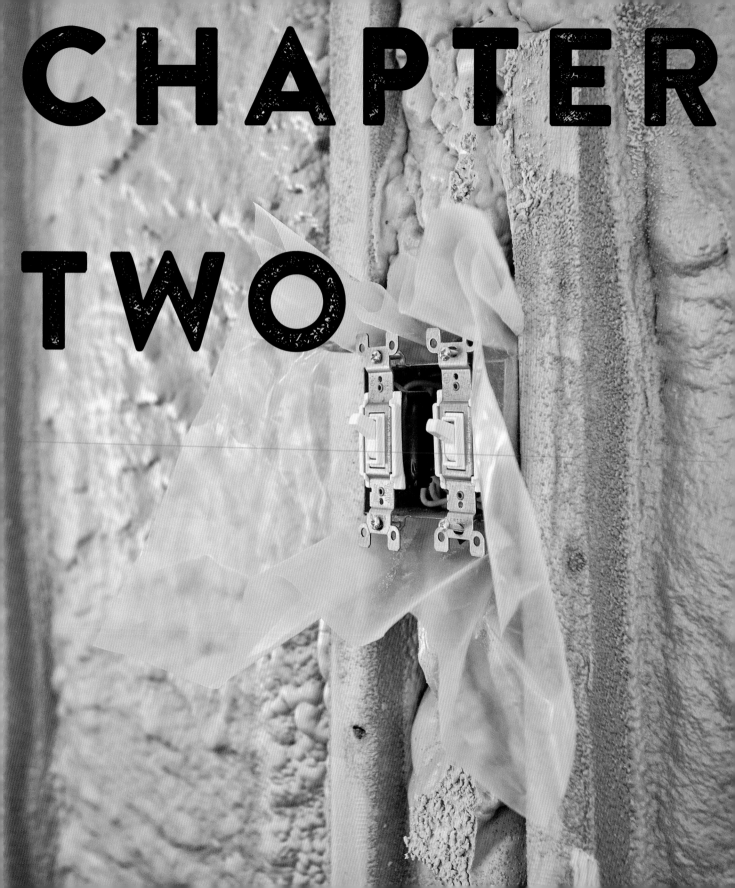

CHAPTER TWO

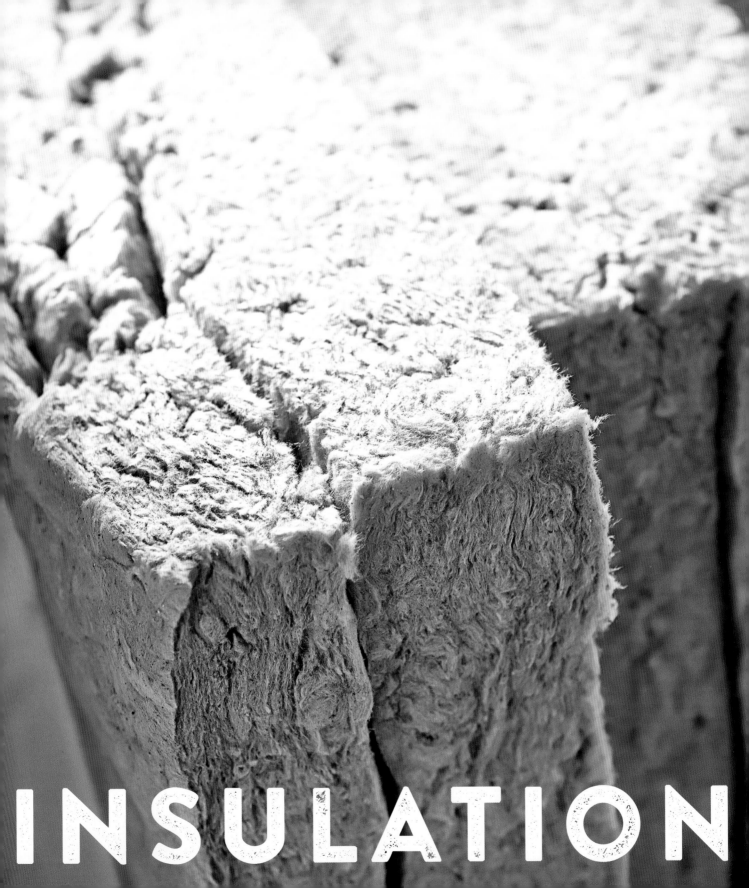

INSULATION

IF YOU EVER FIND YOURSELF WONDERING WHETHER IT'S WORTH SPENDING THE EXTRA MONEY TO INSULATE YOUR HOUSE WELL, LET ME BE CLEAR—IT IS. TO UNDERSTAND WHY, IT HELPS TO THINK OF YOUR HOUSE AS A GIANT COOLER.

We all know if you put your beer and ice in a cheap Styrofoam cooler, in two hours you'll find the ice melted and your beer warm. But if you get a good-quality cooler with a tight-fitting lid, your beer will stay cold for two days. Same goes for a Thermos: the good ones keep your soup hot all day.

The houses our parents grew up in were like those flimsy coolers. With little and poor insulation, and drafts in every place you could think of, it was a constant and expensive battle to keep a home comfortable. Luckily, modern houses are more airtight, just like those thick, high-end coolers and Thermoses. They seal the conditioned air in and keep the outside air out, which makes them much more energy-efficient. Nevertheless, many of those older homes can be made much more cost-effective and comfortable with a bit of spending on the right insulation. Most heat loss occurs at penetration points—vents, plumbing, windows, electrical and so on—so be sure to seal those areas well to eliminate airflow. Think about it this way: it doesn't matter how good your cooler is if there are holes in it or if you leave the lid open.

Retrofitting your entire home with new insulation wouldn't be cheap, and there would be little return on investment for anyone who doesn't live to be 400. But next time you're building or renovating, spend the time and money to get the insulation right while the walls are open. When you're snug and warm on a winter night—and you see your heating and cooling expenses drop—you won't regret it.

INSULATION BASICS

DIFFICULTY: 4 OUT OF 10

Insulation is designed to keep heat where you want it: inside during the winter, and outside when you run the air conditioner in summer. Insulation products are rated with an "R-value" per inch of depth of insulation, which tells you how well the material resists the transfer of heat. Higher R-values are better at keeping heat where you want it. For example, closed-cell spray foam is about R6, while rigid foam (which is used for exteriors or basements) ranges from about R3.7 to R6.7, depending on the thickness of the panel. Building codes set minimum R-value requirements for different parts of a home.

CHOOSING INSULATION

- **Fibreglass insulation** is the traditional pink stuff everyone has seen. It comes in sheets called batts. It's still common, and it works just fine as long as it's installed properly, kept dry and is well sealed against air and vapour transfer. R3 to 3.7

- **Mineral wool insulation** also comes in batts. It's made from crushed stone and keeps its insulating abilities even when it gets wet, so it's often a good choice for basements and attics. R2.8 to 3.7

- **Blown-in insulation** is fibreglass, mineral wool or cellulose material that is chopped into pieces (called loose-fill) and installed between the joists in an attic. R3 to 3.7

- **Extruded polystyrene (EPS)** is rigid foam often used beneath siding or in a basement, where it acts as a vapour barrier as well as an insulator. R3.6 to 6.7

- **Closed-cell spray-foam insulation** is made of polyurethane. It is applied as a liquid and quickly hardens to form both a vapour barrier and an R-value of about R6 per inch.

- **Open-cell spray-foam insulation** is made of varying material. It is also applied as a liquid and quickly hardens to form an air barrier but not a vapour barrier. Requires a vapour barrier. R3.6 per inch.

TOOLS AND MATERIALS YOU'LL NEED

- measuring tape
- utility knife
- sheathing tape (Tuck Tape is a popular brand)
- 6-mil polyethylene for vapour barrier
- mask and gloves
- long sleeves and long pants for working with fibreglass or mineral wool

MISTAKE #9:
NOT FULLY UNDERSTANDING R-VALUE

The effectiveness of insulation is commonly measured and labelled by its R-value. The higher the R-value per inch of a particular insulation material, the more powerfully that insulation can resist the transfer of heat, and the better it is as an insulator. R-value is cumulative: one batt of fibreglass insulates to R3.7, but 10 batts will give you R37. However, a wall cavity wouldn't have enough space to pack batts 10 deep, which is why you'd either need to settle for a lower R-value in your walls or go with an insulation that offers a higher R-value per inch. Remember that your insulation will resist the movement of heat both ways, so insulation helps in all seasons: in winter, it traps the heat inside; in summer, it locks the heat out. But even the highest R-value can't keep your house warm without a vapour barrier. Think of basic insulation as a wool sweater—it'll keep you a little bit warm outside on a frigid day, but if you add a windproof jacket overtop, suddenly you're nice and toasty. Some insulation has the added advantage of an air barrier built right in, which means the wind can't blow through it. It's like having a sweater and windbreaker all in one.

Different parts of the house require different R-values according to the building code for new construction (check the building code in your area). There's no question that properly installed insulation can make a huge difference in how comfortable your house feels. But an equally satisfying payoff comes from smaller heating and cooling bills. By insulating and air-sealing, you'll stop your home from leaking thousands of dollars in wasted heat through the walls, floors and so on. Insulation helps you conserve energy—the furnace doesn't have to work as hard to heat the house when the warm air stays inside where you want it. A two-storey, 2,200-square-foot house built in the 1970s could save up to 28% annually by upgrading the basement walls from zero to R20 and the attic from R8 to R40. I've heard about savings of up to 50% per year on heating and cooling if every wall, ceiling and crawl space is coated with spray foam. If you want to save on operating costs, bumping up your R-value is a no-brainer.

MISTAKE #10:
THINKING IT'S EASY TO INSTALL FIBREGLASS

Fibreglass insulation is made from sand and recycled glass, and comes in batts typically a few inches thick. It's fine as an insulator, with an R-value of about 3 or 4. Fibreglass has to be kept dry to be effective: if it gets wet, it loses some of its R-value until it dries. It also has to be installed so it's fluffy: if it's compressed in any way, it also loses R-value. And you have to install fibreglass with an effective vapour barrier because air will flow right through this kind of insulation. If that happens, it doesn't matter how thickly you line your walls with batts—they just won't keep your house warm.

One of the reasons fibreglass batts are so popular is they're cheap to buy and don't require any specialized equipment to install. However, if you're installing your own batt insulation, you need to be aware that small mistakes can have a big impact—and these mistakes are so common, even builders make them. Let me give you an example: you can insulate almost the whole wall properly, but if you've left a gap in just one area or compressed one batt too much—those are the two most common errors—you can reduce the overall efficiency dramatically.

These are the steps to follow for insulating an above-grade interior wall with batt insulation. To start,

If you're installing your own fibreglass batts, do yourself a favour and avoid the two biggest mistakes that dramatically reduce the insulation's efficiency: (*photo 1*) don't compress the batts; (*photo 2*) don't leave any gaps. Okay, now for the steps: Start by cutting insulation about an inch wider than the width between the studs so it fits snugly without being compressed or creating air gaps. Begin at the top, fitting the insulation against the top plate, working down to fit the batt tightly against the bottom plate. Fill corners without folding or compressing the batts. Once all cavities are filled, cover the wall with a 6-mil poly vapour barrier stapled every 16 inches along the studs and top and bottom plates. Use Tuck Tape to seal each gap, seam and staple hole.

use one of the many insulation calculators online to figure out how much insulation to buy (you'll need the dimensions of your walls). Using a sharp utility knife, cut your batts about an inch wider than the width between studs on the wall cavity you're insulating. The extra inch helps ensure the insulation fits snugly to fill the entire framing cavity, without any air gaps between the insulation and the framing. Start at the top of the wall, pressing the insulation against the top plate of the framing, and work your way down until you fit the batt tightly against the bottom plate. Pay attention when you're cutting and installing insulation in the corners of each cavity: fill them without folding or compressing the batts. You also need to make careful cuts to fit the batts around wiring, electrical boxes or pipes. Remember, a sloppy installation will reduce the overall R-value of the wall.

Once you've filled all wall cavities, you need to protect the insulation from moisture. The warm air in your house contains water vapour. If this vapour passes into your insulation, it could condense, significantly lowering the R-value of the insulation. So you need to install a 6-mil poly vapour barrier on the warm side of the house. In Canada, that means it goes up after the insulation and before the drywall. Staple up the vapour barrier every 16 inches along the studs and top and bottom plates. Patch any rips that happen along the way, since moisture could creep in through even a small tear. Then you have to perfectly seal every gap, staple hole and seam and around penetrations (ducts, pipes, vents, windows) with red Tuck Tape. Using an acoustic sealant (a type of caulking that stays tacky to prevent air from penetrating it) along the top and bottom plates and any areas where the vapour barrier terminates also helps stop air leakage. This is one of those times where it pays to be a perfectionist because any holes will reduce the effectiveness of your insulation. After that,

you can cover the walls with drywall. (If you're insulating a basement, see page 39; the steps are a little different when you're working below grade.)

MISTAKE #11:
IGNORING ALTERNATIVES TO FIBREGLASS BATTS

There are many alternatives to the traditional pink stuff everyone is familiar with.

Mineral wool insulation is made from crushed stone. A product like Roxul Comfortbatt has a similar R-value to fibreglass (up to R3.7 per inch) but with a couple of advantages. If it gets wet, mineral wool does not lose its insulating properties, which makes it a good choice in attics and basements. Another big difference is mice and other rodents, which seem to love fibreglass, won't chew through it. And because it contains no organic material, it doesn't support mould or mildew growth. Mineral wool costs about $1.20 per square foot for R14 or $1.60 per square foot for R22; for fibreglass, you'll pay about $1 per square foot for R14 to R20.

Unlike fibreglass, mineral wool insulation is made from crushed stone, so it doesn't lose its insulating properties if it gets wet, and it won't promote the growth of mould or mildew.

Roxul also makes a mineral wool product called Safe'n'Sound, which is used for interior walls. It has minimal R-value because it's designed to absorb sound, so you can use it to cocoon your bedroom walls to keep out the noise of your screaming kids. I like to use it in all the interior walls in our houses, not just to keep the noise down, but also because it's fire resistant (so are mineral wool thermal insulation and fibreglass). If there is ever a fire in the basement, it travels quickly through wall cavities. If you fill the wall cavities with Safe'n'Sound, there's nowhere for that fire to go.

Extruded polystyrene (EPS) is rigid foam board intended for exteriors or below-grade rooms. Typically, you'll see it installed beneath siding or a basement floor, or around rim joists, which are the ceiling joists in the basement that sit on the foundation wall. You can use it in conjunction with batt insulation on basement walls, since it acts as a vapour barrier and has a higher R-value (about 3.6 to 6.7 per inch) than batts alone. Expect to pay about $3 per square foot for R20; $4.50 per square foot for R28.

Spray polyurethane foam insulation is the new thing everybody is using, and I'm a big fan. You can't beat it for comfort and energy efficiency. Since I foamed my house, we've spent less than $50 a month on heating in the winter, and we stay nice and cool in the summer. Our old, uninsulated bungalow cost over $600 a month to heat in the winter—not good!

Spray foam is applied directly onto the floor or wall cavities as a liquid, and it quickly expands and hardens. The nice thing about closed-cell spray foam is it's actually a two-in-one product, giving you insulation and an air/vapour barrier. That means you won't feel drafts or cold spots from air leaks, and you don't need to install a separate poly vapour barrier as you would for batts or cellulose insulation. And because

Rigid boards of extruded polystyrene are great beneath siding or basement floors. I like to use it with batt insulation on basement walls since it also acts as a vapour barrier.

it stops air movement on both sides of the wall, you won't get vapour condensing in the wall cavity and potentially causing mould and rot. Finally, it gives you a really high R-value: up to R6.7 per inch, compared with R3.7 per inch for batts. It can make a big difference in comfort if you've got a room over an uninsulated space: foaming the roof of a garage or porch can improve the temperature of a bedroom above, for example.

The likelihood of error with spray foam is pretty low as long as it's installed by a certified and experienced professional—you don't want to be putting

I'm a big fan of spray-foam insulation. Not only did we save a bundle on energy bills after spray-foaming our old bungalow, it was also more consistently a comfortable temperature.

this stuff in yourself or breathing the fumes. The good installers are specially trained. They wear tons of protective gear and monitor the mixture and temperatures to maintain consistency. Plan to be out of the house for at least a day while it cures.

But there's a bit of bad news. Prepare for a little sticker shock: spray foam starts at about twice the cost of fibreglass. For open-cell, which needs a separate vapour barrier, the cost is about $2 for R20, $3 for R28, $4 for R40. For closed-cell, expect to pay about $3 per square foot for R20 or $4.50 for R28. But over the long term, installing spray foam throughout a home can reduce your heating and cooling costs by up to 50%, so you will see a return on your investment. Whether you're building new or renovating, I think it makes sense to spend this money.

EIFS stands for **exterior insulation and finish system**. It's an exterior finish with insulating qualities. EIFS has multiple layers. First, insulation board made of expanded polystyrene is attached to the exterior wall. The next layer is a fibreglass mesh embedded in adhesive; these two first layers form the base coat. The finish coat goes over the base coat, and it looks kind of like stucco. An EIFS is an option if you want to retrofit an older home that is poorly insulated but you can't install insulation from the inside without ripping out plaster-and-lath walls. If you are building from scratch, you've got plenty of other choices, but if you're looking to increase the overall efficiency without disturbing the interior of the home, EIFS is at the top of the list. This is definitely not a DIY job.

Sometimes people try to retrofit with insulation by drilling a hole in the wall and injecting low-expansion foam. In most cases, it's a lousy way to insulate. We've done a lot of work in houses where we've ripped out

Think of insulation and vapour barrier like clothing: the insulation is the wool sweater that provides warmth; the vapour barrier is the windbreaker that keeps out the wind.

those walls: there's a big pancake of foam where the hole was and poor coverage in most other places. If you've got anything blocking the foam behind the walls—which you can't see when you're installing the stuff—you'll end up with big empty spots where the foam just can't reach. And sometimes you have only an inch or less of space in the wall cavity anyway, so the most you're going to insulate (in a perfect world) in there is about R3 or R4.

MISTAKE #12:
FAILING TO USE A VAPOUR BARRIER

Remember, think of insulation and vapour barrier as clothing. The insulation is your wool sweater: it provides a layer of warmth but only if you also add a windbreaker overtop to keep out the wind. That same cold air will pass right through batt or cellulose insulation unless you cover that insulation with plastic. That's why we wrap the exterior of new homes in a sheathing membrane before the siding goes up—Tyvek and Typar are two brands you've probably seen in new subdivisions. This kind of house wrap creates an air and moisture barrier that reduces airflow through the exterior walls, which helps maintain the R-value of your insulation and keep your house more comfortable.

We also need to install a vapour barrier on the inside of walls insulated with batt insulation or open-cell spray foam. Here's how a vapour barrier works: in January, when the furnace is humming, you have warm air inside, then you have your drywall, then you've got your vapour barrier behind that and then your insulation batts and your exterior house wrap. So you've got warm indoor air going through the drywall toward the outside. You can't see it, but the air contains vapour from everyday activities (talking, breathing, showering, cooking). The vapour barrier stops warm air from passing through to the insulation and hitting a cold surface, where it would condense (the dew point). So you need vapour barrier to keep your insulation dry and effective and safe from mould. In the summer, insulation plus air and vapour barriers help seal out hot air while keeping cool, conditioned air inside.

People are often unsure about how to layer the vapour barrier during installation. If you're using fibreglass batts, you want the polyethylene vapour barrier between the drywall and the insulation, and the air barrier on the exterior sheathing on the outside of the insulation. But if you're using closed-cell spray foam as a vapour barrier in conjunction with insulation batts (a technique called flash and batt), the order is spray foam, batt insulation, drywall. The spray foam can go against the cold exterior wall because it functions as both a vapour barrier and insulator, but the foam must be at least an inch thick.

MISTAKE #13:
NEGLECTING YOUR ATTIC

There are a lot of insulation jobs you can do on your own. A good one is the attic. Heat rises, so the attic is where you stand to lose most of the heat in a house. If you want to insulate your attic, which will make your house more comfortable and shave a few bucks off your energy bill, you can use loose-fill insulation. You can buy this product ready-made, or you can rent an insulation chopper at most big-box stores: you feed regular batts into the hopper and they get chopped up and blown through a hose to your partner standing in the attic.

Some people get confused about where exactly to put the insulation in the attic. I see how it can be confusing: you might think you're insulating to keep the attic warm, but for most of us with unfinished attics, it's the opposite. You want the attic to stay cool and the house to stay warm. That's why you don't put insulation on the inside surface of the roof—it goes on the floor of the attic, directly on top of the ceiling of the rooms below.

You also need a vapour barrier below your insulation to keep warm, moist air inside the house and out of the attic. This not only helps keep your house warmer, it also protects your roof. If the attic isn't properly insulated and sealed against air movement (with vapour barrier, if you're using loose-fill insulation or batts), the warm air from the home gets up to the roof, where

This old style of mixing fibreglass insulation with a bare concrete wall below the frost line isn't my idea of how to do a basement—spring for mould-proof spray foam instead.

it can cause snow to melt and then run down toward the eavestroughs and form ice dams. If that happens, moisture can start to force its way under your shingles, which can damage the roof. You also don't want warm air from the house to condense in the cold attic air, because that's an invitation for mould and rot. So when you hire a company to top up the insulation in the attic, you'd better make sure they check for a proper vapour barrier installed along the floor of the attic, and make sure your soffit vents and roof vents are clear to allow any warm air to circulate and escape.

How much insulation will you need? In Canada, building codes require you to insulate the attic to R40 or R50, depending on where you live. An inch of insulation should give you about R3, so you'll need to layer it to about 18 or 19 inches deep (it can't hurt to add a little extra to account for settling since insulation can get compressed over time). To determine how much insulation is required, you can get help from the big-box stores, which have online calculators.

Before you start blowing it in, make sure any electrical boxes, pot lights and ventilation fans in the attic are temporarily covered so they don't trap any loose-fill insulation. Some pot lights are actually not designed for attics at all—they can get very hot and potentially start a fire. If you're using pot lights in the rooms below the attic, they should be special pot lights designed for insulation contact. If yours have a sticker that says "IC" (for Insulation Contact), they're safe.

Fill the attic right over the joists. Just don't block any roofing vents with insulation, or that will restrict airflow in the attic. Soffit vents are the ones located along the underside of the roof overhang along the perimeter of the roof. Ridge vents are typically found at the peak of a roof. Our attics are just like us—they need to breathe. So cover the attic floor only as far as the perimeter of the walls.

MISTAKE #14:
USING THE WRONG INSULATION IN THE BASEMENT

If you're finishing your basement, make sure you set aside a line in the budget for the insulation. You can't hang out in an uninsulated basement and watch movies on your big-screen TV—or at least you wouldn't want to because it would be so cold and drafty. Insulating your basement will also help lower your heating bill by up to 20%. Uninsulated basement walls and floors are not just uncomfortable—they're a huge energy suck.

When you insulate down there, you have to think about doing it in a way that deals with moisture. Moisture creates mouldy, rotting basements. First, you've got the vapour created by everyday living: showers, cooking and breathing all create moisture, which flows out through the walls. Below grade, though, you've also got moisture from the soil, and that flows right through the foundation—remember, concrete is porous. That's why we see so many damp, musty basements. If you have *any* moisture coming through your foundation walls, don't finish your basement until the foundation is properly waterproofed and the leak is fixed. Period!

I think the best way to insulate your basement is to use spray foam throughout, but that can be expensive. For a typical four-bedroom, 2,000-square-foot house, installing 3 inches of closed-cell spray foam only in the basement might cost about $3,500. (By comparison, for $1,600, you could have fibreglass batts installed in the basement.)

Another way to insulate a basement is flash and batting: use a minimum of 2 inches of foam in cold climates, and top it up with an R12 of fibreglass insulation. That method would cost about $3,700. With any combination or hybrid system, be sure to use a vapour-barrier sheathing such as 6-mil poly on the warm side. The foam is cooler in temperature because it's insulated by the fibreglass, and if you don't install a vapour barrier on the warm side, condensation can form on the surface of the foam.

If spray foam isn't an option, an alternative would be 1-inch EPS panels with batt on top. EPS panels have rabbet joints, so they lock together, but you have to seal the seams with Tuck Tape to make sure it's airtight and foam the top and bottom of the panels to seal them. You don't need to tape the panels along the top and bottom plates of your framing if you foam the gap. EPS is easy to install along an unfinished basement wall. You can glue the panels directly to the perimeter walls, seal the seams with Tuck Tape, and then frame your walls right in front of the panels and use batt insulation between the studs. Again, it is critical that a vapour barrier be installed properly on the warm side. EPS can be glued right to the concrete, but you have to use the proper adhesive; if you use the wrong type, the glue will eat right through the foam. If you've already framed the basement, you've limited your options: you don't want to be cutting EPS panels to fit between each of the studs. Either way, you insulate after the electrical and plumbing have been installed.

EPS panels can give you the same advantages of spray foam as long as there are no voids. (Convective air flow behind board insulation can reduce the effective R-value by more than 25%.) Costs for this system are significantly higher if you were to hire a contractor, but can be comparable to a complete spray foam.

You don't have to bother with thermal insulation in the ceiling of the basement because it's not exposed to the exterior of the house. However, you might consider installing a sound and fire barrier, such as Roxul Safe'n'Sound, which muffles noise and helps prevent the spread of fire.

The best way to insulate a basement floor is to have your contractor install foam panels on the ground before the slab is poured. If you're not starting a floor from scratch, you can install a subfloor like DRIcore. The 2- by 2-foot panels are tongue-and-grooved on all four sides, and come with a raised polyethylene moisture barrier bonded to the underside. This gives you a thermal break between your basement and the air, soil and moisture outside. I've found that installing DRIcore is quicker and easier than any other product, and it allows for airflow under the floor while warming up the basement and softening the floor all in one step.

What R-value do you need in the basement walls? That depends on where you live. Building code for insulation in below-grade walls can range from R10 to R27. Check with your municipality to find out what code says in your area.

Before you cheap out on the insulation in your basement, consider this: your furnace lives down there! If the air in your basement is cold, your furnace has to work harder to warm up the cold air and distribute it through the house. If the air in your basement is already warm, your furnace (and your wallet) will thank you.

MISTAKE #15:
FAILING TO SEAL AND INSULATE AROUND RIM JOISTS

One spot where you might forget to seal and insulate—and regret it—are the areas around rim joists. That's where the ceiling joists in your basement sit on the foundation wall. In a two-storey house, you'll have a second level of rim joists above the ceiling of the first floor. Many new homes have a handful of batt in the cavity, with a flap of vapour barrier loosely stapled over it. Unfortunately, this isn't effective—the rim joist cavity needs to be completely insulated and vapour-sealed to be effective, just like the rest of the walls in your home.

If your rim joists are not properly insulated, and if your basement has drywall ceilings, cold air can get in between the ceiling joists and create a chamber of freezing cold air. Then what happens is the floor above gets really cold. That's why it's so important to insulate and seal this area properly.

If your basement is already finished, it's hard to do anything about uninsulated rim joists. But if you're planning a remodel, you have three options: seal the batt

Unless you're a fan of cold floors, remember to insulate rim joists, where basement ceiling joists sit on the foundation wall.

insulation properly with vapour barrier, install rigid foam or use spray foam. Taping up vapour barrier around every joist bay filled with batt insulation is labour intensive and leaves your ceiling prone to air leakage if not done properly—but if you're detail-oriented and patient, buy a few rolls of tape and get started!

At up to R6.7 per inch, rigid foam boards are cheaper to buy, but they require more labour than spray foam. Rigid foam is also trickier to install in tight spaces, such as where a rim joist is close to another joist, or where you're working around electrical or plumbing. In a cold climate, you'll want to install at least 3 to 4 inches of rigid foam (you can do this in one thick layer or using multiple thinner sheets). All perimeter cracks have to be sealed with caulk or canned spray foam.

Spray foam has the advantage of sealing air leaks and insulating all in one, with an R-value of up to R6.7 per inch for closed-cell spray foam. In a cold climate, you'll

want at least 3 inches. Like I've said before, spray foam isn't a DIY job. I'd recommend an experienced insulation contractor specially trained to install spray foam.

MISTAKE #16:
OVERLOOKING SIMPLE AIR-SEALING JOBS

If you insulate a house that's got dozens of small cracks and gaps, those holes are pulling heated air outside and letting cold air seep inside. If you seal those cracks, you'll waste less heat, lower your bills and let your insulation do its job. Studies have shown that proper air sealing can save up to 20% on your heating costs, yet most of the materials cost a few bucks at the hardware store.

One way to find out where your home is leaking air is to get an energy audit. The best companies will do a special blower-door test to scientifically measure air leakage in your home and ductwork. During the test, a temporary door with a powerful fan is installed in an outside doorway, pulling air out of the house through all unsealed cracks and openings.

If you don't hire an auditor, you can walk around your house with a candle (air leaks will cause the smoke to change direction or the flame to flicker) or even use your hand to feel for cold zones. Here's a list of common trouble spots and how to fix them.

Caulk cracks and gaps: Where you've got penetrations in walls and ceilings—from windows, doors, mouldings, plumbing, electrical and ventilation— you're likely to have gaps where air seeps in and out. Fill exterior cracks with flexible silicone or polyurethane caulking, which will expand and contract with temperature fluctuations (that's what you want—rigid caulking will crack). Latex caulk is great inside around window and door casings and baseboards since it can be painted.

Once you've got your caulking picked out (read the packaging—that's the only way to make sure you've got what you need), you'll need a caulking gun. The ones with a cradle for the caulk seem to hold the tube in more securely than guns designed with rails supporting the tube. Cut the tip of the caulk straight across: an angled tip limits the positions you can use to hold the caulking gun. Try to push caulk into the crack rather than dragging it, so there's a better chance the caulk will adhere. You can smooth out a bead of latex caulk with a finger made wet with spit (sorry, but it's true) or soapy water. If you make a mess of it—trust me, it happens—you can wipe away the caulk with a damp rag. If you're using a silicone caulk, you'll need a caulk tool (available at building supply stores) to smooth out the bead of caulk.

Cracks and gaps around windows draw out warm air you're paying to heat. Make sure to strip cracked sealant and clean the surface before you install fresh caulking.

Caulk windows: If you feel a draft when you're in front of a window, take a trip outside the house. If there's no caulking or the sealant is cracked or peeling, it needs to be replaced. Start by stripping away the old caulking. In some cases, you can use a sharp utility knife blade; in others, you might need to add a chemical caulk remover that softens old sealant and makes it easier to pull away with needle-nose pliers. Then clean the surface: if it's properly prepared and free of dirt and mildew, the new sealant will adhere better.

Since you'll be working outside, you need a caulk that says "exterior" right on the tube. On installation day, check the weather—you need a dry day that's above freezing, so this is a good project for the spring or fall. Caulk from top to bottom and move the caulking gun at a steady pace so the caulk line looks even. If the hole you cut in the caulking tube is too small for the caulk to seal the crack, don't add multiple lines; it's better to cut a larger hole in the tube. You want to caulk the top of the window (or door) where it meets the outside wall, as this is where water tends to pool. Don't fill the drain holes at the bottom of the window—these need to stay clear to let water drain. If you're not comfortable on a ladder—remember those second-storey windows need to be sealed, too—call a caulking contractor or ask the energy auditor to recommend someone to do the installation. It's not worth risking a fall.

You also need to caulk the interior of the window, which means sealing the edges of your trim. For this, you need paintable interior caulking like DAP. Don't try to caulk large holes or gaps around window or door casings: the caulking will dry and shrink, leaving you with holes. Instead, try using spray foam to fill the larger gaps, repair with drywall compound, or use foam backing rods before caulking.

Install foam gaskets in electrical outlets: Put your hand in front of an outlet on an exterior wall in the winter—if there is no vapour barrier around the outside of the box, or if it wasn't sealed properly, you'll feel cold air blowing in. These outlets are losing heat and allowing warm air to penetrate the wall, but you can reduce the heat loss—and still use the outlet—with foam insulating gaskets purchased for a few bucks from a building centre. Switch off the power to the outlet and remove the faceplate with a screwdriver. Insert the gasket, trimming away any foam that might block the socket, and replace the faceplate.

Seal the attic hatch: Once you've insulated the attic properly (see page 38), don't forget to seal the attic door. If your hatch sits directly on mouldings, it helps to add pieces of wood around the perimeter of the opening to operate as stops. These strips will provide a nice, wide surface where you can attach adhesive foam weatherstripping. The weatherstrip will get compressed (which is what you want) when you close the door, especially if you mount a hook-and-eye fastener to lock the door tightly shut. Put a piece of rigid foam board or fibreglass on the back of the door.

Replace old weatherstripping: Don't run out to replace a leaky front door—you might just need to replace its weatherstripping. The seals on any door will get torn, compressed or bent over time. It might not seem like much, but even a sliver of a gap around an exterior door is like punching a fist-sized hole in an exterior wall. Draft-proofing a door requires weatherstripping around the top and sides, and a door sweep along the bottom. Any hardware store will sell a selection of replacement seals in metal, foam, felt and plastic. The best picks are durable and made of a material with a compression memory so that the weatherstrip springs up when the door is open and seals tightly when the door is shut. It's important to measure correctly: you don't want any gaps, so measure twice and cut once.

You can tell if your door sweep needs replacing—you'll see daylight creeping in under the closed door or a little snow drift forming on the floor in the winter. When you're sealing the door threshold with a new sweep, follow the instructions on the product. Some people trim off the rubber strip at the bottom because they think it interferes with the way the door closes. The only problem is that, without this strip, the product can't seal properly—in order to get a good seal, there has to be a bit of resistance when closing the door.

CHAPTER THREE

DRYWALL

DRYWALLING LOOKS SO EASY, DOESN'T IT? YOU JUST HANG UP A BOARD, SLAP ON SOME MUD, AND IT'S BEAUTIFUL. BUT DESPITE APPEARANCES, THERE ARE ACTUALLY A LOT OF TRICKS TO DOING IT WELL.

Like many things in homebuilding, it's something of an art: you can't boil it down to simple rules. Hanging the board itself is fairly forgiving, as long as your framing has been done properly and the edges of your boards are well supported. You can leave small gaps between the sheets and then fill them before you start taping, so you don't need your joints to be perfect. It's not like finish carpentry, where everything has to fit perfectly: you just want to get that drywall on the wall. The taping and mudding are what will make it look perfect—or not.

The essential skill in hanging drywall is ensuring it's screwed in properly: every 12 inches along the ceiling and every 16 inches on a wall. Getting this right isn't too difficult if you're only putting up four or five sheets in a bathroom or small bedroom, but putting up 100 sheets in a basement is much more complicated—and a basement is exponentially easier than drywalling an entire home. Drywall actually assists in connecting and stabilizing the framing, so if you're going to start a job, it's not something you want to stop halfway through. Chances are you won't go back to it in a timely manner, and you can end up with warped walls and ceilings. So how do you make sure you don't end up with a half-finished project? Start, as always, with the planning.

Whatever you do, don't be tempted to start drilling or cutting into framing members. I know the drywall is the skin of the room, but behind those boards is the structure—posts, beams, lintels, ceiling joists, floor joists and load-bearing walls holding your house up. If you start tampering with the framing, you could end up compromising the structure of your home. I suggest you have a look at the previous chapter on framing so we can both sleep a little easier.

DRYWALL BASICS
DIFFICULTY: 6 OUT OF 10

If you scrape below the paint or wallpaper in your home, you'll probably find drywall underneath. It's what we attach to wood or metal framing to create smooth, firm finished walls and ceilings ready for priming and painting. Also called gypsum board or wallboard, it's made from gypsum (a calcium-based mineral that's also the main ingredient in plaster) covered with thick paper.

Walk through any building centre, and you'll see it lined up in sheets. The standard size is 4×8 feet $\times$ $\frac{1}{2}$ inch thick, but you can also get it in thicknesses from $\frac{1}{4}$ inch to $\frac{5}{8}$ inch and lengths up to 20 feet. You don't need to look for a specific brand—the drywall sold at major retailers is all pretty much the same. Most do-it-yourselfers will get the best price per sheet from 8-foot panels. Since some sheets weigh close to 50 pounds, it helps to work with a buddy.

CHOOSING DRYWALL

• **Regular drywall** is used to construct interior walls and ceilings.

• **Moisture-resistant drywall** (also known as green board) has been chemically treated to make the core moisture-resistant. It's good for humid areas such as bathroom walls, kitchen walls, basements, laundry rooms and utility rooms.

• **Soundproof drywall** is better at muffling sound. You would use it for ceilings and walls in apartments or condos.

• **Fire-resistant drywall** is better at reducing the spread of flames, so you'll find it in garage ceilings, stairwells and halls.

• **Paperless drywall**, such as DensArmor, is covered with fibreglass rather than paper. It's heavy and harder to work with, but it offers much more protection against mould and fire.

TOOLS AND MATERIALS YOU'LL NEED

- measuring tape
- T-square, pencil and utility knife for cutting panels
- 1¼-inch drywall screws
- corner bead (the metal edging used to finish outside corners)
- paper tape for inside corners
- self-adhesive mesh tape for flat joints
- metal-cutting snips for cutting corner bead
- 1½-inch drywall nails for installing corner bead
- drill with Phillips bit that fits drywall screws (or screw setter)
- hammer
- drywall saw or rotary tool for cutting around electrical boxes and recessed lights
- stepladders or drywall lift for installing ceiling panels
- sandpaper
- dust mask

MISTAKE #17:
FAILING TO FOLLOW THE RIGHT STEPS WHEN PLANNING AND INSTALLING

The first step in drywalling is planning out the room. Start by measuring the length and width and use your grade-school math skills—or your smartphone—to calculate how many sheets you'll need for the job. Remember that drywall sheets are laid horizontally on walls, and perpendicular to the joists on ceilings.

Choose the right size boards: Drywall is always 4 feet wide, and a standard sheet is 8 feet long. But you can get longer sheets: 9, 10, 12, 20 feet. These longer sheets allow you to have as few butt joints as possible. Butt joints are where two short ends come together. Along the long edges, sheets of drywall are slightly tapered, so when they come together, they leave a small channel for the drywall compound (or "mud"). But the short ends are flat, so these joints take more skill to mud properly.

Planning can help you avoid too many butt joints. For example, if your ceiling is 12 × 12 feet, you can use three 12-foot boards and have no butt joints at all—which is ideal. The one thing to watch out for: if you're doing a basement and you're working with a narrow staircase, like in many older homes, make sure you can get those longer boards downstairs. You don't want to be cutting all of your sheets before you bring them downstairs—we've had jobs where we've even had to cut 8-foot sheets to get them in. You're down there boarding with 4-foot sheets of drywall, which is not a lot of fun.

Stagger the sheets like bricks: When you're making your plan, if you can't avoid butt joints, you need to

The long edges of drywall sheets are tapered slightly. When placed together, they form a channel to hold the mud.

stagger the sheets in a brickwork pattern. So if you start in the corner with a full sheet, the next row starts with a half sheet; otherwise, the butt joints will extend all the way along the wall or ceiling, which will form a noticeable seam, even after the wall is painted. If you don't stagger them, you'll also have places where four sheets of drywall come together at a joint—you definitely don't want that.

Do the ceiling first: Always start by hanging drywall on the ceiling. Keep the boards perpendicular to the joists, just as you keep the boards perpendicular to the studs when you are putting up a wall. One of the reasons you do the ceiling first is that the sheets of drywall on the walls will then support the edges of the ceiling, so you get a tighter fit and it's easier to mud the corners.

No one wants to see your butt crack! A butt joint is formed from adjacent untapered edges.

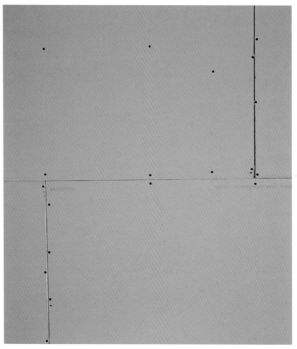

Stagger sheets of drywall in a brick pattern to reduce the length of each butt joint—the crack is more noticeable if it runs the whole length of the wall.

Finish walls from top to bottom: Once your ceiling is up, start at the top of the wall and work down. The reason for that is you don't want to make cuts at the ceiling. Let's say the height of your room is 8 feet. It may not be *exactly* 8 feet, and you may have to trim ½ inch off the width of one of the two 4-foot boards you're using. Because you're probably not going to make a perfectly straight cut, you want to have that cut along the bottom, where it will be covered up by the baseboard. (If you're doing crown moulding, this is less important, because the ceiling joint will be hidden as well, but I'd still recommend starting at the top.)

Hide joints in the least visible spots: If you have an 8-foot ceiling, things are nice and easy: you just stack

Hang drywall on the ceiling first: the sheets you hang on the walls will then support the edges of the ceiling. You'll end up with a tighter fit, and the corners will be easier to mud.

Always hang drywall from top to bottom. That way, if you make an uneven cut at the bottom, the baseboard will cover it. This is what you want to avoid—it will be a mudding job for a pro.

Plan ahead to avoid a vertical joint directly above the corner of a door frame. The constant opening and closing of the door could crack the joint.

two sheets, one on top of the other. But if you have a 9-foot ceiling, you have to use two 4-foot boards plus a 1-foot rip. Put the rip along the bottom to make that joint least visible. I've never understood why some people hang a full sheet at the top and another at the bottom and tuck a 1-foot piece in the middle—that's the most visible part of the wall! I say hide it at the bottom, where nobody's looking. That said, you'll see professional crews using a variety of methods. The key is finding the method that works best for you.

Mistake #18:
PUTTING A JOINT ABOVE A DOOR

Typically, when you're drywalling around a door, you don't want a full sheet butting up against one edge of the door—in other words, you don't want a butt joint directly above the corner of the door frame. With the constant opening and closing of the door, there will be movement, and there's a good chance that joint will crack. So try to plan ahead, but if you get to the door and realize you can't avoid it, you can adjust by cutting the drywall by the width of a stud or two.

There are other tricks you can use when drywalling around openings for doors or windows to make the job easier. If you're going around a doorway that has just been framed and there is no jamb installed yet (the jambs are the vertical pieces of the frame onto which the door is secured), just attach a whole sheet of drywall to the wall and then carefully cut around the door opening afterward. You don't even need to measure. If the jamb is already in place, then you have to measure and cut the sheet before hanging it.

If you're working on an interior partition wall and there's an opening, you can do the same thing. Just hang the full sheet, go around to the other side of the opening, and cut out the drywall from there.

If you're drywalling around a new doorway without a jamb (the vertical pieces of the frame), just attach a whole sheet of drywall to the wall and then carefully cut around the door opening— no measuring required. If the jamb is in place, then measure and cut the sheet before hanging it.

Mistake #19:
USING THE WRONG TYPE OF DRYWALL

There are many of kinds of drywall, but the most popular is a gypsum core faced with paper. Here's one item you don't really need to shop around for: all brands of drywall are going to do the job, so go for the best deal you can find. Your biggest choice will be size, which we've covered earlier, and thickness. A standard sheet of drywall is ½ inch thick, and that's good for most purposes. For a fire-rated wall between houses, you would use ⅝-inch boards. You can also get ¼-inch drywall for use on a rounded wall: use two layers of ¼-inch drywall instead of one layer of ½-inch so you can bend it.

The coatings on green board make it more moisture-resistant than standard drywall. It's not waterproof, though, so avoid using it around tubs and showers.

There are some specialty types of drywall for specific jobs. You've probably seen the drywall with green paper: it has been treated with coatings that make it more resistant to moisture than regular drywall. Most people assume that because it's moisture-resistant you can use it in the shower behind the tiles, but that's wrong. The shower enclosure needs to be completely waterproof before you put up tiles. Green board is water-*resistant*, not water*proof*. It's a better choice than regular drywall on the other walls and ceiling of a humid space like a bathroom, kitchen or laundry room, but don't use it as a backer board around a tub or shower, or you'll end up with mould. Once mould has damp conditions and a food source—organic materials like gypsum and paper—you're in trouble. For tubs and showers, I like Wedi building panels because they're light, waterproof and strong. (Wedi also manufactures complete custom shower kits.) Any backer board used for tile in a wet area needs to be completely waterproof and inorganic.

Paperless drywall, like DensArmor, is becoming more popular. Instead of paper, the surface is covered in fibreglass. It feels a little rougher than standard drywall—you have to sand or skim-coat the entire surface if you want a completely smooth finish—and the boards are a little heavier, but the fibreglass protects against rot and offers greater resistance to mould and mildew. Before painting, you should use a high-volume-solids primer. Unlike conventional base coats, this is a thick primer used to fill and hide minor surface imperfections. I built my last house using fibreglass board throughout. It's probably 25% more expensive and more difficult to work with, but it was worth it to me to know we'd have better resistance to mould and fire than we'd get with green board or standard drywall.

MISTAKE #20:
BEING A PERFECTIONIST ABOUT CUTS

Cutting lumber for millwork is all about precision. Measure twice, cut once—you know the saying—and don't forget to factor in the thickness of the blade. Sawing wood too short may leave you having to redo the cut—and piling up more wasted lumber than you'd care to think about. Drywall is different. You can use a drywall saw or a rotary cutter for internal cuts, but for straight lines, you can do the job just fine with a utility knife and a supply of really sharp drywall blades. You'll also need a measuring tape, a pencil and a T-square that's at least 4 feet long, the width of a sheet of drywall.

When you're making a straight cut on a sheet of drywall, line up the top section of the T with the top edge of the drywall, then run the utility blade along the edge of the T-square. Your cut doesn't have to be precise: if you measure a section of wall to be $47\,^5/_8$ inches, you can cut the drywall to $47\,^3/_8$ inches. This is not fine carpentry. Just get the sheet cut, screw it to the framing and then fill any gaps with mud.

MISTAKE #21:
SCREWING UP THE CUT-OUTS

When you encounter bulkheads and other obstructions, you're going to need to make notches in the drywall to work around them. One trick to measuring these cut-outs is to stand your sheet against the wall in the same orientation you'll be hanging it. Then measure around the bulkhead and transfer those measurements onto your sheet. If you try this when the sheet is upside down or turned around, you're likely to mark it in mirror image and cut it wrong. If it's too awkward, just draw yourself a picture to help you transfer the measurements onto the board itself more accurately.

If you're installing drywall over protruding pipes, place the sheet against the pipe and use a block of wood to tap the surface facing you. This will leave a dimple in the back of the sheet. When you pull the drywall away, you can use a rotary cutter (sometimes called a speed saw) to cut a hole along the dimple. Your other option is to measure to the centre of the opening, transfer the measurement to the sheet of drywall, draw a circle the correct size and cut it out with a drywall saw. But this is hard to do accurately!

I built my last house with paperless drywall. It's covered in fibreglass, so it protects against rot and fire better than standard drywall.

Making cut-outs for switches and outlets is a little different. In these cases, you measure the distance of the switch or outlet from the top and side of the board to the centre of the box, mark the centre on your sheet and then cut out the opening with a rotary cutter.

To cut out an electrical box, start by making sure that the breakers are shut off! Next, mark the centre of the opening on the sheet of drywall. Then stand up the sheet and lightly tack it in place with a couple of screws. The electrical box sticks out ½ inch, so the drywall board won't be flush with the studs. Use the rotary cutter to poke through the drywall at your mark, and then ease the cutter in one direction until you find the edge of the box. (If you're working with ½-inch drywall, you want your bit to extend only about ⅝ inch or maybe ¾ inch: if it goes 2 inches deep, you're liable to hit the wiring.) Trace the outside edge of the box until you've made the full cut-out. That piece will just pop out, and then the drywall will sit flush.

If you're putting in a ceiling with pot lights, cut out all of the openings as soon as you hang the sheet: don't just mark them and plan on cutting them out later. If the drywaller comes in to do the mudding, all of your marks will be covered, and you'll never find where you wanted to place your lights. Some pot lights are designed to extend slightly from the framing, like an electrical box, so they won't sit flat until you make the cut-out, but most pot lights don't protrude. Again, find the centre of the light and use a rotary cutter to poke through the drywall, slide it over until you find the edge of the fixture, and then cut around the outside of the pot light.

We once saw a house that had been drywalled without cutting out any of the heat registers. That's fine in theory—they had been marked out—and if you're mudding and sanding, it's sometimes better to leave the registers covered to prevent dust from getting into the ductwork. The problem was that the painter had come in and primed everything, so none of the markings were visible. In the end, we had to crank up the furnace and use an infrared camera to locate all the heat vents.

My best tip to prevent problems like this is to take pictures of the walls and ceilings before you start hanging drywall. If you happen to lose an electrical box or a pot light behind a sheet, and you can't find it just by measuring, a photo may allow you to avoid having to take the sheet off.

Before you make cut-outs for switches and outlets, turn off the power! Then measure the distance from the centre of the outlet box to the top and side of the board, and mark these on your sheet. Lightly screw the sheet in place. The electrical box sticks out 1/2 inch, so the sheet won't be flush with the wall. Use a rotary cutter to poke through the drywall at your mark, and then ease the cutter around until you find the edge of the box. Trace around the outside edge of the box until you've made the full cut-out. That piece will pop out, and then the drywall will sit flush.

Mistake #22:
TRYING TO DRYWALL A CEILING BY YOURSELF

Some experienced drywallers can hang a sheet on the ceiling by themselves. They take a couple of 2 × 4s and cut them about 2 inches shorter than the height of the room. Then they nail or screw a shorter piece of 2 × 4 to one end of each of the first boards, ending up with a pair of T-shaped pieces. They stand up one T, lift the piece of drywall into place on the ceiling, resting it on top of the T, and then use the other T to hold up the other end of the drywall. They don't stand the Ts perfectly straight on the floor, where they would be likely to fall over; they angle them so the drywall is level but the Ts are wedged tightly between the floor and the ceiling.

But as I said, that's what some experienced dry-wallers do. It's not something I would recommend to a do-it-yourselfer. It's too easy to end up with wallboard falling on your head or knocking you off a ladder.

Here's what I recommend instead: invite a buddy or two over, offer them pizza and beer, and get them to help hold the drywall in place while you put in a couple of screws. Failing that, you can rent a drywall lift. They're worth their weight in gold, especially if you're working on your own: you'll be able to do the work in about a quarter of the time. And it will save your neck, since you won't have to hold up the sheets with your head. Prevents a lot of swearing, too.

Mistake #23:
USING THE WRONG TECHNIQUE FOR CUTTING

You always want to cut the front of the drywall, not the back, so that the cleanest cut is on the front. If you tear any paper on the front, you have to cover the tear with mud or you'll see that rough paper on the finished wall—it's just work you don't need to do.

Sometimes when cutting drywall, people try to go all the way through the sheet with a knife. But you just have to score the paper and then hit or bend the board, and it will break along the scored line. (If you're trying to cut only an inch or so, you need to cut a little deeper.) It's a good idea to then run your knife along the paper on the back of the drywall to finish the cut—although experienced drywallers can detach the piece by slapping the piece in the other direction. Pros who have been drywalling for 20 years can cut pieces so fast, it would make your head spin.

The way you hold your knife is important, too: if it's perpendicular to the sheet, it will wobble all over the place. If you hold it at a less steep angle, you're more likely to keep it straight. You can practice on your scrap pieces if you want.

If you're cutting a long sheet and your T-square doesn't reach all the way, you can use a chalk line. Stretch the string out along your T-square, hold it taut, and then snap the string to leave a perfectly straight line of chalk marking your cut.

Mistake #24:
FASTENING THE SHEETS IMPROPERLY

You can use a regular drill with a Phillips head to put in drywall screws, but you have to be careful. If you drive the screw in too far and you break the paper, you risk cracking the gypsum beneath. So you don't want the screw to break through the paper, but it has to sink in far enough that you won't hit the screw head with your taping knife when you cover it with mud.

A drywall screw setter is an attachment that prevents you from inserting the screw too far: the bit automatically

Drywalling a ceiling alone (not recommended!) requires a couple of these homemade Ts made from 2 × 4s.

The T should be a little shorter than the height of the ceiling. Lean one T against the wall and place the sheet against it.

Lift the drywall into place on the ceiling as it rests on top of one T. Keep the drywall as level as possible.

Now place the second T under the opposite side of the drywall and slide the drywall into place. Then screw it to the framing. Adam dropped the board twice here, so again, doing a ceiling this way isn't easy. But it's better than leaving it unfinished!

Adam's cuts look clean even when he cuts the front of the drywall, not the back. If you tear any paper on the front, you'll have to cover that with mud, or you'll see the rough spot on the finished wall—it's just work you don't need to do. Don't try to cut all the way through drywall. Score the paper and then hit or bend the board so it breaks along that line. Run your knife along the paper backing to finish the cut.

USE THE RIGHT SCREWS	
Type of screws	**When to use**
1¼-inch screws	Installing ½-inch drywall on walls: holds securely without too much extra length; can be bought affordably in big tubs
1⅝-inch screws	Installing ⅝-inch drywall or ceiling drywall: the extra length gives additional strength against gravity
Coarse-thread drywall screws	Installing drywall to wood framing: large threads provide a strong hold
Fine-thread drywall screws	Installing drywall to steel framing: sharp points allow for easy penetration

disengages from the screw when it gets to the right depth. You can get one that fits on any drill. You could also rent an actual drywall gun that does the same thing. These help you put screws in a lot faster, which makes a big difference if you're working on a large space but might not be worth it for a small bathroom. You can even get drywall guns that you load with strips of screws, so it's multiple rapid-fire. But again, if you're hanging a few sheets, you can probably just use a regular drill and be careful about how deep you drive the screws.

Drywall screws come in many lengths with coarse or fine threading. The choice comes down to preference. A fine thread is good if you're going through metal studs, but other screws will work with both metal and wood. The standard for walls is 1¼-inch. The main danger is using screws that are too long. If you're covering a pocket door (one that slides into the wall cavity), then you don't want to use 2-inch screws, or they will go right into the door. Believe me, people do it. Another danger of using long screws is hitting plumbing or electrical lines running through the studs. While they should both be protected, you can't be sure, so better safe than sorry.

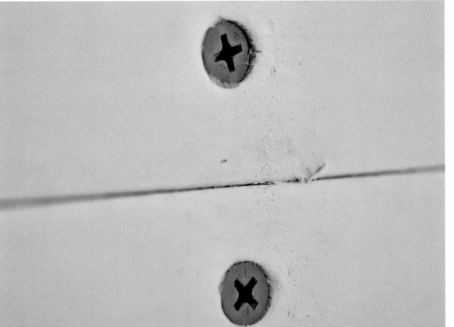

This drywall screw setter (*top*) prevents you from inserting the screw too far. If you don't have a setter, look to sink the screws through the drywall by about the width of a dime (*left*).

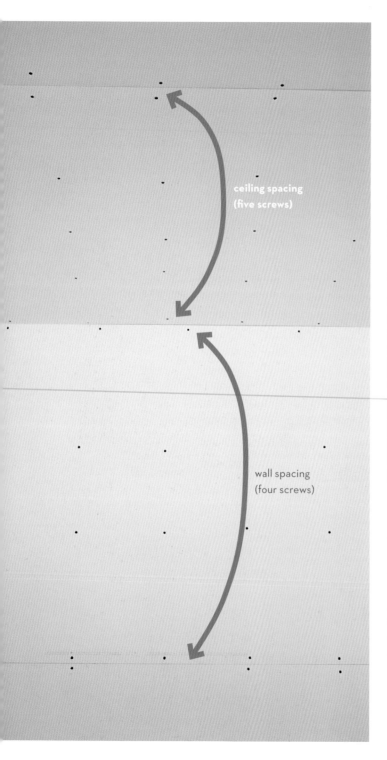

ceiling spacing
(five screws)

wall spacing
(four screws)

When attaching drywall to studs, insert a screw at each edge and two in between, each about 16 inches apart.

To fasten drywall to the ceiling, insert four to six widely placed screws, starting from the first joist in from the corner. Fasten the sides and ends first and then the middle.

After that, plan on five screws per 4-foot span on the ceiling, with a screw on each edge, one in the centre and one between the centre screw and each outer screw, all about 12 inches apart.

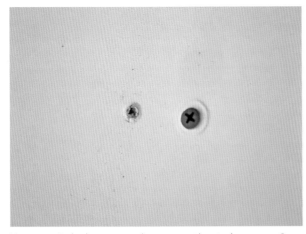

You weren't thinking it was okay to miss the stud, were you? I didn't think so.

When attaching drywall to studs, use four screws per 4-foot span: that's one at each edge and two in the middle about 16 inches apart. On the ceiling you should space the screws about 12 inches apart on each joist so you have five screws per 4-foot span: one on each edge, one in the centre and one between the centre screw and each outer screw.

To fasten a sheet to the ceiling, start with four to six widely spaced screws to take some of the weight off you and your buddy: fasten the sides and the ends first, then do the middle. This is not a science, but what usually happens is you put in a couple of screws while your buddy is taking all the weight on the head—swearing and trying to get another screw in to take the weight off—so the screw just ends up wherever it lands and hopefully doesn't miss the joist. (Then you realize you forgot to mark a pot light, so you have to take it down and start over.)

Which brings up another point: before you hang the sheets on the ceiling, you want to make sure you know where the joists are because you won't be able to see them once you have the drywall in place. Locating the joists on the ceiling is easy: look for the screws

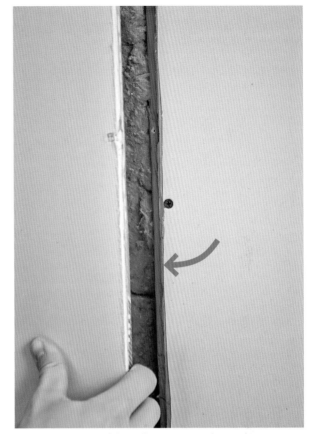

Where two pieces of drywall meet at a stud, you've got a 1½-inch face of stud behind the joint, which leaves just ¾ inch per sheet (*above, arrow*). Be careful! Putting the screw too close to the board edge will crush the gypsum.

on the adjacent piece of drywall! If you're putting up drywall on an exterior wall that's insulated, put a black mark on the vapour barrier along the ceiling that will stick out beyond the drywall sheet; then when you hold up the sheet, you can put in a screw where the black mark is. (At the other end of the sheet, you will see the studs or joists extending, so you can just put in a screw there.) You should be able to eyeball the other screws. You'll know if you miss the framing because the screw will go right through the sheet with no resistance. Just pull it out and try again. You can always mud those empty screw holes.

In the corners, if you've done your three-stud corner properly (see Mistake #8, page 24), you'll have 1½ inches of backing for both sheets. But since you're putting one sheet perpendicular to the other, one of the boards will have the full 1½-inch backing, and the other one will have only an inch, but that's enough.

If two pieces of drywall meet at a stud, then you have only a 1½-inch face of stud behind the joint, which is only ¾ inch per sheet. You have to be careful not to put the screw in too close to the edge of the board, or you'll crush the gypsum, so the screw needs to be at a slight angle to make sure you're engaging the wood. Do your best not to break through the paper, though a lot of the time you won't be able to avoid that—just put in another screw a couple of inches away to make sure the board is secure.

If your framing is crowned (that is, the studs have a slight bow) and you're trying to suck a piece of drywall in so it sits flush on the stud, some of the screws are going to break through the paper. You can even end up with five or six screws in a row all trying to hold that board in place. Don't worry—over time the drywall will lose some of its flex, and it will stop resisting.

The important thing is to make sure the sheets are secured to the framing in the corners and at the joints. They don't have to look pretty—you could have a ½-inch gap between them. That's not ideal for the person doing the taping, but it'll work. You can fill that gap with a pre-coat of mud before taping and mudding. But you do want a little bit of a gap between the sheets at the butt ends so the mud can get in and hang on to that joint. If there isn't space, you'll end up with a very thin coat of mud that is susceptible to movement and cracking along the joint.

MISTAKE #25:
MAKING BAD CORNERS

After you've fastened your drywall, but before you start taping, you'll need to install corner bead. This is the long L-shaped piece that caps the outside corner. Corner bead also adds reinforcement so the corners of your room are less likely to get dented or damaged when you bump them with a chair.

There are many different kinds of corner bead. The screw-on metal type is what is usually used and is probably the strongest, although if you hit the metal with something, you'll end up with a dent that's there to stay. For a rounded corner, we will use plastic, which is glued on.

The key with corner bead is to put it in and make

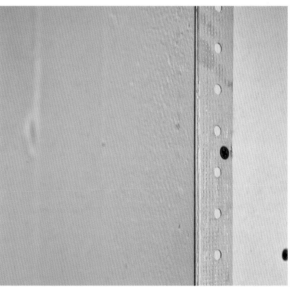

Metal or plastic L-shaped pieces of corner bead are used to cap and reinforce outside wall corners—the ones you can bump into. I prefer metal corner bead secured with screws because it's the strongest, though it will dent if you hit it. If we're doing rounded corners, we'll glue on plastic corner bead. The key is to make sure the corner bead is slightly raised so it sits a little farther out than the rest of the wall. That way, there's space for the mud.

sure the corner itself is slightly raised so it sits a little farther out than the rest of the wall. That way there's space for the mud. You want to create an acute angle with the corner trim, meaning that the finished corner will be slightly less than 90 degrees. The way to get the angle right is by slightly pinching the metal band so the outside corner spreads and is not actually in contact with the drywall.

If you have to use two pieces of corner bead, just cut them with tinsnips. When you butt the two pieces together, make sure they're not overlapping, or that joint will be visible. One trick is to put a small piece of corner bead behind the two larger pieces to help keep them aligned. Plastic corner bead often has tabs to link them together.

Metal corner bead has large holes all along its length, but those are not where you put the screws—those are for the mud. Look for the smaller holes along the edge: those holes are where you put the screws.

For inside corners, the pros use paper tape, which has a scored line in the middle indicating where to crease it to form the corner. But if you're doing a small area, a great option is to buy paper-faced corner bead: it's available in both inside and outside corners. Although it's a little more expensive, it creates a very crisp line so is a great way to make your inside corners look perfect.

Whether you're using tape or paper-faced metal corner bead, put a thin layer of mud in the corner, push the paper against it and then use your knife or trowel to gently smooth the paper into place and squeeze out the excess mud. If using the paper-faced corner bead, apply mud in a thin but uniform layer, about 2 inches out from the inside corner. Embedding the paper in mud holds the metal corner in place. Let it dry fully before you go over it with the next coat of mud.

Professionals can take a whole roll of tape, run it through some watered-down mud and then slap it on the wall and smooth it out immediately. But that's messy as hell, and if it's your first crack at this, that technique will cause nightmares. You're better off just using some setting compound (more on this later) to hold the tape in place.

CORNER JOINTS

Outside corners: The joints where two walls form an external angle, or one you can walk around.

Inside corners: The points where two walls form an internal angle, as in the corner of a room.

MISTAKE #26:
THINKING MUDDING AND TAPING IS AS EASY AS IT LOOKS

Mudding walls is an art. It's also a lot more difficult than it looks, so unless you're doing a very small area or you have a lot of expertise, I suggest hiring a professional. You can hang the drywall, and you can prime and paint afterward, but get a pro to do the mudding and taping. To do a small basement will cost about $1,500. Trust me on this—that $1,500 will make you look like a DIY star.

That said, some pros won't do the mudding if you've installed the drywall yourself, or they'll charge you extra. That's because if you've done a poor job of hanging the drywall—screws sticking out, joints not lined up, corner bead not on properly—they will have to fix all that stuff before they tape.

Typically, the first coat is a setting compound. (On the job we just call this 90, because it dries in about 90 minutes.) Setting compounds are faster-drying, harder compounds that help prevent shrinkage and cracking. Use a drywall trowel to fill any large gaps in the corners or joints with mud and let it set so you've got some backing for your future coats. If you've got areas around electrical outlets that have big chunks of drywall cut out, put 90 in there as well. Less is more on your setting coat: you don't want to use too much. After your first coat, you should not have to sand—your goal here is to create a flat surface

It sounds obvious, but start by reading the label: it'll tell you exactly how much water to use (*photo 1*). When you're mixing the mud, add dry to wet: measure the water into a bucket (*photo 2*), then add the powder (*photo 3*). If you add wet to dry, the compound is going to be lumpy. Mix it with a mixing paddle and a strong mixing drill (*photo 5*). If you don't have a mixing paddle and drill, you can use a large paint stick or something similar to mix by hand—but don't forget, you want the mixture perfectly smooth with no lumps, about the consistency of heavy whipped cream. This stuff starts to set up the more you work it, so stir it only as much as needed to get the right consistency.

Believe me, taping and mudding is harder than it looks. On inside corners, crease the paper tape to give it a nice, sharp edge. I mix drywall compound to different consistencies depending on what I'm using it for. To fill holes, I mix it a little stiffer—like cake icing. When I'm taping in the corners, I make the compound like pudding so I can squeeze it out and set the paper into it. Feather out the edges as you mud.

while applying a thin layer of compound, not to use the entire container and spend hours sanding it smooth! If you do end up with some globs, use a trowel and taping knife to knock or scrape them off. As we say to novices, "It's called mudding and taping, not sanding and scraping."

You can also get setting compounds that harden in 45, 20 and 5 minutes. You're not going to do a whole room with 20: it will set before you have a chance to smooth it out. But on a Friday afternoon, if you're doing a little repair and you need to do a coat or two quickly, 20 is the way to go.

Be careful when you're mixing setting compound. If you mix too much, it will dry before you have a chance to use it, so you want to mix only a little at a time. You might think you can just add more water if the compound starts to harden, but that won't work for more than a minute or two. When you're first mixing the water and powder, the more you stir, the quicker it will cook, so stir it only as much as you need to get it to the right consistency.

It takes a while to get a feel for mixing any kind of drywall compound. You don't want it to be too stiff or too runny, but the right consistency depends on what task you're doing. If you're filling holes and gaps, you don't want it sliding off your trowel. It needs to be a little stiffer, like icing for a cake. But if you are using it to attach tape in the corners, the mud should be a little more runny—more like pudding—so you can squeeze it out and set the paper into it.

When mixing the mud, add dry to wet—in other words, pour the powder into a bucket of water. If you put all the powder in a bucket and then pour in water, it's going to be lumpy. All the bags tell you exactly how much water to use, so follow the instructions carefully. The pros can just eyeball it, but if you're a novice,

To hold the mud while I work, I use a hawk, a square of sheet metal with a handle. Use a trowel or taping knife (it looks like a spatula) to scrape mud from the hawk.

you'll want to measure at least the first few times. You can buy ready-mixed drywall compound in a pail or in boxes—the mud itself is in a plastic bag—but that's not first-coat stuff. You can also buy ready-mixed compound in buckets, but you'll need to add water to get a smooth consistency—again, not for the first coat. If you were to use that as your setting compound, it would probably crack.

Cover all the screw holes at the finish coat stage. Look for protruding screws and give them a tap to make them flush.

It doesn't matter if you work one by one or throw mud on three or four at a time as long as you plug those holes and smooth everything out.

Scrape off the excess mud and feather the edges.

Paint will highlight all the rough spots, so pay attention!

When you're applying the compound, you can use a large trowel or a taping knife, which looks like a spatula. The knife is easier for beginners to use, but a wide trowel will be faster if you know what you're doing. It also helps to have something like a drywall mud pan, which is a personal 12- or 14-inch trough for holding and scraping compound. Or you can get a hawk, which is a square piece of sheet metal with a handle. It's a bit like an artist's palette, but instead of dipping your brush into paint, you use the hawk to supply your trowel or knife with mud.

Three coats are usually necessary: the first is your setting compound, used to fill in your big holes and set the tape and corner bead (use the 90 here). The second coat, called your fill coat, is where you fill in the divot at your factory edges. For this, use an all-purpose drying compound, which hardens through evaporation (you'll need to wait about 24 hours between coats) and isn't as strong as a setting compound. Then there's the finish coat. Manufacturers make light and ultra-light compound for this last coat. Honestly, if you're doing only one job, you probably won't notice any difference between the two. But pros who have been taping for many years sometimes prefer the ultra-light for the finish coat.

For joints in the middle of a wall, you can use paper tape or fibreglass mesh tape, which acts like rebar—it strengthens the drywall compound. Fibreglass tape is self-adhesive, so you don't need to put a setting coat of mud on before attaching it: just put the mud on top when doing the fill coat.

On a butt joint (where there is no taper like on a factory edge), cover the first setting coat and extend it maybe 6 inches on each side of the joint. After that compound sets, you will have to sand it lightly just to get rid of the really rough spots. At this point you don't need to sand it to feather the edges at the joints (see Mistake #27, below).

For your third coat, or your finish coat, you're going to extend that butt joint about a foot on each side using the all-purpose compound. And at the factory edges, just fill in that trough and feather the compound out a little.

Make sure you cover all the screw holes at the finish coat stage. The pros will often just throw a line of mud across the wall and get three or four screws all at the same time, but I've noticed homeowners often just coat one screw at a time. It makes no difference as long as you cover those holes and smooth everything out. The paint will highlight all the rough spots you'll wish you'd paid more attention to.

MISTAKE #27:
SANDING TOO MUCH

Some sanding is inevitable, but you really want to do as little as possible. Use a very light touch when sanding mud. Don't even think about using a palm sander or any kind of power tool. Just use a sanding block and move lightly in a circular motion, feathering out so the joint kind of disappears at the edges. (To sand the ceiling or higher spots on the wall, it helps to have a sanding pole.) You might start with 80-grit sandpaper, and 120 is probably as fine as you need to go. Primer is pretty thick, so it's going to fill in those micro scratches. When you think you're finished, shine a lamp on the walls and ceiling to highlight any dings or pits.

You never want to sand the face of the drywall—you don't want to damage the paper. If you do, you need to cover it with mud again.

Any time you sand, wear a mask and turn your furnace off. Cover up the return air ducts, or your furnace will suck in all that dusty air and distribute it throughout

Fibreglass mesh tape strengthens the drywall compound, so it's best for joints in the middle of a wall. It's self-adhesive, so just roll it out like normal tape over all your joints. I like to use the handle of my trowel to hold the tape so it unrolls smoothly then cut the tape off using the blade. Do one thicker pass of mud to fill the crevices, and then smooth it out.

your house. Also cover any door openings with plastic. If the room has an external window, you can put a fan in the window blowing outside to create some negative pressure that will suck the dust out.

By the way, don't get too excited if your building supply store sells "dust-free" compound. It sounds great, but it's not completely dust-free: it's just made of slightly heavier material that settles to the ground faster.

MISTAKE #28:
CLUMSY DRYWALL REPAIRS

There are a few different ways to patch drywall. Let's say your teenager has put his fist through the wall. Cut a square piece of drywall that is bigger than the hole; hold the square over the damage and trace it on the wall; and then cut out the piece of wall marked by the trace line. The square of drywall will fit perfectly in the square hole you've just cut and removed. You can put some backing—either a couple of shims, drywall repair clips or 2 × 2s—inside the hole and screw it to the framing on each side. Then insert your new piece and screw it to the backing.

Another trick is to take your newly cut patch and cut around the paper only on the back, so the paper on the front is larger than the actual patch itself. You can mud the wall and embed that paper instead of using tape. Then you don't need backing. However, in the time it takes to master this trick, you could probably do three patches with backing!

One other way to patch is to use drywall repair clips, which actually stick on the drywall. What you do is cut a rectangle around the hole to remove the damaged section. Make the edges straight with a utility knife. Then attach each of the clips to a corner of the remaining drywall, making sure the two spring tabs on each clip face out. To cut a new piece of drywall that fits neatly into the opening, trace the piece you removed and cut it out. To secure the new piece, drive two drywall screws into each mounting clip. With pliers, pull the tab off each clip. Now you're ready to mud, tape, sand and paint.

If you've got a really large damaged area, you can cut the drywall from stud to stud. Find the studs using a stud finder, then just cut back to them so you still have ¾ inch, or half of the stud, to use as backing. Then attach a new piece of drywall.

Remember, any time you're replacing a square piece of drywall, you're going to end up with four butt joints. It takes some skill to feather out those seams so they're not visible after you paint. You will probably need to apply two or three coats of mud, feathering out at least 12 inches: the farther out you go, the less you're going to see. Then, of course, you'll need to sand before you prime and paint.

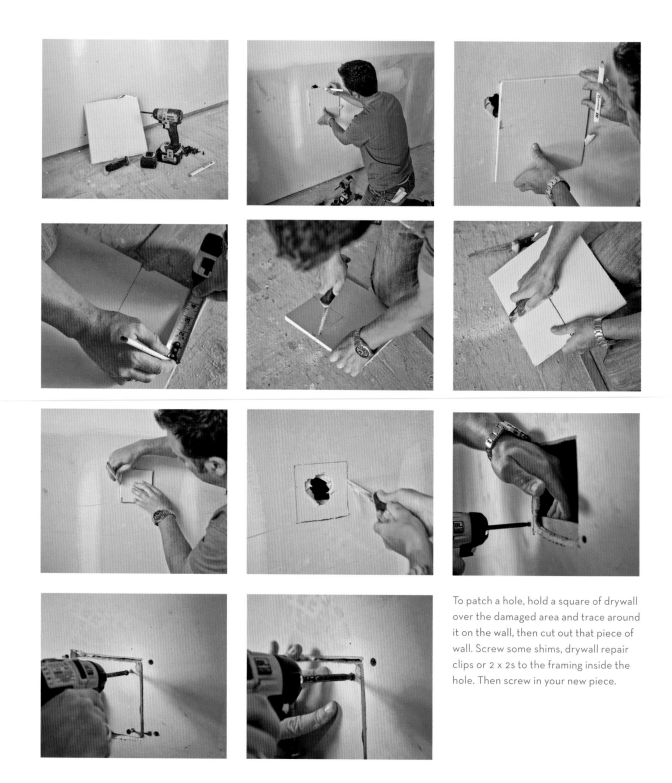

To patch a hole, hold a square of drywall over the damaged area and trace around it on the wall, then cut out that piece of wall. Screw some shims, drywall repair clips or 2 x 2s to the framing inside the hole. Then screw in your new piece.

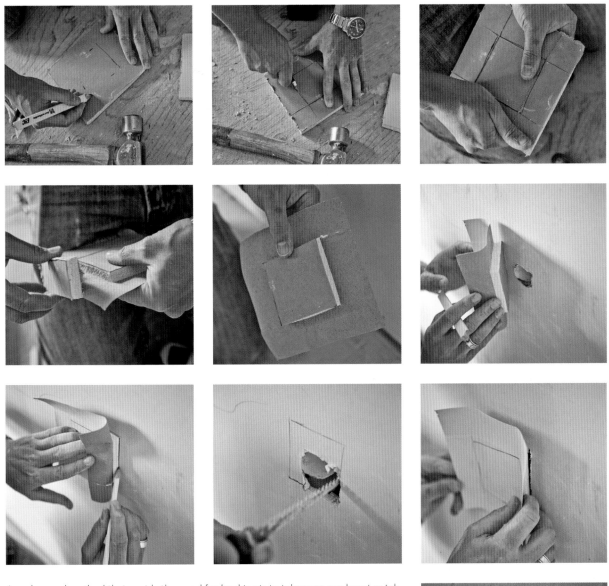

An advanced method that avoids the need for backing is to take your newly cut patch and cut around the paper only on the back so the paper on the front is larger than the patch. Instead of using tape, mud the wall, embedding the extra paper.

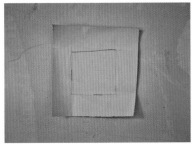

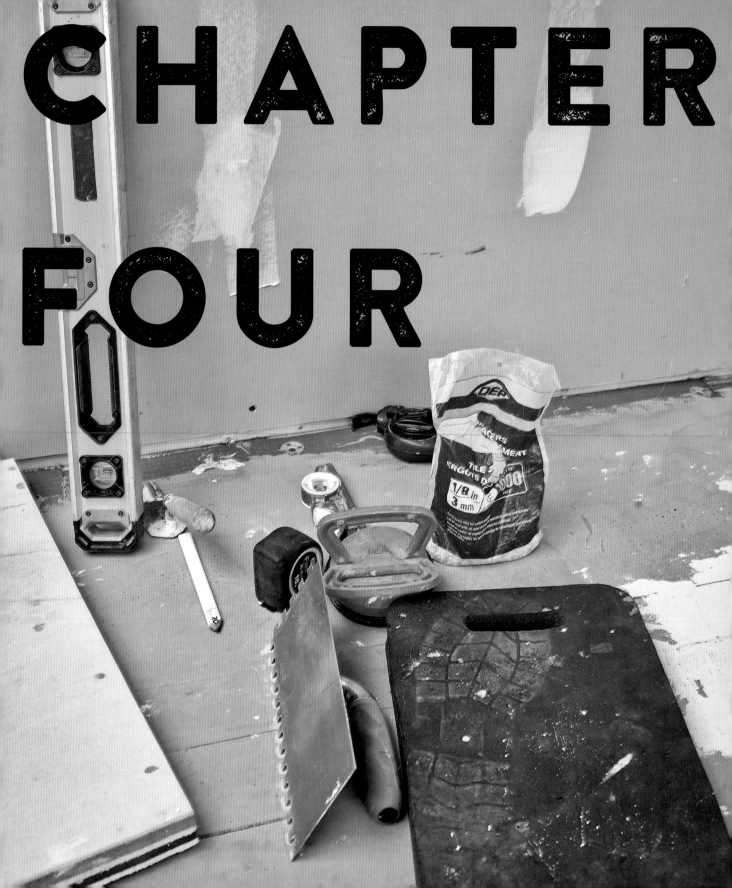

CHAPTER FOUR

FLOORING AND TILING

THERE ARE A LOT OF DIFFERENT TYPES OF FLOORING THESE DAYS. BEFORE YOU DECIDE WHICH ONE IS RIGHT FOR YOUR NEXT PROJECT, IT HELPS TO KNOW WHAT YOU'RE GETTING SO YOU CAN MAKE AN INFORMED CHOICE.

Ceramic and porcelain tile stand up to high-traffic areas like a bathroom, kitchen or entranceway. Ceramic is typically cheaper than porcelain though not quite as strong since porcelain is denser and fired at higher temperatures. Natural stone tile costs more, but nothing compares to the look and feel of marble, limestone, slate and travertine. Tiles can feel cold, but you can put heating mats directly underneath for radiant warmth.

Laminate floors are made to look like hardwood. The surface is created from a detailed photograph of hardwood. The core of laminate flooring is medium-density fibreboard (MDF), which is made from wood scraps bound together with adhesives. Laminate is the least expensive option, although price and quality vary according to brand.

Then you've got natural, beautiful hardwood. Typically, you'll see ¾-inch-thick boards of oak or maple in 3- or 5-inch strips. You can also find specialty woods, from ash and walnut to reclaimed barn board. Each one has its own look in terms of colour and graining, and some are harder than others. There's even bamboo, which is technically a grass but has the same hardness as oak.

Engineered hardwoods are becoming more popular. These have a ⅛-inch veneer of real hardwood applied to a base of MDF or plywood, a more stable base than solid hardwood. Engineered woods are moisture-resistant and won't shrink or expand as much as solid hardwood. Plus, you get the look of real wood and better performance for about the same cost. Both engineered and laminate floors can be installed as floating floors, which means they don't need to be nailed or glued to the subfloor.

FLOORING AND TILING BASICS

DIFFICULTY: 9 OUT OF 10

You might see a style of flooring that you love the look of, but you need to think beyond aesthetics. If flooring isn't suited to the conditions you're subjecting it to, you'll run into problems. A glossy, non-textured tile on a front porch will be too slippery whenever it rains or snows. A big Labrador retriever might be able to scuff cheap laminate with its claws. Hardwood looks great, but I would never put it in a basement because it swells in moist, humid conditions.

CHOOSING FLOORING					
Material & cost (/sq. ft.)	Pros	Cons	DIY degree of difficulty	Tools & materials	Where to install
Ceramic tile ($1 to $8)	Durable, long-lasting, inexpensive; waterproof; easy to maintain; easier than porcelain to cut	Cold; hard on the legs; harder to install than laminate or hardwood	8.5	• Measuring tape • Framing square • Chalk line • Safety glasses • Rubber gloves • Knee pads • Buckets • Drill and mixing paddle • Spray bottle • Trowel • 2 × 4 • Rubber mallet • Sponges • Tile cutter • Tile nipper • Grout and grout float • Tile spacers • Thin-set mortar for ceramic or porcelain • Painter's tape • Grout haze/film remover • Cheesecloth	Almost everywhere: kitchen, bathroom, entryway, laundry— anywhere with moisture; can use below grade
Porcelain tile ($2 to $12)	Dense, durable, long-lasting, non-porous, waterproof; easy to maintain	Same as above	8.5	Same as above; use mortar specifically made for porcelain	Same as ceramic

Natural stone ($5 to $12+)	Natural, luxurious; some more durable (slate, granite) than others (marble)	Most are porous—absorb moisture, spills, stains; require sealing for protection (how often depends on traffic); among the hardest to install	8	Similar to above, plus: • Thin-set, modified and unmodified • Penetrating stone sealer • Sanded grout	Same as ceramic, plus often used in hallways or around a fireplace
Hardwood ($6 to $15)	Natural, beautiful; durable: can be sanded and refinished numerous times for long lifespan; available in dozens of types of wood, finishes, etc.	Not suitable for basements; expands and contracts with temperature fluctuations; poor moisture tolerance; floor may squeak over time	7	• Measuring tape • Tapping block • Nail set • Chalk line • Hammer/nail gun • Floor mallet • Level • Saws (mitre, table, jig saw, jamb saw) • Countersink bit • Flooring nails • Wax paper or felt paper • Drill with 1/16" bit • Transition strips	Living room, dining room, bedroom; kitchen if you're careful about mopping up spills
Engineered hardwood ($5 to $20)	Moisture-resistant; combines beauty/durability of hardwood surface with strong engineered base; more installation options (can be floating floor or nailed/stapled in place); depletes fewer forests than solid hardwood	Can be sanded only once (veneer is not as thick as solid hardwood)	7	Same as hardwood for nail installation; for floating floor, you don't need nails, but you do need: • 6-mil poly sheeting • Foam underlayment • Adhesive • Transition strips • Flooring filler	Same as hardwood, plus basements
Laminate ($3 to $10)	Very affordable; floating, click-together floor is easy to install; best-quality laminate can last up to 25 years; resembles hardwood, stone or ceramic	Not recommended for bathrooms or other damp areas; can't be refinished; poor-quality is less resistant to scratches, etc.	6	• 1/4" spacers • Adhesive • Foam underlayment • Carpenter's square • Utility knife • Safety glasses • Saw (circular, table and/or jig saw) • Pull bar • Chalk line • Hammer • Measuring tape • Tapping block • Level	Living room, dining room, hallway, bedroom

MISTAKE #29:
USING CHEAP FLOORING

Lots of homeowners tell me they love the look of solid hardwood. But when they see the price tag, they discover their budget for a bedroom or a living room renovation wasn't as generous as they'd imagined. Suddenly, their love of hardwood turns into a search for entry-level laminate as a way to save a few bucks and leave enough for a new sofa, rug and crown moulding. I'm all for sticking to a budget, but not when it means choosing a poor-quality product. Get the hardwood and save up for the sofa next year.

Laminate varies massively in quality. You can find it from 6 mm thick right up to 16 mm or more. Usually the thickness and cost are a good indicator of quality in terms of how easy it will be to install, how uniform the pieces are and how the surface looks and feels. Some brands are extremely resilient and resistant to moisture and scratches, which makes them a good option for someone with kids or pets. Because laminate floors are floating floors (meaning that they are not nailed down and are relatively easy to install, uninstall and reinstall), they are also the best choice for homeowners looking for an interim floor. If you decide to put the laminate somewhere else, you can pull it all up without damaging the floor.

Be wary of the very cheap laminates, though, because the off-gassing can be worse with lower-quality products. Materials that contain chemicals (e.g., adhesives) can release volatile organic compounds (VOCs) into the air over time—you don't want to be breathing that stuff. If you're buying something for $0.69 a square foot, it's probably not made of healthy stuff—it's repackaged garbage. Laminate is graded for quality: good, better and best. Ask the salesperson about the manufacturing process—high-pressure

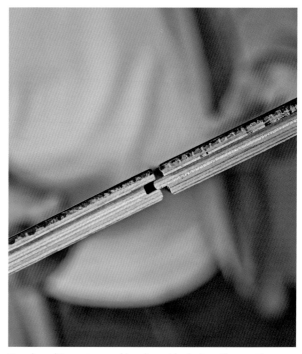
Good-quality engineered hardwood locks together easily.

laminate is often of better quality than direct pressure. Check out the sample in the store—the good stuff locks together seamlessly and easily without gaps or buckling. Examine the pattern on the surface—more variety typically means a more natural look. Expect to pay $8 per square foot and up for higher-grade products.

You will definitely notice the difference between good-quality laminate and cheap laminate when it comes to installation. If you choose the product that is $2 a square foot over the one that is $6, you might save money, but it's going to cost you a lot of pain and require more tools. That four bucks a square foot is going to beat you up! Your knees and hands are going to hurt because you'll be kneeling while hammering on a tapping block to force the pieces to click together properly. You'll also need a knife to trim off the shreds and burrs of MDF you'll find stuck in the channels. The good stuff is manufactured and finished at a higher quality, so you won't find bits that need to be trimmed or removed before the planks can click together cleanly. It's not just the financial cost—there's the human cost to consider. Working with poorly made laminate is like trying to learn how to play guitar on a cheap instrument: your fingers get shredded. That's just the way of the world: more expensive materials tend to be easier to install. With good-quality laminate, you may be able to install it with nothing more than a pencil and a chop saw (also called a mitre saw), which is a motorized saw that makes it easy to cut multiple pieces of wood. As with any of the tools I talk about, you can get one at a building supply centre.

Sheet vinyl is another cheap, quick option if you've just moved in somewhere and can't afford your dream floor just yet. The same goes for an income property you're renting out. Vinyl surfaces can take a bit of neglect. You can wander in and out wearing your shoes without worrying about dirt or scuffs. Sheet vinyl is sold in 6- and 12-foot widths, so you can cover a smaller room with vinyl and make it seamless.

Sheet vinyl gets installed much like carpet: in one big piece (or more if the dimensions of the room are larger). First, you have to remove any obstructions such as a toilet. There are two ways to cut sheet vinyl. The first is to measure the floor area, cut the vinyl 3 inches wider than the space on all sides and then trim the vinyl after you lay it in place. This works best in rooms with a simple shape and few obstacles to work around. If your space has lots of recesses or angles, you can make a template of your room on builders' paper and then transfer it to the vinyl to mark and cut. Either way, know that the flooring will expand, so leave about ⅛ inch of space between the wall and

Engineered hardwood (*top*) maintains the beauty and durability of traditional solid ³/₄ inch hardwood (*bottom*) but can also be installed as a floating floor and in moisture-sensitive areas like basements.

the new flooring. Vinyl is attached to a subfloor with adhesive, which you apply with a trowel. Then you nail the baseboard to the wall. If the vinyl flooring is in a bathroom, caulk around the edges of the baseboard by the bathtub and toilet to keep water out.

Probably the cheapest way to cover a big area of floor is carpet. On the one hand, I love carpet: it reminds me of my childhood when I spent hours on my hands and knees playing with toys. It's still popular in rooms where you want some warmth, such as bedrooms. But not all carpets are ideal over the long term. Like laminate, they can off-gas. Chemical finishes and fire retardants are woven into the fibres, backing and underlayment to help repel stains and dirt. Fumes from these chemicals can trigger headaches, nausea or issues with asthma or respiratory illness.

Even with stain resistance, carpets inevitably get dirty. Sure, you can have them cleaned, but anything that gets through the carpet ends up in the underlayment, which you can't always get at. Carpets are not great in areas with moisture, and they can trap mould, so don't carpet an entranceway, bathroom or kitchen.

One more thing: don't even think about laying carpet yourself. The carpet has to be stretched properly, and that requires special tools. It has to be fastened around the room just the right way, and you will want to make sure the seams don't show. It really is a specialized skill. By the time you buy or rent the tools and wrestle that giant roll into the room, get the tacking strips down (those are the wood strips pre-nailed with pins that grip and secure a carpet in place) and figure out where to cut the corners when you're working with a giant fold—it's not worth it. If you cut carpet or sheet vinyl too short, you're done. Suddenly your cheap fix isn't so cheap.

MISTAKE #30:
OVERESTIMATING YOUR DIY SKILLS

If you're going to be installing your own flooring, it's important to consider your skill level when you're choosing which type of flooring to buy. Overestimating your skills can cause a lot of headaches down the line. Be realistic, or the end result will not match your expectations.

Floating laminate and engineered hardwood floors are very popular with do-it-yourselfers, and they're relatively easy to install. Some people do real hardwood themselves, too, but you need to have decent carpentry skills to do a hardwood floor well. Installing individual pieces in the middle of the floor is not that difficult, but when you get to the edge and you need to finish it and trim it, it's very difficult to make it look professional. You don't want to spend $10 or $12 a square foot on material and then install it yourself and have it look like hell. It's just such a waste.

It's hard to determine what level of quality a homeowner is shooting for. If you want to walk into a bathroom and say, "Wow, I feel like I'm staying at the Ritz-Carlton," it's going to be a professional-level, painstaking and expensive installation. If you want to walk into the bathroom and say, "It looks nice, nothing is cracking, and it looks like Uncle Bill did it," that's a different story. If you're looking for a world-class installation, you need to make sure those floors are perfectly level and flat and every wall tile in the shower sits perfectly plumb.

I like to install my own tile. When we've built our own houses, I've always tiled my bathroom floors myself because every morning, I'm going to be in there feeling the floor with bare feet, and if I feel even the tiniest edge of a tile, it will drive me nuts, so I want to make it absolutely perfect. So if you're like me, save yourself the annoyance of a hack job and hire a pro.

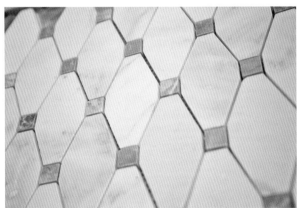

Laying 12 × 12 tiles in a grid is something many DIYers can handle. But if you want your bathroom to feel like a fine hotel, you're going to need a professional—and expensive—installation.

You need some skill and experience if you're going to install your own tile. The difficulty level depends on the number, size and arrangement of the tiles and what they're made of. Laying one 12 × 12 tile is easy, but laying 20 of them in exactly the same plane is tricky. It can take 15 or 20 minutes to install one tile—you're not just throwing them down. Ceramic tile is the easiest to install. Porcelain looks good, but it's really difficult to cut. You need a tub saw (also known as a wet saw) with a diamond blade, and there are a lot of tricks to learn. It's also very hard to drill through. I'm not sure why

people choose porcelain; you can often get ceramic tile that looks exactly the same, and it's a lot easier to work with.

Keep in mind larger tiles are more difficult to work with than smaller tiles, because they're less forgiving. When one corner moves, the opposite corner moves as well. Plus you need the tile to sit at the proper height off the subfloor to match the one next to it—it's a challenge. If you want to try tiling, start with a backsplash. The tiles are typically smaller, and often they come in sheets, so they are manageable, and you won't be working with a giant space.

In my experience, it's easiest to lay tile in a grid pattern. As soon as you start offsetting the tiles in a brick or subway pattern, tile placement really gets critical. If one tile is too high, the next one has to come up to meet it; the adjacent tile could be low in the middle but high on the ends. It can get out of control very quickly.

You can also make your installation easier with some prep. The flatter the surface you begin with, the easier it is to do an installation. When you have a floor with high and low spots, you have to fix the unevenness by varying the amount of mortar you use and how high off the floor you're setting the tiles. That's pretty difficult, and it takes a lot of practice to get it right. If, after reading this, you're still up for the challenge of tiling, keep reading for more information about how to avoid common tiling installation errors.

MISTAKE #31:
THINKING WOOD FLOORS DON'T WORK IN KITCHENS OR BATHROOMS

As I mentioned off the top, choosing the right type of flooring has a lot to do with where you want to put it.

Hardwood is becoming more popular in kitchens. It comes in so many finishes, and it looks great when you carry a single type of flooring through an open-concept house. But some people won't put hardwood floors in a kitchen because they're worried about water damage. I think these people are missing out.

It's true moisture can cause problems for hardwood. If we want to get scientific about it, the cell structure of wood allows it to take on and give off moisture depending on humidity in the home. When the air is humid, wood swells. When it's dry, wood shrinks. Shrinking or swelling can sometimes cause the boards to warp. Narrower boards tend to expand and contract a little less than wider boards—but they are all going to move a little one way or another. The key to preventing or minimizing these changes is first to acclimatize the wood to the indoor environment where you're planning to install it. That means letting the boards sit in the house for at least three or four days before installation. Otherwise, moisture shouldn't be a problem for hardwood in a kitchen. You're not showering in the kitchen, so you typically don't get significant amounts of water on the floor. And the clear urethane coatings now in use are very resilient. If you spill something on the floor, just wipe it up before the liquid has a chance to penetrate the joints and cause damage.

In bathrooms we're seeing more and more laminate and engineered hardwood. If you're thinking of installing solid wood or engineered wood floors in the bathroom, you really need to consider carefully the way it's used. If you've got kids who are going to be taking baths and splashing copious amounts of water on the floor, then you're going to end up with some damage. You'll need to wipe up spills quickly so the water doesn't pool for too long and hang soggy bath mats to dry so as to limit the amount of water on the floor.

Whether or not wood floors will get wrecked in the bathroom largely depends on the quality and the finish of the hardwood and how well it is sealed and maintained. Some brands are treated just on the top with a polyurethane coating, while others are water-resistant all the way through.

You also don't necessarily have to write off wood if you want heated floors in the bathroom. However, you need a water-based radiant heating system or one that's low-voltage. Otherwise, you'll dry out the wood so much that you'll shrink it. You can use electric heating mats under some laminate, but definitely check with the manufacturer to be sure.

If you're the type who'll cringe every time your kids climb into the tub or someone spills milk, maybe hardwood isn't the right choice in your bathroom or kitchen. If you still want the look of wood without the moisture worries, you can buy ceramic or porcelain that looks like hardwood.

MISTAKE #32:
USING HARDWOOD IN THE BASEMENT

No matter how much you like hardwood, I wouldn't recommend it in a basement. The higher humidity and temperature fluctuations from season to season will cause it to expand and contract more dramatically than it would in other parts of your home.

Engineered hardwood or a high-quality laminate is a better choice. Because of the engineered base, they're more stable and less susceptible to expansion and contraction due to changes in humidity. Both of these options can be installed as floating floors, which means they don't have to be fixed to the subfloor with glue or nails—they click together or get glued into each other on top of the subfloor.

However, floating floors can be noisy: every time you put a little weight on them, they can slap against the subfloor. A foam underlayment or a product called QuietWalk, which is made from materials such as recycled jeans and is designed to absorb sound, will be a little softer underfoot, and it will reduce the noise. Check with the manufacturer to make sure you choose the right underlayment for your floor.

MISTAKE #33:
GETTING CONFUSED ABOUT UNDERLAYMENT

Underlayment is typically the middle of a flooring project, where the top layer is the finish floor and the bottom layer is the subfloor. Underlayment is typically a ¼-inch or ½-inch layer of plywood, fibreboard or cement board. It provides a smoother and more forgiving surface on which to lay your flooring than the subfloor does (most subfloors are made of plywood or oriented strand board). It makes the whole floor more stable by beefing up the flooring structure. And if you're tiling, it gives you a better foundation than just the subfloor.

Underlayment can be confusing because it isn't always needed and because the proper underlayment depends on the kind of floor you're installing. Plus, sometimes the subfloor and underlayment are basically the same thing. (Soft underlayments like foam and cork are different, and I'll get to those.) What you need to know is that remodelling typically requires underlayment because the subfloor may not be in pristine condition, whereas with a new build, the subfloor may be in mint condition, and you can just install the finish floor. If the flooring is hardwood or engineered wood, all you need is wax or felt paper on top of the subfloor. For dry rooms, ¼- or ½-inch AC-grade ply-

wood is smooth enough on the A side for hardwood, engineered wood or laminate.

Foam or cork underlayments are completely different. They float, meaning they're not attached to the floor. They offer a sort of buffer, protecting the finish floor from protruding screw heads on the subfloor. Some may also have insulating qualities.

One thing underlayment won't do is fix structural issues with your floor. If you've got problems with your subfloor or joists, you need to fix those before thinking about underlayment.

MISTAKE #34:
POORLY PLANNING A FLOORING PROJECT

As always, once you have decided on the type of flooring you want, the first step in a flooring project is proper planning. Start by determining how much flooring you will need. To do this, simply measure the square footage of your room: get your length, multiply by your width and add 10% to 15% for waste and breakage. If you're measuring an irregular space, break it down into individual rectangles.

If you're measuring a piece of laminate or hardwood to see how many strips you will need to lay across the floor, remember not to measure the tongue, or you will throw off your calculation. Only measure the top finished piece, which is the part that will be visible. Laminate pieces will be all the same size, whereas a box of hardwood usually contains strips in different lengths. With hardwood or laminate, you often have a baseboard and maybe quarter-round going on top of it, so you have a little bit of wiggle room around the edges. Leave a ¼-inch gap or so, which will allow for some expansion. Remember, the gap will be covered by the trim.

MISTAKE #35:
GETTING THE LAYOUT WRONG

After you've got your measurements worked out, you need to consider how to lay out your flooring. With hardwood or laminate, you should generally run the boards parallel to the longest wall. There is no law about this—you can run it whatever way you like—but running wood floors the length of the room means fewer cuts and an easier installation. If you have two walls that are parallel and two that aren't, it's probably best to run the floor lengthwise between the two walls that are *not* parallel. Sometimes there are just no perfect options—that's where the science of renovating gets pushed out of the way and the art comes in.

When you measure the room, often you'll realize you're on track to end up with a tiny strip of flooring at one end. For example, say your hardwood strips are 4 inches wide, and the room is 97 inches wide. You'd have room for 24 full boards and 1 inch left over. The general rule is you don't want to end up with anything less than half the width of the original piece. First, it looks terrible. Second, it's hard to cut and install a really small piece, so you're making your job more difficult than it has to be. (See page 91 for how to make accurate cuts.) So this takes some planning.

With a floating floor, you also want to leave about ¼ inch around the edges to allow it to expand and breathe. If the pieces are rammed up against the wall, the floor is going to move and start squeaking, and they could even pop if they expand too much.

Let's continue our example with the 4-inch boards and a 1-inch strip at one end. If you are planning to install cabinets against one wall, then it doesn't matter what it looks like underneath those cabinets—there's

no need to put in that tiny strip because the cabinets are going to cover that area. So plan to put the ugliest finishing point of the floor under a fixed feature like a built-in cabinet or some other place where it's not visible. (Don't plan for it to fall under your sofa: if you rearrange the furniture, your eyesore pops right back out in full view.) The biggest pieces should be placed in the most prominent and visible areas.

Another option, especially if you don't have a built-in in the room, is to split the difference at each edge. For example, if each board is 4 inches wide, you can rip an inch off the first board to make it 3 inches wide, and that will make your final board 2 inches, which will look better than a really narrow strip.

With laminate, laying out pieces perfectly the first time isn't so important because the floor is going to move around so much as you're installing the first few rows. I tell homeowners just to get the first three or four rows together and then adjust and measure where it's going to be. Since that floor is always moving around (remember, it's floating; it's not anchored to the subfloor), you need to have enough of it installed in order to get a real sense of where you're at. Typically, we roll out our first strip of underlayment, which is probably 4 feet wide, before we worry too much about whether or not the flooring is parallel with the far wall. Since it's not nailed down, you can always move it.

Things are always going to change a little bit as you go along. It's not like you can precut the width of the last row before you lay the first board. You can measure carefully, but it's going to change a little bit as you get closer to the end, so you just have to adjust as you go.

MISTAKE #36:
FAILING TO WORK IN TRANSITION STRIPS

When you're laying out a hardwood or laminate floor in a large area—say a couple of bedrooms and the hallway—you can't just install a million square feet all attached together. That's true whether you're nailing it down or installing a floating floor. It's going to move around too much, and there will be different areas of stress where it is going to buckle and may come apart.

In a hallway you'll have foot traffic that goes parallel to the boards, and the floor will move a little bit. And then in the bedroom you might have a kid who's running in a perpendicular direction to that, so the boards are going to be pushed around in different ways. If all of your boards are clicked together without a transition piece, the hardwood joints that fall in the doorway could eventually start to open up or fail altogether.

So when you're installing wood floors across several rooms, you need to glue or nail down transition strips. These are pieces used to join two areas of wood flooring in doorways or thresholds. If the wood flooring in the two areas is the same height, you'd use a wooden T-mould transition. If you've got two areas of flooring sitting at different heights, you'd smooth out that transition with a reducer strip. There are lots of products available, and the right one depends on the type of flooring you're installing, but the general idea is the same. They allow you to leave room for sections of the floor to move independently.

MISTAKE #37:
NOT FOLLOWING THE RIGHT STEPS TO INSTALL HARDWOOD

First, cover the subfloor with wax paper or felt paper. Always find the centre point of the room, and then figure out the layout from there. Start by making two chalk lines that are perfectly perpendicular to one another in the centre of the room—measuring from each line to the wall will tell you if the room is square. Then you can take your measurements and determine where the boards or tiles are going to fall from there. If you discover that you're going to end up with a little piece along one wall, you know you're going to have the same thing against the opposite wall because you're working from the centre of the floor and moving outward. So now you can adjust that centre line to whatever is going to work best. If there will be cabinets along one wall, you can move that centre line a few inches one way or the other so you end up with a full strip of hardwood on the most visible wall.

Mark the location of the joists on the walls, because you'll need to know this when it comes to nailing boards in. Most boards are nailed in through the tongue only, but the first and last rows of flooring along the long edges of the room have to be nailed through the face of the boards. To avoid splitting the face-nailed boards, use a $1/16$-inch drill bit to drill holes an inch from the grooved edge, and then countersink all the nails. (To countersink nails, you tap them with a countersink bit: a small metal piece with a tip. This inserts the nail just below the surface of the wood so it's not sticking out and getting in the way of two boards fitting together nice and tight.) Unless the hardwood manufacturer suggests otherwise, it's smart to space the face nails so they hit a joist.

To install hardwood, first cover the floor with wax paper or felt, then mark the centre of the room to plan where boards will fall as you move toward the walls. Install boards by sliding the tongue of one into the groove of the next. Tap them into place, then nail the boards through the tongue—except the perimeter boards, which are nailed through the face.

When you're putting in boards, you're going to seat the ends into one another—slide the tongue of one board into the groove of the next—and push them together tightly to close up the seam. Move down a row of boards, nailing the tongue every 8 inches or so until you reach the wall. Remember to leave a gap of ¼ to ½ inch against walls to allow for expansion.

When you start the next row, make sure the first board you select (or cut) is at least 6 inches shorter or longer than the one it'll be lying beside. Seams that are too close together look bad and create weak spots in the floor. Use a spacer (a narrow piece of wood) against the wall to make sure you're leaving an expansion gap, then put down that first board in the new row. Snug the new board up to its neighbour, using a floor mallet to tap the boards together. Then continue nailing, working one row at a time.

Sometimes if you look down the length of newly installed hardwood, you see that the boards curve. When you tap the boards in place, it's possible you'll end up moving them ever so slightly because there's nothing to resist that movement. This is more likely when starting installation at the midpoint of a room without a face-nailed row to resist movement. To prevent this from happening, I screw down a 2 × 4 on one side of my chalk line so when we tap a board in place, it's got something to hit that will keep it in place. That first piece along the chalk line is then solid, so you can nail and tap against it and nothing will move around as you go along.

Once you've installed your floor, you typically install the baseboard. But if you are installing a new floor in an old room and have really nice existing trim that you want to leave in place, you may be able to install the new floor against the baseboard. Depending on what the flooring is and how high the old floor was compared with the new one, you might be able to slide the new floor underneath, or you may need to butt it up against the baseboard. In the latter case, you're probably going to want to finish it with a shoe moulding or quarter round.

MISTAKE #38:
MAKING INACCURATE CUTS WITH HARDWOOD AND LAMINATE

Laying a full tile or a full piece of hardwood is relatively easy. The skill in installing flooring comes when it's time to make cuts. Part of the solution is using the right tools, but there are also some tricks you can learn to make cleaner, more accurate cuts.

First, when you need to rip a piece of hardwood or laminate (that is, when you're cutting with the grain), make sure you measure from the end of the board, not the end of the tongue. If you measure from the end of the tongue, then when you click that board into place, it's going to be too narrow.

There are even some tricks for making accurate cuts without using a measuring tape. For example, when you get to the end of the row of a wood floor you're laying and you need to cut the last piece to fit, just grab a full piece and turn it around so the tongue is facing away from you; snug it up tightly against the installed row and slide it until it's about ¼ inch from the wall (remember, you're leaving that small gap to allow for expansion); and then make a pencil mark on the bottom of the piece at the appropriate spot. I suggest also making an X on the waste side so when you get to the saw, you'll know which piece is which. Make the cut with a mitre saw, cutting into the waste side—otherwise, your piece will be too short by the width of the blade.

In most cases, you'll have to use a jig saw to cut into your new hardwood to make room for vent holes or other cut-outs. You can use the register cover as a template: just trace around the part that penetrates below the floor, use a ½-inch drill bit to make a hole, and then insert the blade of the jig saw and cut along the lines. (You might need to trim the edges of your hole just a little until the register cover drops in smoothly.) An even easier way is to simply mark the corners of the vent holes on the piece of flooring, and cut out each piece before it's installed. This also ensures you won't forget to open up any vents later! There's usually a ½-inch tolerance around the edges of vent covers, so don't panic if you cross the line.

MISTAKE #39:
IMPROPERLY SPACING JOINTS WHEN INSTALLING LAMINATE

When you're laying laminate, and all the pieces are the same length, you need to stagger the joints. I've seen floors with all the pieces lined up, but this arrangement makes the floor weak along that joint, and it doesn't look great. Joints should be at least 4 to 6 inches apart as a general rule. Some people like regular patterns and arrange the laminate so that half pieces and full pieces alternate, but I prefer a random look. So what I do is take a stack of five pieces to the saw and, with no measurements, just cut them randomly at different lengths. Then I use one of those to start each of the first five rows (starting with the longest). The offcut from the other end will be used to start the next row after that.

Doing this can actually make a floor look pretty random even though most of the pieces are the same size. If you're working with a box of pieces that are all the same size, your very first piece determines where everything else falls. If you're working with a product that's all different sizes, cut the one that is closest to the length you need. That way, you'll waste as little as possible.

Most products come with instructions that explain this stuff. If you buy a box of laminate, it comes with a how-to book that tells you exactly how to lay out the floor. I've been in other people's houses and they've said, "I just have no idea how to do this," and I say to them, "There's an instruction manual right in the box." It's amazing how many people don't read it.

MISTAKE #40:
POORLY PLANNING THE LAYOUT OF A TILE FLOOR

At our cottage we tiled a 100-foot hallway in stone. We ran a chalk line from end to end and then laid an entire row of tile right down the middle. We based everything from there on that centre line. That's what you need to do in a large room, but in a small bathroom, you can probably just dry-lay a row of tiles and see what makes sense. The bigger the room, the more important it is to plan everything out; with a smaller room, you can often figure it out on the fly.

I like using DRIcore panels as a subfloor in the basement. They're made of particleboard with a moisture barrier on the bottom, so they go down over bare concrete and keep your feet warm and dry.

When you're planning how to lay out tiles, another trick is to use a story pole. This is basically a homemade ruler with tile and grout widths marked. To make one, just lay out five or six tiles, spacing them evenly to leave room for the grout. Then place a straight piece of wood (a 1 × 2 works well) next to the tiles and mark each corner of the tile on the wood. This will help you play around with the location of the tiles until you find the best layout.

A story pole can be really helpful, because sometimes the box says your tiles are 12 × 12, but they're actually $11^7/_{16}$ inches square—plus you have to account for the grout between each tile, so you can't just assume six tiles are going to cover exactly 6 feet. If you do, any mistake you make will be compounded with every tile, and pretty soon you will be off by a wide margin. So instead, use your story pole to see exactly where the tiles would fall. It helps for walls, too—making it easier to calculate how high to place a recessed niche or a strip of contrasting decorative tiles so you can minimize tile cuts and maximize the use of full tiles.

MISTAKE #41:
LAYING TILE ON A SHODDY SUBFLOOR

If you're building a subfloor you plan to cover with tile, you need to build it carefully. The success of a tile installation is directly related to the strength and solidity of the subfloor. If your subfloor is anything but rock-solid, when you put any weight on it, that movement is going to be transferred to the tile. Ceramic, porcelain and stone tiles don't want to move, and neither does mortar. As soon as they move, they crack.

I really like DRIcore panels, which are made from particleboard with a high-density polyethylene moisture barrier on the bottom. They're particularly good over concrete in the basement because they keep your feet warm and dry. DRIcore can go under carpet, laminate, engineered hardwood, tile and vinyl flooring. But if you use it under tile, you've got to use five Tapcon screws per panel to lock it all down to prevent movement.

If you're putting down a laminate floor over concrete, use a foam underlayment that will act as a moisture barrier. Concrete is always wicking moisture, so the foam will prevent the moisture from going up into the floor and ruining it. It will also provide some give under the floor so it doesn't feel like you're just standing on concrete.

In theory, you can install tile directly onto a plywood subfloor as long as it's at least $1\frac{1}{4}$ inches thick. Unfortunately, builders in the average subdivision like to save money on costs, so many will install a $\frac{5}{8}$- or $\frac{3}{4}$-inch subfloor. If you're installing tiles over a thin subfloor like that, you need an underlayment to isolate movement from the tiles.

This theory for underlayment goes back to ancient times: for tile beds, roads or sidewalks, they used to put down a layer of compacted sand and then put the tile on top of that; the sand absorbs movement so the tiles won't move, crack or come apart. The idea is to avoid sticking a solid surface to a surface that is going to flex and, instead, put something in between that will act as a buffer.

Not too long ago most tile was installed on wire mesh with a scratch coat of mortar on top. Today there are a lot of engineered backer boards (fibreglass-reinforced concrete boards used for laying tiles) and underlayments designed to be installed under tile in place of a scratch coat. The problem with a scratch coat is that it takes a lot of skill and experience to install it and to maintain a flat surface for tile installation—not easy for the average DIYer. These new underlayments are more expensive than wire mesh and mortar but much easier and faster to install. I've recently found a product line from Wedi that includes underlayments, backer boards and shower systems: rigid, waterproof foam panels with a cement-like coating act as a great underlayment, insulating and isolating the tiles from movement.

MISTAKE #42: FAILING TO PREP THE SURFACE BEFORE TILING

Surface preparation is everything when you're tiling. Take the time to adjust the subfloor or backer board until it's perfectly flat before you start tiling. That's easier than trying to make the walls and floor look flat by adjusting the angle of every single tile. The flatter the surface, the less mortar you have to apply. If you are installing tiles larger than 12×12, use a $\frac{1}{2}$-inch-square notched trowel to lay down and spread out a thicker bed of mortar on the floor. The extra mortar will help you manage the less-forgiving nature of larger tiles and any imperfections in the subfloor. If your subfloor happens to be perfect, consider yourself one of the lucky few—you can use a $\frac{1}{4}$-inch-square trowel to lay down mortar.

Before you install tile, get a really long level and find the highest spot on your floor or wall. (Professionals will use a 12-foot or 16-foot piece of aluminum with a level on top.) Your first tile has to be placed at the high spot, or at least in the same plane: it's relatively easy to pack a little more mortar under a tile to lift it up, but it's hard—okay, impossible—to push one down into the subfloor.

You have to get the consistency right when you're mixing mortar to lay tiles. If trowel lines are breaking apart as you pull, the mortar is too dry. If they slump into soupy piles, it's too wet. When applying you want those nice square lines to maintain their form.

If the floor has a lot of high and low spots—and this is a common problem—there are a couple of ways to manage that. (It actually doesn't matter too much whether the floor is perfectly level—it's more important for it to be flat.) You could pour self-levelling cement to bring up the lower areas. Self-levelling cement is almost the consistency of water, so when you pour it on, it will run to the low spots. But beware—it starts to harden very quickly, so you have to mix it and pour it within about 20 seconds. It helps to have everything ready to go so you're not reaching for tools or moving things off the floor. The trick here is to work quickly, pouring thin layers around the low areas and then feathering them out with a trowel as the mixture starts to harden. If you wait too long before you pour, it will look like an elephant came along and left you a big gift in the middle of the floor!

Professional tilers will use dry pack, which is a sand-and-cement mortar mix. They'll pack that onto the floor to create a perfectly level base and then tile over it. This produces better results than self-levelling cement, but it's much harder to install.

If your floor is very close to flat, you can just rake the mortar, "back-butter" the tile—apply a thin layer of thin-set mortar to the back of the tile with the straight edge of the trowel—and then make minor adjustments. But if your floor is uneven, you'll need to use a margin trowel to put more mortar in specific places to account for any lower spots in the floor. (A margin trowel has a narrow rectangular blade and is used for working in smaller spaces. It is also great for getting mortar out of your bucket and onto your trowel.) This is really painstaking, and the margin for error is huge: you have to make adjustments tile by tile. In some spots where you might have ¾ inch of mortar underneath the tile, you can go through a bucket of mortar every five or six tiles. That's why it's better to take the time to make sure your subfloor is flat before you begin.

A wet saw or tub saw grinds through tile using a moist diamond blade.

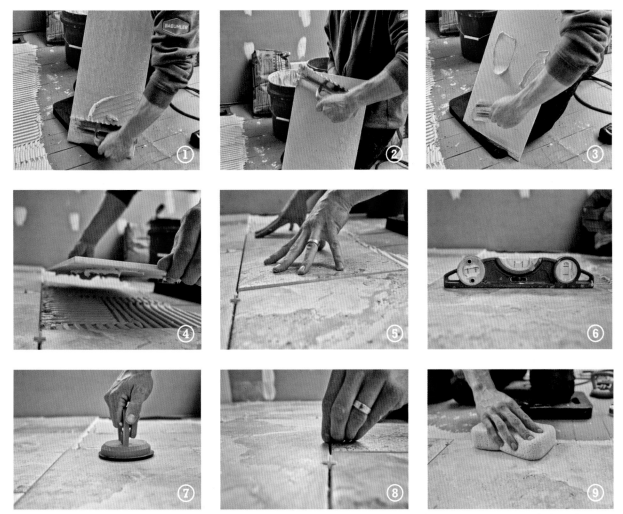

Rake a layer of mortar on the floor with a notched trowel. Lightly back-butter each tile with mortar using the trowel's flat side (*photo 1*), then scrape it off (*photo 2*). You're priming the surface so the tile will stick. Add a few extra dots of mortar for extra adhesion (*photo 3*). Set a tile next to the existing one (*photo 4*), tap it down so they are on the same level, and then slide the tile away into the right spot (*photo 5*)—this prevents mortar from squeezing up between the tiles. Tap the tile into place and double-check that it's level (*photo 6*). Use a suction tool to pull up any tiles you pressed down too hard (*photo 7*). Insert spacers around the tile (*photo 8*), then wipe off any extra mortar on the tile (*photo 9*).

MISTAKE #43:
USING THE WRONG TILE ADHESIVE

There are a lot of confusing options for tile adhesives. Cement-based mortar, also called thin-set, can be modified or unmodified. Modified mortar has additives that make it adhere better, but it needs air to gain strength. Unmodified mortar sets even if you are using it between two nonporous surfaces, like a waterproof membrane and a porcelain tile—it will dry even if you install it underwater!

For most jobs, modified mortar is preferable, especially if you've got a plywood subfloor. However, some product and tile combinations require unmodified mortar because it's going to sit between two impervious surfaces and won't be able to air-dry. As always, check the manufacturer's instructions to be sure.

Mastic is a different product that's more like glue. You can get mastics for a wall application like a backsplash, and they've developed some for floors as well. Five or 10 years ago, nobody would use mastic in a shower because of mould, but now some are designed to work well in wet areas. Mastic also sets quickly, which is an advantage if you're working with

If you see well-formed grooves like this when you rake mortar with a notched trowel, the mortar is the right consistency.

heavy tiles—you can get the project completed faster. It's also incredibly strong—you can use it with stone. Some people find it easier to use than mortar because it's thinner and spreads out evenly. The key difference is that mastic has to cure fully before it comes into contact with water. Mastic comes premixed in buckets and is generally more expensive than mortar, so we'll typically use it only for smaller jobs.

The point is there are lots of products out there—too many, in my opinion. If you get confused, don't just buy a random bag, or you'll find yourself using the wrong thing and your tiles will fall off the wall. Read the label carefully on your adhesive product and follow the manufacturer's instructions. I can't say this enough: there are lots of ways to tile a wall or floor properly, and there are lots of ways to mess it up. Reading the instructions or not is usually the best indication of which way you're headed!

MISTAKE #44:
IMPROPERLY MIXING AND APPLYING MORTAR

Mortar binds tiles to another surface, either the wall or the underlayment. Since working with mortar requires some skill, it helps to have all your tools and materials organized before you start. Typically, the bigger the tile, the bigger the trowel. For floors with 12-inch-square tiles or larger, use a trowel with ½-inch-square notches. You can go down from there: for smaller tiles or flatter floors, you might use a trowel with ³⁄₈-inch or ¹⁄₄-inch notches.

For a backsplash, use a V-notch trowel. V-notches are used for vertical surfaces because you don't want to get too much mortar on the wall or it just slides off. You can use the same mortar on walls that you use on the floor, but you have to be certain it's not too wet.

When you're laying tiles, have your mortar bucket nearby, along with a margin trowel. I use a margin trowel to load up the notched trowel I'm using to apply the mortar. It's the easiest way to get mortar out of the bucket without making a huge mess, and it's great for back-buttering small tiles or working in small areas.

You should also have a bucket of clean water and a sponge nearby to clean up any mortar you get on the tiles, because once it hardens, it's really difficult to clean up. Take two seconds now to avoid hours of frustration later.

When mixing your mortar, you have to get the consistency right. Whether you're using modified or unmodified mortar, the consistency should be such that you see well-formed grooves when you rake the mortar with the notched trowel. When applying, if the lines of mortar are pulling apart or are hollow in the middle, then you don't have enough on the trowel. If the lines are breaking apart as you pull, your mortar is too dry. If they aren't nice and square, and they're starting to slump into soupy piles, your mortar is too wet. You want those nice square lines to maintain their form.

Before you rake out the mortar with the notched edge, prime the area by spreading some of the mortar on the floor using the flat side of the trowel. If you don't do that, some areas won't get any mortar. Don't worry about which direction you're raking: the point of the notches is just to help you control how much mortar you apply to the floor. If you use ½-inch notches and push the trowel down firmly, you can get only a certain volume of mortar on the floor, and it will be consistent every time. If you don't push the trowel down—if it's just floating over the mortar—then you might end up with different thicknesses.

If you have a perfectly flat floor, you don't need a thick layer of mortar to set the tile (½ inch is fine). But

Use a V-notch trowel to mortar vertical surfaces like walls and backsplashes so the mortar won't slide off.

make sure you aim for 80% to 90% coverage to avoid air pockets. If someone walks on the tile with high heels, and all the weight is on that one small point, you don't want it to be a corner where there's no mortar—the tile will crack.

With floor tiles, it's best to back-butter them using the flat side of the trowel—just apply a skim coat and scrape it off. This primes the surface and gets some moisture onto the tile, which is important because wet things stick better to wet things. Ceramic and natural stone suck up a lot of water, so if you just put a dry tile onto the mortar, the tile will suck out all the moisture too quickly and it won't form a good bond with the mortar.

When you're setting tiles in place, don't slide them *into* the right spot. If you do that, you're going to squeeze mortar up between them. Instead, set the next tile close to the existing one, then tap it down with a fist or a rubber mallet (using just enough pressure to set the tile in place without breaking it) so they are on the same level, and then slide it *away* until it's in the right spot. It's better to pull tiles apart than to squish them together.

As you're installing tiles, don't put down any more mortar than you can work with in 10 or 15 minutes. If you're experienced, that can be quite a few tiles' worth of mortar, but if you are new to this, you might spread out a patch just big enough to lay one tile. You can still mix the mortar in a fairly large bucket because it won't dry too quickly. But once you've put that mortar down, make sure you get the tile into it before a skin forms on the surface. If a skin forms, remove the mortar with your trowel and work it back into the mortar in your bucket with a little water. Remember, the more you stir it, the faster it cooks—especially with modified mortar. If you've ever worked with drywall compound, it's like that: if you keep mixing it and adding water, it'll dry more quickly.

If you're putting in-floor heating beneath tile, that process can get pretty technical: the couplings and wiring have the effect of raising the floor in certain sections. If you're laying this kind of heating system, you have to install an insulating underlayment panel (like a Wedi construction panel) before the heating mat or wires go down, then another layer of scratch coat on top of the wire and finally your tiles. But don't tile right away after installing the scratch coat: let the mortar set up before you start tiling. You should also let the mortar cure for at least 48 hours before you turn the heat

on—it might even need more than that, so check the heating system's instruction manual. Otherwise, you will dry out the mortar before it has a chance to cure, and it will be brittle.

Generally, you will need an electrician to install a dedicated circuit for a heated floor, and depending on the size and complexity of the room, you may want to bring in a pro to install the heat mat or cables, too.

Mistake #45:
CUTTING TILES THE WRONG WAY

Cutting tile is a little different from cutting hardwood and laminate, and there's a technique you can use to cut the last tile in a row. Say you're laying 12-inch tiles, and your last full row will be 7 or 8 inches from the wall. Take a full tile and place it so one edge is about ¼ inch from the wall and the opposite edge is overlapping the last row of full tiles. Now mark the tile at the place where it meets the top edge of the tile underneath. You can now cut the tile at that mark, and it will fit perfectly in the last row. When you get really familiar with this method, you can even use it to make complicated cut-outs around door jambs and other obstacles.

If you are doing a really simple installation with ceramic tiles, you may be able to use a snap cutter, which scores the tile and then snaps it along that line. Or you can use a carbide saw, which looks like a hacksaw but has a carbide blade and can be used to cut shapes and lines and corners. Tile nippers can also be helpful for biting off little pieces. For cutting holes, you can get fluted or carbide drill bits.

But the most versatile tool by far—and the one that gives you professional-looking cuts—is a wet saw, or tub saw. (It's not worth buying one if you have to tile just one room, but you can rent one at a building

Making a cut-out to fit around a corner isn't easy, but here's a trick that doesn't even require a measuring tape. Place a full tile on top of the last full row so that its edge is about 1/8 inch from the wall. Mark the tile where it meets the edge of the tile underneath. You can now cut the tile at that mark, and it will fit perfectly.

supply store.) Wet saws grind through tile using a diamond blade and a pump that keeps the blade and tile wet while you're cutting. The water recirculates continuously to cool the blade and reduce tile dust and flyaway particles. This isn't a toy: there's a very real chance bits of sharp tile could go flying. Safety goggles are a must. First, get the water flowing. If it's not pouring around the blade, don't start cutting, or you could break the blade or the tile. Then power up the saw. The blade is in a fixed position, so you manoeuvre the tile into the blade using the sliding tray. If you like your hands as they are, keep them out of the line of the cut!

MISTAKE #46:
IMPROPER SPACING ON A TILE FLOOR

When is it appropriate to use plastic spacers between tiles? I've done entire floors with no spacers—usually in a room where the walls are all over the place. If I go into an old house and none of the walls are square, I will often do the tile with no spacers, because there is no sense in installing perfectly straight tiles in a room where nothing else lines up—it will just make the flaws more visible. So in cases like that, it's often better to go in and massage things in a way that looks just right—though that takes a little experience.

An eighth of an inch is pretty standard spacing between tiles. You might see joints as wide as $\frac{1}{4}$ inch in commercial bathrooms or in homes that are 30 years or older. The problem with wide joints is that the grout you fill them with gets dirty, so you end up with these giant dirty lines. That's one of the reasons I prefer a tighter grout line. On a big floor, spacers can help keep things consistent, because after you've been staring at the tile for a while, your joints will start to get a little tighter or a little wider. Spacers are also important if you've got two

or three people tiling: everybody has a different eye, so everybody's $\frac{1}{8}$ inch will be slightly different.

MISTAKE #47:
IMPROPER SPACING ON A TILE WALL OR BACKSPLASH

If you're tiling a wall or backsplash, you definitely need to use spacers, or gravity will squeeze the tiles together—unless they have built-in spacers (subway tiles, for example, typically have these). There are also backsplash tiles that are grout-free; they're just installed tightly together. The challenge with them is there's no room for adjustment. Cheaper tiles can be a little inconsistent—one might be $\frac{1}{16}$ inch too narrow or too wide—so you end up with small variations across the backsplash. If your grout line is too small (or nonexistent), you can't adjust for these tile imperfections as you go along. You don't have to worry about spacers if you're using tile sheets on mesh unless you want to use them between sheets to ensure consistency.

When tiles meet in a corner, they should line up. If you're doing a shower, and the tiles are not perfectly level when you get to the corner, you need to make little adjustments. This is where you back up 2 or 3 feet

along the wall and start to use plastic levelling wedges. You can use the wedges to bring up the edge of a tile, say, 1/16 or 1/8 inch. You may have to bring the level up slowly over four or five tiles so it's not visible, and if your joints are really tight, it's hard to do that without trimming the tile. Also, make sure the tiles are tight in the corner—within 1/8 inch or so. After you grout there, you can even put in a bead of silicone caulking to give the corners an extra layer of sealant against moisture.

Tiling a wall from floor-to-ceiling, like in a shower, for example, is a little more difficult than laying a floor. On the floor, remember, you need to find the high spot and build up to it to make everything flat. That's harder to do on a wall or ceiling. It doesn't much matter if the wall is leaning in or out or is twisted one way or the other—that's fine. But if it's not perfectly flat—and often you've got a big hump in the backer board—that's

going to be very visible when you try to tile over it. (Some backer boards are more flexible than others, so with some products, any variations in the framing can transfer through to the tiling surface.)

The first challenge is you can't use self-levelling cement on a wall. Second, on the floor you can place a tile down and use a level to see if all four corners are flat. But on a wall, no level will tell you if all the corners are on the same plane as the wall's. It will tell you if you're plumb (perpendicular to the horizon), but it won't account for that third dimension. So walls are typically a lot harder—and the higher up the wall you go, the more weight you have messing up the tiles below.

I remember in my younger days, I tiled a whole wall at one time. I came back to find there were no grout lines because all the thin-set had slipped down and squeezed the spacers so tight that I couldn't get them out. What you need to do with bigger tiles is put in a couple of rows and let them set up and start to dry before you move on to the next few rows. I also prefer hard plastic spacers for these jobs over the rubbery ones because the rigid plastic won't compress and move around like the rubber does. The other thing you can do is drive in nails or screws to take some of the weight and just pull them out after the tile sets. (But don't do that in a shower because you don't want to create holes in the backer board that could lead to water penetration and mould.)

MISTAKE #48:
MESSY GROUTING

I have a trained eye, so I can tell if a floor is going to look good even before it's grouted. But it's funny, sometimes a homeowner sees a tile floor before it has been grouted and worries because they think it looks terrible—they can still see all the mortar between the tiles. Grout is the finishing touch, and it makes a huge difference.

Grout comes in two main types: sanded and unsanded. The one you need depends on how much space you're leaving between tiles. The sand in grout acts as a reinforcement—it's kind of like rebar in concrete. It gives the grout added strength and volume. The rule of thumb is if your joints are 1/8 inch or more, use sanded grout. If you use unsanded grout in a larger joint, it will shrink and crack and fall apart. If you use sanded grout in a tiny joint, squeezing it in will be tough.

I prefer the look of sanded grout just because of the texture. Any time you've got a smooth surface, every flaw is noticeable, and that's the case with unsanded grout: it's very smooth, so any imperfection is going to be visible. Sanded grout is more like a travertine or a tumbled marble: there is some texture to it. It doesn't hide problems, but it does blend inconsistencies or changes in depth or level. If the installation isn't perfect, unsanded grout will make minor inconsistencies more obvious; for example, you'll notice if two tiles aren't exactly the same height.

For applying grout, you need a grout float, which looks like a trowel but has a flexible edge made of rubber or soft plastic, almost like a squeegee. You use it to squeeze the grout into the joints and smooth the surface. It also helps to have two buckets ready for wiping the grout: one for clean water and one for dirty.

Mix the grout so it has a kind of wet sand consistency—drier than mortar. It always seems a little bit wet at first, but if you give it 10 or 15 minutes to slake (a chemical process that causes the grout particles to crumble and disintegrate as they mix with water and air) and then mix it to loosen it up again, you'll have the right consistency.

For a floor, fill your trowel with grout, put it on the floor and, with the grout float, push it down until it completely fills the void around the tile. Then drag the excess off using the edge of the grout float, always on a bit of an angle to the grout line (if the float is parallel to a grout line, when you hit the joint, it will dig right in). Then you just work the float back and forth to completely fill those joints. Grouting is not a difficult job, but you do need to get the hang of it. It's the angle of your hand and the angle of the float that people have a hard time getting used to. But after 10 or 15 minutes of doing it, you'll get a feel for it.

Once the joints are filled and you've cleaned the surface with the edge of the grout float, wipe off the excess grout with a wet sponge and let it sit for 5 or 10 minutes. Then use the wet sponge to "tool" the grout: gently wipe in circles over the lines to dig out the grout just below the surface of the tile and give it a smooth finish. During this stage, you'll have to clean your sponge about a thousand times, so that's where those two buckets that I mentioned earlier come in. Once the lines all look nice, use the sponge to wipe as much grout off the surface of the tiles as you can. Wait until the dirty water on the tile hazes over, and then take a dry rag and buff that haze off the tile.

MISTAKE #49:
SEALING STONE TILES AT THE WRONG TIME

If you're working with a natural, porous stone, you may want to seal the tile before you grout. If you don't seal the tiles first, you could get grout in the holes, and you probably don't want to muck up your expensive tiles like that, depending on the look you're going for. Sealing the stone first also makes cleaning off the excess grout later a lot easier. But if you're putting down something like a shiny ceramic or porcelain, you don't need to worry about sealing them first. Just brush them with a liquid tile sealant (available at building supply centres) or apply the sealant with a spray bottle and wipe the tiles down with a damp sponge after a few minutes.

While we're talking about sealant, there is some debate about whether or not grout needs to be sealed. Some people say you have to seal it to keep the moisture from getting behind the tile, but others point out that sealing grout doesn't make it 100% waterproof, so there will always be a bit of moisture getting in there, and if the grout is sealed, the moisture has a tougher time getting back out; over the years it may accumulate and eventually cause more damage. If you leave it unsealed, the walls can breathe, and moisture or humidity can go in and out of the seams at its leisure.

To be honest, we do both. We will often seal the grout on a floor in a high-traffic area where people are coming in with dirty boots, and the grout would get dirty pretty quickly. In a shower, if we're doing natural stone like travertine or marble that needs to be sealed anyway, then we will seal everything. If we're doing a ceramic with really tight grout lines, often we don't bother. Make a call based on the kind of tile you're installing and the location.

I'll tell you this: people get really passionate about these sorts of things! On the show when we've tiled, we might get 100 emails from people who install tile for a living. Fifty of them will say, "Great job, that's the way you do it," and the other 50 will say, "I was taught this way, and that's the only way to do it." So even professionals disagree on a lot of this stuff. I always tell homeowners there are 10 different ways to flatten the wall or install a tile—the best way to do it is often the way that makes sense to them and works well.

MISTAKE #50:
FAILING TO WATERPROOF THE SHOWER

A lot of people think that the tile and grout form the waterproofing layer in a shower. The truth is, it should be completely watertight before any tile goes down—you should be able to shower in there with no tile at all! You've got space between the tiles and mortar, which isn't waterproof, and vapour going through grout and porous tiles. The tiles offer a level of protection, but they are not the last line of defence against water.

For a waterproof shower base, there are a couple of options. You can build a mortar bed from scratch for about $50 for a bag of mortar and a PVC waterproof membrane. Mix up the mortar, pre-slope the base, install the membrane, and then painstakingly apply the mortar over the membrane with a trowel, shaping a sloped floor that you'll later fit with a drain. But you need a high level of skill to slope the base properly to the drain so it looks good and feels good on your feet when you tile it. Not only that, but you have to get the slope right so water goes down the drain and doesn't pool in the membrane under the tiles—it's often a two- or three-day process. Or you can spend $700 on a pre-sloped shower kit from Wedi and install it in less than a day. There's comparatively little skill required, and there's way less room for error—but you've spent $700. At the end of the day technology costs money, but that upfront expense will often save you money in the long run.

I've seen many DIYers using green drywall as backer board for tile in a shower. Don't! That green drywall *is* designed for high-humidity areas, including bathroom walls, but it's not waterproof, and you should never use it in a shower unless it's covered by a waterproofing system. You can use cement board, but you have to remember to put up a vapour barrier behind it because it's porous and water vapour can pass through. It's also really heavy, so it's unwieldy to install, and you need a carbide blade to cut it. A lighter option is a fibreglass-faced board such as DensShield, but it still needs to be installed and waterproofed correctly.

My preferred product is by Wedi: it's a 3' × 5' × ½" backer board with an extruded polystyrene foam core, reinforced with fibreglass and coated with a waterproof cement resin (about $40 per sheet). It's strong, light-weight, insulated, easy to cut and 100% waterproof. It's easy to install, and once you seal the joints, you can tile right over it. There are lots of foam products out there, but I've never found one that is waterproof throughout and as easy to work with.

Installing a completely waterproof shower might look easy, but think long and hard before you tackle this as a DIY project. This is often one of those projects that warrants calling in a pro if you're not ready to put in the time to learn.

MISTAKE #51:
IGNORING TILE REPAIRS AND MAINTENANCE

Let's say you're doing a small job in the bathroom or the laundry room, and you drop your hammer on the tile floor. You crack one of the tiles and curse yourself because you can't fix that, right?

It's actually pretty easy to replace a broken tile, which is why I recommend saving a few leftover tiles when you finish a job. But you have to think of it like this: once you install tile and grout it, you no longer have a bunch of individual pieces—you now have one big plate of solid, brittle material. So to get one tile out, you need to isolate it from everything else, because if you take a hammer and chisel and try to break out that tile, chances are you're going to crack the surrounding pieces.

So first you need to remove the surrounding grout. You can use a handheld grout saw if it's just one tile, but the best thing out there for this job is an oscillating multi-tool. If you attach a carbide-grit grout-removal blade (they come in different thicknesses to work on various joint widths), you can grind the grout from the joints, whether between floor or wall tiles. Once you've removed that surrounding grout, use a screwdriver or sharp chisel, and just hit the tile until you break all the pieces out. The oscillating multi-tool also comes in handy after you've removed the tile: it can sand off all that mortar. (If you don't have a multi-tool, use a carbide blade or old chisel to clean up the subfloor.) Then you just apply more mortar to the floor, back-butter a tile and put it back in place. Let it dry, and then finish with grout, and you've got your perfect floor back.

CHAPTER
FIVE

CABINETS, COUNTER-TOPS AND FIXTURES

IF YOU'RE LIKE MOST PEOPLE, YOU CAN'T HAVE TOO MUCH STORAGE. WE'VE GOT BUILT-INS TO HOLD THE ELECTRONICS, KITCHEN CABINETS TO STORE DISHES AND GLASSES, VANITIES TO SUPPORT THE SINK AND CONTAIN THE SHAMPOO AND TOILET PAPER, AND DELUXE LAUNDRY ROOMS WITH FOLDING STATIONS. TODAY'S GARAGES ARE SO WELL ORGANIZED THAT THERE'S OFTEN EVEN ENOUGH ROOM FOR A CAR!

Installing a kitchen or bathroom is one of the tougher projects in a home. The type of cabinets selected can determine not only how the finished room looks but also how much of the installation you can realistically take on. A handy homeowner can install pre-assembled or build-it-yourself cabinets with a simple laminate countertop. But DIY is not really an option if you're going with custom cabinets—beautiful pieces of furniture built to your dimensions and specifications—or a high-end stone countertop.

An experienced DIYer should be able to handle installing kitchen and bathroom fixtures. If you need new supply lines or drains, though, you should definitely hire a professional plumber. But replacing an old faucet, laundry tub, toilet or dishwasher is probably within your abilities. As always, use good judgment, and don't be afraid to call a pro if you've bitten off more than you can chew.

CABINET, COUNTERTOP AND FIXTURE BASICS

DIFFICULTY: 8 OUT OF 10

Installing cabinets, countertops and fixtures requires some decent carpentry skills and a basic familiarity with plumbing. It also helps to understand the lingo:

- **Backsplash:** The wall above the kitchen or bathroom sink takes abuse from soap, water and dirty dish splatters. Covering this part of the drywall, typically with tiles, gives it character and protects it.

- **Cabinet box:** This is the foundation of cabinetry where items are stored. Cabinet boxes are covered with doors or fitted with drawers.

- **Main water line:** This pipeline enters from outside to supply a home with water and is typically a faucet or lever found by the water meter. It should be turned off before attempting plumbing work if the fixture you're working on doesn't have a local shut-off valve (see definition below).

- **Plumb:** True vertical. Kitchen and bathroom cabinets should be installed perfectly plumb so items don't slide out. Test for plumb by holding a level against a vertical surface of the cabinet.

- **P-trap:** This sideways-P-shaped fitting under kitchen and bathroom sinks catches debris to prevent it from forming a clog deep within the plumbing system while also preventing sewer gases from entering the home.

- **Shims:** These thin, tapered wedges are usually made of wood. They're used to prop under or behind cabinets, vanities and dishwashers to help level them.

- **Shut-off valves:** Shut-off valves are located under the sinks (and on toilets) to allow you to turn off water near the fixture itself instead of shutting down the water for the whole house.

- **Toe kick:** This recessed hollow at the bottom of a kitchen base cabinet or bathroom vanity allows room for your feet so you can work closer to the countertop.

- **Work triangle:** The most functional kitchen layout minimizes the distances between the sink, stove and fridge to allow for more efficient work. The general rule is to draw an imaginary line linking these three zones; the sum of the triangle's three sides should not exceed 26 feet or cut through an island or peninsula.

TOOLS AND MATERIALS YOU'LL NEED
- measuring tape
- level
- mitre saw, table saw, hole saw and/or jig saw for countertops
- carpenter's square
- drill
- screw gun
- wrench
- hacksaw for ABS pipe
- ABS cement
- plumber's putty
- Teflon tape for pipe threads

Mistake #52:
PLANNING CABINET PLACEMENT POORLY

There are a lot of good online resources you can use to plan your kitchen cabinet layout. Through Lowe's, for example, you can go online or to a store and use a computer program to get a 3-D drawing of what your kitchen could look like. These visualization tools can help you imagine different variations of your future kitchen. If you're planning a major project like a kitchen, however, it's important to take the planning one step further. I recommend sitting down with an expert who can work with you to design a functional space. Kitchen cabinets are a big expense, so you want to get it right.

A lot of people think kitchen planning is just about deciding where you want your sink, stove and fridge to go. But it's much more involved than that—there are a lot of factors to consider when designing a convenient kitchen that suits your lifestyle. You have to decide which drawers will hold cutlery, which cabinets will hold plates, where the spice rack should go—you name it. It's helpful to know what kinds of items you need to store, how much space they take up and how often you need to access everything. For example, if you're a person who loves baking and owns a dozen cookie sheets, then you can make sure in advance that there's enough room to store them and they're in a handy location (maybe near the oven). Everyone needs daily access to cutlery, dishes and glasses, so these are often kept in drawers and cabinets within reach and fairly close to the dishwasher for easy unloading. Maybe you use your slow cooker only once a month, so you'd tuck that away on a high shelf. There are so many cabinet options nowadays—shelves, pullout pantries, drawers with built-in organizers, recycling stations—that it's no

I think it's worth getting a professional designer to plan a new kitchen. Their experience will give you a more functional space.

longer just about saying, "Put a cabinet here." You need to think about exactly what that cabinet will contain and how those items are best organized and stored. And then the sum of all those parts is the kitchen.

Designers tend to follow certain rules about how kitchens should be laid out. For example, many suggest allowing for counter space on either side of the sink and on either side of the stove so that you have workspace where you need it most. Likewise, if the fridge and stove are placed at the opposite ends of the room, you'll be complaining each time you have to run back for one more ingredient while you're in the middle of cooking something. But every space is different, so the rules are not set in stone.

Keep in mind that plumbing labour and material costs will be lower for kitchens that reuse existing hookups for the sink and dishwasher instead of radically relocating them. The same goes for a vent hood over the stove—it's an easier installation for the HVAC specialist if the stove is located on an outside wall. Venting is possible from inside walls, but it will cost more to install.

If you're installing the cabinets yourself, plan to install upper storage before lower cabinets, whether you're using pre-built cabinet boxes or flat-packed boxes of the Swedish variety. Here's why: with a base cabinet on the floor, it's harder to hold the upper cabinet in place when the space below it is blocked and there's nowhere to position your feet; you'll end up leaning and twisting your body awkwardly to work around that lower cabinet. Upper cabinets also require more hardware and engineering to hang, which will be a whole lot easier to deal with if you have full access to the floor and wall.

Some homeowners argue they want to install the base cabinets first so they can measure from the top of the base to decide where the bottom of the uppers should be. (The standard height for a base kitchen cabinet is 34½ inches, plus an extra 1½ inches for the countertop, so from the floor to the top of the counter is 36 inches.) But these measurements are easy to get with a tape measure—you don't need the lower cabinets installed to figure that out.

The most common height for hanging upper cabinets is 54 inches (measured from the ground to the bottom of the upper cabinet), but don't be afraid to play with that if you are taller or shorter than average. A similar guideline says to hang them 18 or 19 inches above the finished height of the countertop. You can mark this measurement on the wall with a pencil and install the uppers using that mark as a guide. Cabinets above the sink are generally smaller, and hung higher, for a reason: so you don't bump your head while washing the dishes. Plan on 68 to 78 inches off the floor, depending on the height of the owners.

MISTAKE #53:
THINKING CUSTOM CABINETS ARE THE ONLY WAY TO GO

The quality of the material in your cabinets may not matter as much as you think. The lowest-quality option is particleboard cabinet boxes surface-wrapped with a plasticized paper. But these days the boxes of a lot of custom cabinets are just particleboard covered with veneer. You don't need solid wood cabinets. You might want solid wood *doors,* but even then it's possible to get laminated wood or wood veneer doors that look great. If you want something like walnut, the problem is you just can't find a walnut tree big enough to make boards that size, so it's all veneer.

Custom cabinets are made to order, allowing you to choose the style, design, materials, size, finish

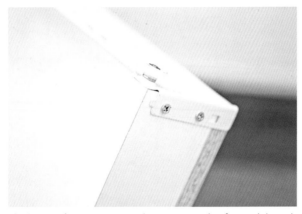

The boxes of many custom cabinets are made of particleboard covered with veneer. You can improve the look with solid wood doors.

and hardware according to your needs, space and taste. This is the most expensive option when it comes to cabinetry for kitchens and bathrooms, and fabrication and delivery of the cabinets can take up to four months. I guess this is why people are often shocked to learn that some of these high-end cabinets are made of top-grade particleboard and veneer—they're not necessarily solid wood. The benefit of particleboard over solid wood is that it's engineered to be very dense and stable. The doors aren't going to warp, shrink and crack when your house becomes humid. The magic of custom cabinets is in the nuances and small details: the doors feel a little heavier, but they don't slam; the drawers close quietly—you can even tap some drawers, and they open themselves. And, of course, everything is built from scratch to fit your space perfectly. I'm a big proponent of custom kitchens, and I like details like crown moulding and trim, which make a big impact.

On the opposite end of the spectrum are **stock cabinets**. These are ready-made cabinets manufactured in a factory. They are sold in modular units with no option to customize, though you'll get some choice in cabinet heights, door styles and finishes. Stock cabinets are the most affordable and quick to ship. You can buy them pre-assembled or flat-packaged depending on the store and manufacturer.

Semi-custom cabinets sit somewhere in the middle in terms of price and delivery time because they combine custom and stock components. For example, we'll make custom doors to fit stock cabinet boxes. We'll get maple veneer hardwood, cut it into

The magic of custom cabinets is in the nuances—solid wood drawers have beautiful joints and slide closed without slamming. But there's a cost: custom work is the priciest and can take up to four months for delivery.

door sizes and then cover the exposed edges and stain it all the same. When we're done, it looks like a solid piece of maple. Or we'll use detailed crown mouldings to make a range hood look like it was made from custom materials. Quite often we will do this kind of work if homeowners want a great look but can't afford custom cabinets.

MISTAKE #54:
RIPPING OUT A KITCHEN WHEN YOU JUST WANT NEW CABINETS

To reface or replace—that's a question many homeowners ask themselves. It all depends on your budget and what you really want. If the layout of the kitchen works, maybe you don't need to gut it. But it's pretty rare that we go into a kitchen and hear the homeowners say they just want to change the colour of the cabinets. We do 90% of our kitchen renos because the layout isn't practical or the room is too small. There's always more than one thing that needs fixing.

But refacing cabinets is definitely a cost-effective option. The doors themselves can just be removed, sanded, primed, painted and then reattached if you want to stick with the same style. Even the plastic veneer finish on some low-quality cabinets can be painted, and so can the interiors. If you want, you can spray the inside of the cabinet a different colour from the doors, but ideally the inside should be a light colour—it will look brighter and will reflect light into your cabinets.

You could also reface cabinets with new veneer. The most common option is wood veneer, a durable covering made of wood strips and applied to the surface of cabinet doors and frames to update their appearance (vinyl and plastic laminate veneers are also available). The process involves removing exist-

Take your pick: Do you want the cabinet face to be visible around the doors (*top*), or do you prefer that the doors cover the cabinet face (*bottom*)?

ing doors, drawer fronts and hinges, and then applying and trimming matching veneer to all visible exteriors of the cabinet. I'd recommend this option only if your doors and boxes are in good condition—it's harder to work with cabinets that have swollen or warped due to humidity damage. You can have this done with laminate veneer for less than half the cost of replacing all of your cabinets. Of course, if you decide to reface with all wood veneer, the price starts to increase. Refacing your entire kitchen with veneer isn't a job for the uninitiated, though, so the better cost-effective DIY solution is to paint the doors and the face of the cabinets.

Another option is to keep the cabinet boxes and replace the doors. With some cabinets the closed door will cover the whole cabinet face; with others the cabinet box will be visible when the door is closed (see photos, page 117). If we're retrofitting a white kitchen with new mahogany or walnut doors, we take all the doors off and paint the cabinet faces dark. That way everything ties in when the new doors are in place.

MISTAKE #55:
INSTALLING CABINETS BEFORE FLOORS

If you're doing a big kitchen reno, always install flooring before the cabinets. Working with an empty space will make the floor installation much easier because you won't need to make nearly as many difficult cuts.

If you're replacing the floor in a kitchen and you don't want to rip out the cabinets, it's usually possible to remove the toe kicks so you can install one row of new tile or hardwood slightly underneath the cabinets. Once you reinstall the toe kicks, you won't see the unfinished edges of the flooring because everything will be hidden.

You've got a different problem if you want to install new flooring without removing the old flooring. Let's say the cabinets are sitting on a ceramic floor, and you decide to put hardwood on top of that. Now you may not be able to get the dishwasher out. Murphy's law says as soon as you put the new flooring in, there will be a leak or some other breakdown, and the dishwasher will absolutely need to be taken out. So I'm warning you now that this shortcut might end up biting you in the butt.

If a homeowner wants a new floor, most of the time we will remove the base cabinets and the dishwasher, install the new flooring and then put everything back.

Mouldings can give base cabinets the look of furniture (*top*), but a recessed toe kick (*bottom*) makes standing at the counter more comfortable.

Chances are there aren't too many base cabinets and it just takes a couple of hours to remove all the stuff, which will save a lot of headaches.

MISTAKE #56:
STARTING YOUR BASE CABINET INSTALLATION IN THE WRONG PLACE

A lot of people installing cabinets will just start in a corner and work their way out from there. That sounds sensible enough—unless the corner ends up being a low point in the room. If that is the case, your cabinet will sit fine in that spot, but as you move along the wall, the cabinets won't be level. You'd have to cut the bottoms off to align the tops, which would be way too much work. That's why you have to start by finding the highest point of the room. It's a lot easier to raise a cabinet up than to push another into the subfloor.

To find the high spot, use a long level and a straight edge to make a reference line on the walls where you're planning to install cabinets. Then go around the room with a measuring tape and find the spot with the shortest distance between the floor and your reference line: that will be the highest point in the room. Once you find it, measure from the floor to 34½ inches (the standard height for lower cabinets), and make a mark on your wall. Now use the level to extend that line all the way around the kitchen, wherever you're planning to install base cabinets. The floor may not be level, but your line will be, and that's what matters.

After an accurate line has been drawn, measure the backsplash. The standard space between the countertop and the bottom of the upper cabinets is 18 inches, but that's by no means the maximum. If your upper cabinets are 42 inches and go right to the ceiling, the backsplash can be a little bigger. But for the sake of argument, let's say you're going with an 18-inch back-splash. Measure 19½ inches from your line, because you have to account for the countertop. Then draw another line to mark the bottom of the upper cabinets. Locate the studs using a stud finder and mark them on the wall; you'll fasten the upper and lower cabinet boxes into the studs.

Once I've got my line for the upper cabinets, I screw a 2 × 4 into a couple of studs right below that line, like a shelf, as a temporary support for the cabinets. When I put in the uppers, I can just rest them on that 2 × 4. This works especially well if you're working

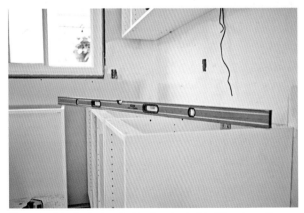

Use a stud finder to locate the framing behind the drywall, which you'll fasten the upper cabinets to (*top*). Next, install base cabinets, working from the highest point along the floor (*middle*). Use a level to make sure cabinets are plumb and level before securing them (*bottom*).

alone—it's like having an extra set of hands. Once the cabinets are installed, you just unscrew the 2 × 4, and if you're going to tile the backsplash anyway, you don't even need to patch the wall.

Now you can start installing the base cabinets, making sure to shim them up to the line and making sure the top is level and the face is plumb (see more details on this below).

USING A STUD FINDER

All jokes aside, a stud finder (also known as a stud detector or sensor) is a handheld gadget used to locate framing studs behind walls. Press the button on a stud finder and slide it along the wall until the gadget beeps or activates a red light. Stop immediately and mark this spot with a pencil or scrap of masking tape; this marks one edge of the stud. Repeat to find and mark the other edge.

MISTAKE #57:
INCORRECTLY INSTALLING BASE CABINETS

After marking reference points (see Mistake #56, page 118) and installing wall cabinets, you can switch to lower cabinets. Start in the corner and progress to the end of the row, not the other way around. If you start at the end of the row and discover once you get to the corner that you've measured wrong and don't have enough space, there's no way to make the boxes fit since you're dealing with a fixed wall and cabinet boxes that can't be resized. You'd have to tear everything out and start again.

Make sure the cabinets are plumb and level before you attach them to the wall (more details on this below). If the floor is uneven, you may have to raise the cabinet with shims so it meets your 34½-inch

line. Shims are thin tapered wedges of wood used to fill gaps or spaces between objects (in this case, the cabinet base and the floor). You may also need to use shims to make the cabinets vertically plumb (which means perpendicular to the floor). At the high spot in the floor, as long as you found it and measured properly all the way around the room, the cabinet there shouldn't need any shims.

To fasten each cabinet to the wall, drill a hole at each stud, going right through the shims if you used any. (Marking stud locations on the wall between the upper and lower cabinets before you start installing will make locating them easier.) Drive screws partway into the drilled hole, check again that the cabinet is level, and shim at the floor or wall if needed. This first step isn't the final fastening; that comes in a minute. Set the adjoining base cabinet in place. Pull the two cabinet frames tight together and clamp them in place. Level in all directions; make sure the cabinet faces are flush (you might need to shim). Repeat all steps with all cabinets, levelling and screwing cabinets to the wall studs one at a time. For each cabinet, use at least two screws in the wall studs, and use four screws to secure cabinets to each other, pre-drilling to prevent the cabinets from splintering when screwed. Use a utility knife to cut off any shims sticking out.

MISTAKE #58:
NOT SECURING UPPER CABINETS PROPERLY

Remember when you put up cabinets that you're not just hanging a painting. Even if they're just made of MDF, but especially if they're solid wood, the cabinets themselves have some serious weight. Then, of course, you'll be filling them with dishes and glasses or canned and dry goods—this stuff isn't light. So make

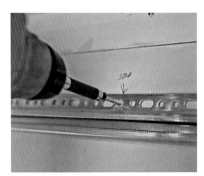

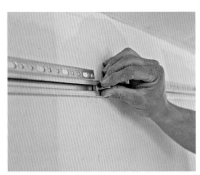

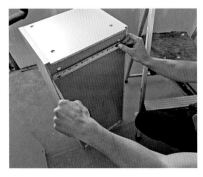

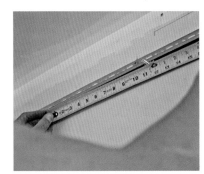

Some cabinets, like those of the Swedish variety, are fastened with a rail system screwed to the wall. These cabinets come with precut reinforced holes at the back. Measure the spacing of those holes, then attach the cabinet to the rail system. Level and plumb the first cabinet, then use clamps to keep the remaining cabinet faces flush.

sure the cabinets are well secured so they won't come away from the wall after a few years of opening and closing and loading and unloading.

The specific technique for securing the cabinets to the wall will differ depending on the manufacturer. Most flat-packaged cabinets, for example, have two holes in the back where you attach the cabinets to a rail system. The rail goes horizontally along the wall and is screwed to the studs, and then you just attach the cabinets to the rail.

We sometimes use a similar technique with other types of cabinets. If we're doing a complete kitchen renovation and we're going to tile the backsplash, we might put a horizontal strip of plywood on the walls instead of drywall. Then we can attach the cabinets anywhere on that plywood wall, and we don't need to search for a stud. If you're not using a rail system, always attach your upper cabinets at the top to studs in the wall. If you don't, you're asking for trouble.

Once you fasten the tops of the cabinets into the wall, some will protrude a little more than others. Align them so they are all flush by clamping the frames together with the faces in line. Some cabinets come with little bolts. For these ones, you drill through the sides of the cabinets and then bolt them together on both sides, which locks them all in line as one big assembly. Just make sure you clamp the cabinets tightly before you start pre-drilling and fastening, or the act of drilling will move the cabinet out of position.

Now you've effectively got one big cabinet, and you can shim behind the wall until everything sits plumb—or as plumb as possible. If your wall has a pronounced bow, make the cabinets lean back a little bit rather than leaning forward, so your glasses won't slide out. This happens more often than you think—

sometimes a tape joint (where a seam between drywall sheets has been taped) will really stick out in the middle of a wall. But fortunately, kitchens don't normally have a full run of upper cabinets; often, something breaks up the uppers, like a window or range hood, and makes any irregularities in the wall less obvious. That's where the art of kitchen design and experience comes in: finding the right combination of cabinets can minimize the problem.

For safety reasons, it's also important to set the range hood at the correct height above the stove. The amount of clearance depends on the capacity of the hood and type of range, so check appliance manuals and building code for guidelines. All stoves need a vent fan to extract humidity and cooking smells, but fans are especially important with gas appliances to

Once the cabinets are fastened to the wall, line up the faces and use clamps to keep them tight and flush. Then bolt the cabinet boxes together from both sides.

prevent exhaust fumes ending up inside your home. Follow installation instructions carefully. Microwaves with built-in ventilation fans are a good space saver if the capacity of the fan is high enough for the range (again, check manuals). Cabinets and any other finishes need to sit at least 30 inches above a gas cooktop.

Once all the uppers are hung, and the faces are all lined up, attached and shimmed, only then do you put in the shelves, hang the doors and attach all the hardware.

MISTAKE #59:
SPENDING TOO MUCH ON THE COUNTERTOP

Everyone's obsessed with countertops these days, and some people are spending five figures on them. That's fine if you can afford it, but there are great options at much lower price points.

Laminate is the cheapest if you go for standard particleboard covered with a plastic or some other kind of manufactured veneer. But there are high-end laminates out there, too: we've installed some that look just like marble—but you can tell the difference when you run your hand over them. As with laminate floors, you can get cheap garbage, or you can spend a little more and get something that looks almost natural. Cost: about $20 to $80 per square foot.

Laminate countertops are relatively easy to install—at least compared with granite. You buy them in lengths of 8, 10 or 12 feet, cut them on-site and then just glue veneer on the ends. You can also buy corners that are already assembled, and I would recommend doing this because putting together a corner on a laminate countertop is actually very difficult—you have to make a perfect mitre joint. You may also be able to

custom order the countertop so there's only one factory seam right in the corner.

I've been into so many kitchens where it's a dead giveaway that the homeowners have installed the laminate countertop themselves because the end of the countertop is all chipped. To avoid damaging it, flip the countertop over and cut it from the bottom; otherwise, the saw teeth will chip the laminate off the surface. A saw blade with more teeth will also do a better job, but one crack and your counter is garbage, so if you're doing the kitchen yourself, be careful. You can also ask the countertop fabricator to cut the counter to size.

Laminate countertops seem like a great deal—until they get chipped.

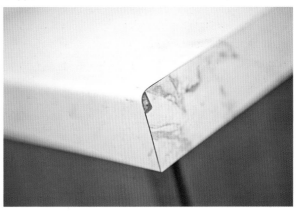

MARBLE
2cm GREYSTONE
Origin: Iran

PER SQUARE FOOT
$69
INSTALLED

MARBLE
2cm BLANCHE NOIR
Origin: China

PER SQUARE FOOT
$59
INSTALLED

Granite (*top*) is pretty bulletproof, but like marble, it needs to be sealed. Some engineered quartz (*bottom*) is translucent, so it can be lit from below.

If you're installing your own laminate counter, fasten it by driving screws up through the base cabinet. Make sure your screws aren't too long, or they'll go right through the countertop—I've seen it happen a million times. The right length depends on the type of countertop: some are 1½ inches thick and will overhang the front of the cabinets a little bit. Others are ⅝ inch thick and have a ⅝-inch lip around the front. In

Marble countertops (*opposite*) are pure luxury but are prone to staining.

that case, use ⅝-inch plywood or MDF strapping along the top of the cabinets to lift the countertop off the cabinets. Otherwise, the front lip will hang over the doors and block them from opening.

Marble counters are pure luxury. You can't see it, but they sometimes contain steel rods for reinforcement because marble often has quartz veins, which are weak spots that can crack easily. Some marble countertops are attached to a sheet of plywood for the same reason, though most are a solid 1¼ or 1½ inches. Marble can stand up quite well to water if you seal it properly (you'll have to do this yourself after installation unless you arrange for the installer to seal it). But walking on marble with wet feet in a bathroom is not the same level of abuse as chopping food, throwing plates, juicing pomegranates and spilling red wine on it. The kitchen counter is a pretty violent place and sees lots of foods that can stain, so marble doesn't usually look the same after a few years in a kitchen. Cost: about $125 to $250 per square foot.

Granite is pretty much bulletproof. The problem with any stone countertop is if you drop anything breakable on it—your grandmother's soup tureen or the crystal glasses you got for your wedding—your item will be destroyed. Like marble, granite needs to be sealed. Cost: about $100 to $225 per square foot.

If you want the look without the maintenance, granite veneers are available. They can be attached to an existing countertop or a piece of ¾-inch plywood. This has never really been a DIY project, although materials will soon be available that could change that.

Engineered quartz is a very cool design feature: you get the look of natural stone without any of the maintenance. There's even semi-opaque quartz that can be lit from below. It's used a lot in hotel bathrooms,

With stone and engineered countertops, you get to choose how the edge is finished. Eased and squared edges are more popular these days than the old bullnose.

where the nightlight comes up through the countertop. Cost: about $100 to $185 per square foot.

Soapstone is another material that looks great. It scratches, but you can sand and shape it with sandpaper and rub in some mineral oil or beeswax. And when soapstone is treated with linseed or tung oil, it darkens up, making the blue and white veins really visible. Cost: about $100 to $125 per square foot.

With stone and engineered countertops, you can choose how you want the edges finished. The bullnose style used to be really popular but isn't so much anymore; now we see more squared or eased edges.

I love **butcher block** countertops. They age well—they get that patina over the years—and they're pretty easy to repair because they can be sanded. But they are very porous, so don't cut raw chicken and fish on there without giving the countertop a thorough cleaning afterward with soap and water. Regular maintenance is important, which means oiling every month for the first year, then every six months after that. Cost: about $75 to $200 per square foot.

MISTAKE #60:
SCREWING UP THE SINK CUT-OUT

If you want an undermount sink, you'll need to choose a countertop made from real or engineered stone. As soon as a laminate countertop is cut, there's an exposed edge, so you need a rim-mounted sink to cover up that cut.

One of the trickiest parts about installing a countertop is making the sink cut-out. When you buy a sink, it comes with a template for tracing the cut-out onto the countertop. The installers who come to measure for your stone countertop will typically take the sink template and make the cut-out for the sink at the factory. In fact, you can just give them the sink so they can see exactly what they're doing.

If you're installing a laminate countertop on your own, you have to make this cut. First, tape along the line you're cutting or tape the feet of your jig saw so you don't damage the counter surface (painter's tape is fine for this purpose). Then trace the template onto the countertop or onto the tape. Drill a hole for the jig-saw blade, and then cut out along the template line. Use a hole saw to cut the hole for the faucet. Some faucet sets require one hole; others need two or three depending on the style of the taps. You might need a fourth hole if yours comes with a soap dispenser or

If you want the clean look of a rimless undermount sink (*top*), you'll need a countertop in real or engineered stone. Rim-mounted sinks (*bottom*) hide the exposed edge of a laminate counter.

hose. Once the holes have been cut, hook the fastener (which comes with the faucet set) into the channel that's usually located under the lip of the sink. The fastener will pull the sink down and hold it against the countertop when you tighten it. Seal underneath the lip of the sink with a bead of silicone, because the last thing you want is to get water under there. If particle-board gets wet, it swells up and looks like hell.

With stone countertops, undermount sinks are attached with epoxy and 100% silicone. The epoxy cures in about five minutes, but the silicone takes longer, and that's what holds the sink for the long term.

Installers usually lay a piece of 2×4 on the countertop across the top of the sink hole and insert a threaded rod that extends down through the drain hole. By tightening that rod, they can pull the sink up toward the countertop and clamp it in place until the adhesives cure.

MISTAKE #61:
IMPROPERLY REPLACING A SINK

Replacing an undermount sink is a pretty delicate procedure. First, you have to remove the P-trap from the plumbing. Start by turning off the shut-off valves under the sink (they resemble odd-looking faucets) in case someone tries to turn on the water while the trap is removed. Place a bucket under the trap to catch water. On a plastic trap, unscrew the nuts: grip the trap in one hand and rotate each nut counter-clockwise. If turning by hand isn't loosening the nuts, unscrew them with pliers. If you're dealing with a metal P-trap, you will definitely need pliers because of corrosion. Slide the nuts out of the way and pull down on the part of the trap connected to the pipe extending down from the sink (have that bucket handy). Once that end is free, the other end of the trap should detach easily from the plumbing.

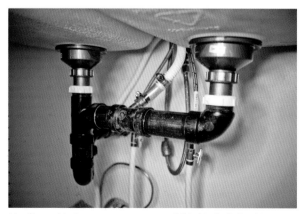

You'll need to know your way around this kind of plumbing to replace a sink.

When you're dry-fitting a P-trap, press the pieces together fully and then mark each side of the joins with a white crayon so you can easily match up the marks later.

Then get a very sharp knife that can fit between the countertop and the sink and use it to cut away the silicone bond all the way around the sink lip. There are also chemicals that will dissolve silicone, which you can use to clean the bottom of the countertop before installing the new sink. Make sure you prep the surface well, removing all the old silicone so the bottom of the countertop is good and clean. Otherwise, the new silicone won't adhere properly.

If you're installing a laundry tub or another single sink, it's not very difficult to install a new P-trap. You can buy kits that have everything you need to build a P-trap and attach it to the drainpipe in the wall. You just have to piece it all together. First, dry-fit everything (put the pieces in place without adhesive to make sure it all fits), and then glue it all together. The P-trap has all kinds of angles and turns, so when you're dry-fitting, screw the pieces together fully, then use a white crayon to mark each side of the joins so you can match the marks up later.

It's also possible to install a new sink and use an old P-trap (as long the P-trap is in good shape and not too corroded). Usually there is a threaded copper or chrome neck inserted into the top of the P-trap that you can unscrew so the sink pops right out. You can then attach your new sink to the old P-trap—but that's assuming the hole in the new sink is in the same spot. If it's not, you may be able to loosen the P-trap and swivel it, or you may just have to modify the drain using one or more plumbing adaptors, which are sold at hardware stores or plumbing suppliers.

It's important to note that once you put glue on the P-trap pieces, they'll slide more and they may go in farther than when they were dry. The glue slightly melts the ABS (that's the plastic used to make drain pipes), so the pieces will fit together much easier, and all of a sudden the joined pieces may be shorter than you expected. The obvious solution here is to squeeze the pieces together as tightly as possible when dry-fitting, but the danger is you might never get them apart! A better fix is simply to measure properly. Inside each fitting there's usually a kind of stopper that prevents the pipe from going in more than about ½ inch. So measure the distance between the stopper and the edge at both ends and then measure the pipe in the middle. You can use a hacksaw to cut the ABS, or a chop saw if you're doing a lot of cutting. (Plumbers often have a wheel cutter that clamps on the pipe and spins around. That gives you a nice edge, so you'll get a better dry fit.) A hacksaw can leave really rough edges that may not fit together well, so you may have to sand them smooth to prevent burrs from getting jammed into the fitting.

MISTAKE #62:
INSTALLING A DISHWASHER IMPROPERLY

Installing a dishwasher is not particularly hard, although you do have both electrical and plumbing to worry about. Some of the new models now come with plugs, but others still need to be hard-wired, which is a little more difficult. All dishwashers require three basic connections: attach a water supply, connect a drain line and hook up the electrical. I won't go into detail on the electrical and plumbing because there are tons of websites that describe the steps in detail. But I will share a couple of tips.

One of the trickiest parts can be securing the dishwasher in place so it doesn't tip forward when you open the door. There are usually two straps at the top, which fasten the dishwasher into the countertop—you'll likely have to open the dishwasher door to do this. If you've got a stone countertop, there should be strapping across there that you can screw into.

To drain the dishwasher, an ABS fitting hooks into the same drain as the kitchen sink. If you're just replacing a dishwasher, the fitting is probably already there, but if you're adding a dishwasher to a kitchen that didn't have one before, you'll need to install it—or call a plumber. If you're installing the ABS fitting yourself, remember that it goes in before the P-trap. If it goes in after, you could get sewer gases backing up into your dishwasher.

MISTAKE #63:
ASSUMING YOU CAN FIX ANY LEAKY FAUCET WITH A NEW WASHER

When the kitchen or bathroom faucet leaks, it's tempting to think you can just buy a new washer or replace some other worn-out part. And in many cases you can: replacement parts for expensive faucets are usually easy to find. When purchasing faucet sets, look for models with metal and ceramic parts, not plastic. And if you just bought a new faucet, hang on to the instruction manual and the warranty in case someday you need to replace a worn component. If you can

get the right part at a hardware store or directly from the manufacturer, you may be able to remove the tap handle, take out the cartridge, valve, washer, O-ring or whatever is worn out, and replace it with a new one. (Make sure you shut off the water first!)

Unfortunately, more and more we're finding you need a specialty shop if you just want a new part. With a lot of the lower-end faucets out there—the ones you find in most entry-level homes—you won't even find parts. The sad reality is that these faucets are cheaper and easier to replace than they are to repair: you might pay $40 or $50 for a cheap new faucet, whereas you would pay $30 for the part.

By the way, if you're buying a new faucet, consider looking for a model that uses less water. Many come with internal aerators that mix air with water. You won't feel like you're sacrificing—you still get the same pressure and flow—and you'll pay less for your water bills. Actually, with a high-efficiency faucet, you save twice since you also save on water heating. Standard faucets use 2.2 gallons per minute (8.3 litres); high-efficiency faucets use 1.5 gpm (5.7 litres) or less. Look for products with a WaterSense label (epa.gov/watersense), which is similar to the Energy Star sticker you find on electrical appliances.

MISTAKE #64:
NOT INSTALLING A BATHROOM VANITY CORRECTLY

Bathroom vanities take a beating from daily use and humidity. It's no wonder they start to look tired and might need replacing after several years. Fortunately, they're easy to replace with a process much like the one used to install kitchen cabinets.

Start by turning off the water supply to the house and removing the faucet, sink and vanity. Next, bring in the new vanity. Vanities typically come with a removable countertop and sink. Move the complete vanity into place where it will be installed and trace its shape on the wall. Locate the studs and mark them just above the top of the vanity—you're going to screw the vanity to the studs to secure it.

Next, measure, mark and drill holes in the back of the vanity (if it has one; some vanities are open at the back) for drain pipes and supply lines, which will be protruding where you removed the previous vanity from the wall. Place a level on the vanity. Shim it at the floor until the vanity is level. Place the level against a vertical edge of the vanity and shim it at the wall until it sits plumb.

Now you work from the inside of the vanity to attach it to the wall. Use 3-inch wood screws through the back of the vanity's top mounting rail and drill right into the studs. Check again for level; you might need to shim a second time at the back and/or sides. Don't forget to trim the shims with a utility knife. Sometimes after a vanity is installed, you'll notice gaps between the vanity and the floor or wall. Cover those gaps by installing quarter-round moulding along the wall or floor, or fill with paintable caulking.

Put the vanity top in place and install the faucet and drain assembly (see Mistake #65, next). To secure the vanity top, most installations call for a small bead of silicone caulking on the top lip of the cabinet. Press the top into place, checking that it's level, looks evenly placed and sits flush to the wall. If there's a big gap between the vanity top and the wall, you'll lose toothbrushes and lipstick behind the cabinet.

Finally, reconnect the faucet supply lines to the water supply and connect the P-trap. Turn on the water supply and test for leaks. Follow the faucet instructions to install the pop-up drain.

MISTAKE #65:
THINKING IT'S TOO HARD TO REPLACE A FAUCET OR TOILET

Normally I don't recommend DIY plumbing. But changing a faucet or swapping out an old toilet are fairly straightforward DIY jobs, as long as you have local shut-off valves, which are actually required in new homes now. Look under the counter. You should have hot and cold supply lines coming up from the basement, and ideally there's a shut-off valve that

You don't need to shut off the water main to replace a faucet: just find the local shut-off valves.

links to a ⅜-inch coupling that's threaded to accept a braided hose. (A heads-up before you leave the store: not all faucets come with these braided hoses, especially if you buy a cheaper one, so you may have to buy the hose separately.) Same with a toilet: there should be a shut-off valve near the floor, and you can simply unscrew the hose that attaches to the tank.

Here's a tip: even if you have shut-off valves under the sink or near the toilet, it's still important to know where the main shut-off is. We've been in houses where something has gone wrong—either a fitting has broken or somebody has nicked the pipe with a saw—and we're running around trying to find a shut-off valve because the homeowner isn't there.

One thing I wouldn't recommend is putting in a new shut-off valve if you've never touched plumbing before. It requires using a propane torch in tight quarters—not a great idea if you don't have any experience. Plus, if you try it and have a problem, you need to shut the water off and it has to stay off until a plumber can come in and fix it.

Once you locate and turn off the local shut-off valves, make sure your new tap fits your countertop: faucets require one, two or three holes. Some fabricators drill these on-site, and others use the template that came with your faucet to do them before the counter is delivered and installed. (It's possible to drill these holes yourself but it takes a fair amount of skill and a diamond-coated hole saw bit if you're working with stone.) Place the new faucet into the pre-existing holes and use the washer, metal ring and nut assembly that comes with the faucet to fasten it securely to the countertop. Put a bead of plumber's putty under and around the base of the faucet (or silicone caulk if your sink is marble) so water can't get underneath it. Some faucets come with a rubber gasket and don't require putty or caulking—as always, read the instructions and follow them!

The faucet will come with instructions for you to follow. But what they don't tell you is that once you get everything in place, there is a danger of over-tightening. You can actually crack the countertop or break a solder joint or a fitting if you tighten too much. Normally the connections have a good solid rubber washer, so you need to go only about a quarter turn past hand-tightening: you don't have to crank them down. If you turn the water on and there's no leak, you're fine.

One final tip: many a colourful word has been uttered under the sink by someone trying to install a faucet on his or her own. When you're under the sink, it helps to have a second person making sure the faucet is in the right spot.

Replacing the toilet is a little harder than switching a faucet—and the consequences of doing it wrong are a little more unpleasant. I would put it at a 4 or 5 on a difficulty scale of 1 to 10. The hardest thing about replacing the toilet is making sure you have a good seal underneath. But even without a perfect seal, you're not going to get a ton of leakage. Under the toilet bowl, there's a protruding lip that sits inside the 4-inch sewer pipe and a wax ring that creates the seal. The best wax rings have a plastic flange that extends down into the sewer pipe. That way, for anything to leak, it would have to go down and come back up around that flange. If you do have water under the toilet, it's probably coming from condensation under the tank. The supply line carries cold water, and if it's really humid in your house, it can condense around the tank, run down the bowl and onto the floor.

You might be tempted to attach the bowl to the floor before you attach the tank, but it's actually easier

The bowl is attached to a rough-in in the floor. Make sure you have a good seal underneath the toilet, which is created by a wax ring that sits between the bottom of the toilet and the top of the toilet flange.

if you assemble the whole toilet first. If the tank isn't attached to the bowl, it will be hard to tell whether the toilet will line up with the wall. Between the tank and the bowl, there's a pretty large rubber gasket, so you don't need to tighten the bolts too much: there's a danger of breaking either the bowl or the tank if you over-tighten.

Once the toilet has been assembled, begin the installation by turning it over and attaching a new wax ring. (Warning: The area under the rim of the toilet can be razor-sharp. Once, I grabbed there to pick up the bowl, and it sliced all my fingers. So use caution when you're first lifting it just in case there are sharp edges.) Now that the new wax ring is attached, turn the toilet back over and place it on top of the rough-in—the part that connects the toilet to the sewer pipe. Make sure the bolts in the rough-in come up through the holes on the sides of the toilet. The rough-in has guides on both sides—elongated holes that are adjustable—so you can turn the toilet a little bit to align it. If you're replacing an old toilet, get rid of the old bolts and replace them with clean new ones. Toilet bolts sometimes come with little

plastic covers—you may need to use a hacksaw to cut away part of the bolt to allow those covers to fit. Don't cut all the way through—just get it started and then bend it back and forth until it breaks off.

The new toilet will probably not sit flat, so just sit on it and wiggle around a bit until the wax seal is compressed and fits tightly. Once it's in snugly, then you can tighten those bolts to secure the toilet to the floor. But be careful: again, if you really crank it, you can break the bowl. That's especially true if you've got an old-school copper rough-in—they can be really strong. You can't fix a cracked toilet bowl; you just have to buy a new toilet. All it takes is one extra turn. I've seen people do it immediately after I told them to be careful not to tighten too much. To be fair, it's hard to know you've gone too far until it actually breaks. So just tighten it until the toilet stops wobbling.

With a lot of new toilets, the mechanism in the tank is all plastic. We're getting away from the big float on the arm and all those bigger moving parts. Now there's basically just a tower in the centre, so it's a lot simpler. If those parts break, you can replace them, and they're relatively standard sizes. If you've got a toilet that's not working, pull the guts out and just take the pieces to the hardware store, where you should be able to find some sort of kit to match it. In a worst-case scenario, if there isn't a replacement, you're already at the hardware store, so you can buy a new toilet, a new wax ring, toilet bolts and the whole deal.

Now, there are a few mistakes people make along the way—other than breaking the toilet. You can damage the rough-in, in which case you will need a plumber to replace it. If the wax ring isn't sealed properly, you can end up with sewer gas coming up through the hole. You can also cause water damage if the supply line is leaking or if there's condensation.

We had a customer who replaced his own toilet, and it dripped for months from the supply line. Five drips a minute is a pretty slow leak, but it amounts to about one litre a day. Over a year, that's about 20 full bathtubs. In this case, the water ran along a grout line and then down into the floor. Well, the area underneath was full of water, and we had to rip down the whole ceiling in his kitchen. Plus, the wall was full of mould. He didn't notice because it was very subtle, and that ended up being an expensive mistake. The thread where the supply line connected to the shut-off was fine; the culprit was the other end that connects to the tank. That connector is just plastic, so you have to hand-tighten it. He had tightened it a little too much and it cracked. It was an expensive mistake!

Any time you've installed a new fixture or faucet, check it carefully over the next 24 to 48 hours to make sure there isn't a slow drip that could turn into a huge problem. The best way to do that is to wrap the connections with some toilet paper. In a day or so, if the paper is still dry, you know you're okay.

MISTAKE #66:
CALLING A PLUMBER TO INSTALL A NEW SHOWERHEAD

There are few things better than a new showerhead. But before you replace yours, try soaking it in a cleaner that dissolves hard-water stains (like CLR) or tying a bag of vinegar around it for a few hours. Over time, minerals in your water can accumulate in the tiny openings of your showerhead and reduce the flow. A good cleaning can make it spray like new.

If cleaning doesn't help, or if you're updating the look, changing your showerhead is an easy DIY job, and it can make a big difference. Even converting a standard showerhead to a rain showerhead is something many homeowners can do on their own.

On the shower arm—that's the pipe that sticks out from the wall—there's a male thread. Just turn the showerhead counter-clockwise, and it will come off. Then wrap the male thread with Teflon plumber's tape and screw on a new showerhead—it couldn't be easier.

Installing a rain showerhead is a bit more difficult, but you don't have to get behind the wall to do it. Inside the wall is a 90-degree brass coupling with a female thread on it. That's what holds the shower arm. (This coupling should be secured to a stud so it doesn't flop around, although I've certainly seen homes where that wasn't done properly.) If you want to install a longer shower arm for a rain showerhead, first remove the escutcheon plate that covers the hole in the wall and then unscrew the old shower arm from that coupling and replace it with a longer one. Again, use Teflon on the thread.

Finish by sliding the escutcheon plate over the rough hole. But before you tighten it, turn on the shower and take a peek in there to make sure you haven't got any leaks behind the wall.

CHAPTER

SIX

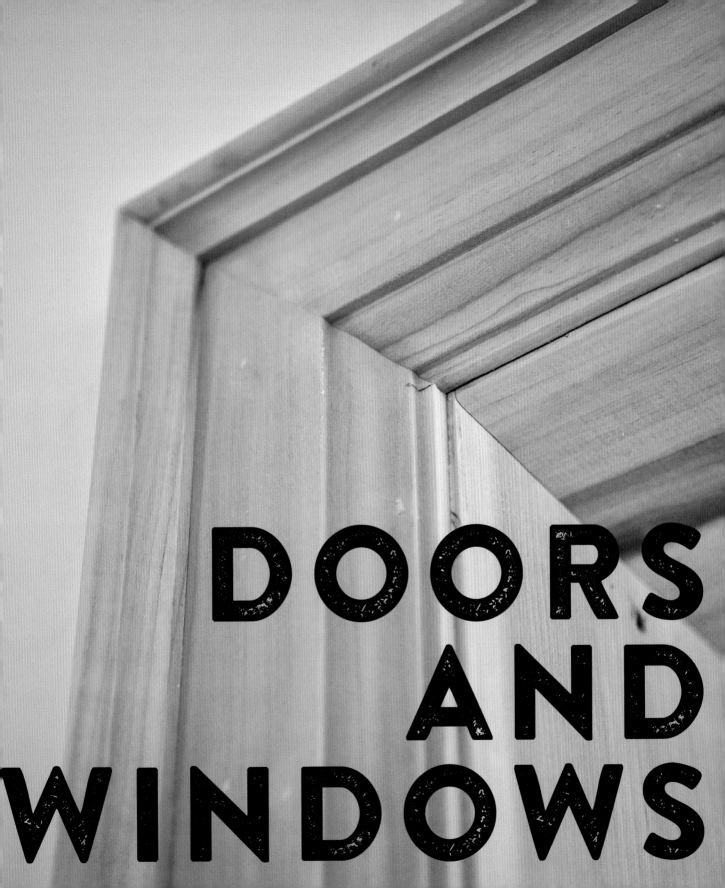

DOORS AND WINDOWS

DOORS AND WINDOWS MAKE A BIG IMPACT ON THE CURB APPEAL OF YOUR HOME. YOUR FRONT DOOR, ESPECIALLY, IS A FOCAL POINT, SO THIS ISN'T A PLACE TO SKIMP.

Unfortunately, many new subdivision houses have doors and windows of less than stellar quality. Not only does this affect the appearance of your house, it also leads to poorer insulation (and higher energy bills) and more street noise. The same goes if you live in an older home that still has single-pane windows or an uninsulated wood door.

Upgrading your exterior doors and windows is an expensive job, but it's probably necessary if you have noticed the warning signs: condensation between panes of glass, moisture causing rot around wood frames or windows and doors that don't open and close properly.

Changing interior doors and upgrading trim is just as powerful as fresh paint—these changes will instantly improve the appearance of your home. Replacing trim is a relatively easy DIY job, and the wider designs look a lot classier than the entry-level MDF many builders use. Replacing the door hardware (the knobs and hinges) is another simple weekend job that gives your home a quick facelift.

However, if you're someone who doesn't have a tool box and has never operated a saw, installing new doors and windows yourself is a bad idea. On the surface this kind of job looks fairly easy—at least it's not dangerous like wiring or roofing. But as you will quickly realize, there's a lot going on when installing a door or window because you're working in three dimensions, making adjustments from top to bottom, front to back and left to right. It's quite difficult to keep everything plumb, level and square—you almost need to be an octopus.

DOOR AND WINDOW BASICS
DIFFICULTY: 8 OUT OF 10

In a newly built home, the builder will usually stick to the minimum door and window requirements laid out in your local code: interior doors on the main floor must be at least 32 inches wide, for example, except for closets and bathrooms, which may be as narrow as 24 or 28 inches. Egress windows (those you may have to climb out of in an emergency) also have a minimum size. If you're building a custom home, you can make many of your own decisions as long as they meet code.

If you're doing any work on doors and windows, make sure you understand the lingo. The **jamb** is the wood frame surrounding a doorway. Doors and windows are usually surrounded by **trim**, which can also be called **moulding** or **casing**.

CHOOSING DOORS AND WINDOWS

- **Exterior doors** typically come in steel, wood, vinyl or fibreglass. They need both strength and insulating properties.

- **Interior doors** are lighter and thinner; they are rarely made from solid wood and are much more likely to have a hollow core filled with a structural paper.

- Windows come in many types, including **single-** or **double-hung** (the panes slide up and down), **slider** (the panes slide right to left), **awning** (the pane is hinged at the top and swings out at the bottom) and **casement** (the window swings open like door). These days the most common material for window frames is vinyl, which is weather-resistant and won't rot like untreated wood.

TOOLS AND MATERIALS YOU'LL NEED

- measuring tape and pencil
- level
- low-expansion spray-foam insulation
- mitre saw
- nail gun
- brads (for attaching trim)
- shims
- screw gun and screws

MISTAKE #67:
USING THE WRONG TYPE OF EXTERIOR DOOR

The ideal front door not only looks good but is also strong, secure and long-lasting and has some kind of insulation value. For example, whereas interior doors have a gap underneath the bottom to allow for airflow within the house, an exterior door is a completely different beast. The whole idea is to prevent air leaks, which will help keep your heating and cooling bills under control.

There are a few things to consider when looking at different door materials. Steel has a lot going for it: steel doors are very heavy, secure and resistant to break-ins. A **steel door** is not going to expand and contract as much as wood throughout the seasons, so it is good for sealing your home against air leaks. The insulation value is around R5, which isn't bad (for a complete explanation on R-values and what they mean, turn to page 30). But steel also conducts temperature, so the door will feel warm to the touch in summer and cold in winter. It also is more prone to denting. If a steel door gets banged up, those dents are there for good. If the door gets scratched, the scratches can rust.

Everybody loves the solid feel and natural look of a **wood door**. It's generally a high-end look that can work with many styles. Scratches can be fixed pretty easily. But while they have a warm look and feel, wood doors don't offer a great insulation value. A standard wood door that's 1¾ inches thick has an R-value of about 2.5, which means it's not going to do a great job of keeping warm air indoors and cold air out.

The other challenge with wood is it expands in the summer and shrinks a bit in the winter, which is going to mess with the weatherstripping around the perimeter. We've installed wood doors in the summer,

A steel door won't expand and contract as much as a wood door, so it helps guard against air leaks.

and they fit perfectly. Then we get a call in the winter from the owners saying there's a gap: when they close the door, they can see sunlight peeking under it. When we install wood doors in the winter, they call in the summer saying, "My door's too tight."

Sealing a wood door properly can reduce the amount of moisture that gets in under the wood so it doesn't expand and contract as much. For raw wood doors, some manufacturers recommend a stain-and-sealer as the first coat, which colours the wood and seals the surface. Make sure you coat all edges and surfaces—you have to remove the door from the hinges to do this properly. After the first coat dries completely, you can follow with an oil- or water-based finish.

Oil-based finishes have the advantage of drying faster. They become harder and more resistant to water, and you can apply them under most weather conditions. The problem is they break down faster in UV light, so they're not as durable. Water-based finishes are more flexible and stand up better to UV light. The problem with these products is they can't be applied in cool weather and can take weeks to fully cure. If you want to paint over that coat of sealant, you'll need to wait up to 45 days.

Fibreglass doors are great because they can mimic the finish of wood and the strength of steel with the added bonus of energy efficiency. Fibreglass entry doors have a polyurethane foam insulation core that can give them an insulation value of about R5 to R11. Plus, they've got a magnetic strip that acts as weatherstripping and seals in the same way a fridge door seals magnetically. If you install a fibreglass door properly, you don't need any other weatherstripping. They're low-maintenance because they won't rot, deteriorate, warp or twist like steel or wood. The big drawback of a fibreglass door is the price tag. If you want a highly insulated door and that natural wood look, be prepared to pay for it.

Doors with glass inserts are great at bringing in natural light, but they have two disadvantages. For one, glass has poor insulation value, which affects the overall R-value of your door (the reduction in R-value depends on the amount and type of glass). If you want more light inside without sacrificing heat waste, look for double- or triple-glazed window panes (that means two or three panes of glass) filled with gas. These two features help boost the R-value of the glass and the door. The second drawback of glass is security. It's a lot easier for thieves to break a pane of glass to gain access to your home. Consider using shatterproof glass or installing a grille using non-removable screws. There are also sheet coatings available that, when applied, reduce heat loss and increase security.

MISTAKE #68:
NOT KNOWING WHEN TO USE A PRE-HUNG DOOR

Swapping one interior door slab for another doesn't require advanced carpentry skills, but if you plan on replacing the entire kit and caboodle, you do need to know a few things.

First, you can choose a pre-hung door. Like the name suggests, the jamb (the one horizontal and two

I love the look of wood doors, but they can require more maintenance than steel or fibreglass doors.

Pre-hung doors come with the jamb already in place, which can make installation a lot easier.

vertical pieces that frame the door) arrives already built with the door itself (called the slab) hanging on hinges. A pre-hung door is one option when your existing jamb is so warped that it would be hard to hang a new slab and get it working properly. If you're in an 80-year-old home where the footings are sinking and your doors are on an angle or the jambs are out of square, you might want a pre-hung door. If you're not changing the size of the doorway, you can leave the frame and all of the trim in place and just replace the old door with a new slab. Stock doors come in standard sizes (typically 80 inches high by 32 inches wide, though 28-, 30- and 36-inch

doors are also common), so fitting a new door in an old home won't be a problem. If you're moving the door opening or making it bigger, obviously the whole frame has to come out, and that's a bigger job.

I definitely think pre-hung is the way to go for exterior doors. These units are built to be weather-resistant, so you don't have to do anything to make them tight-fitting. I wouldn't recommend trying to install a slab entry door—most homeowners will have a tough time because the job requires advanced carpentry skills.

Pre-hung doors aren't perfect, however. They're quite heavy, and this is especially true of exterior doors. Two strong people are needed for this installation (interior doors are generally lighter because the slab is often hollow). And I wouldn't describe them as easy to install. While you don't need to be a finish carpenter, you need some skill and experience to properly shim a pre-hung door, which involves inserting tapered slivers of wood to get a good fit. If you screw that up, you'll wreck the way the slab sits in the frame, and the door won't open and shut properly.

I've seen a lot of people trying to install a pre-hung door with the slab still hanging on it. That's making the job more difficult than it needs to be. Instead, remove the pins in the hinges so you can detach the slab without unscrewing the hinges from the jamb. Attach the hinge side first and make sure it's flush with the drywall on both sides. Everything should be plumb and not twisted—the jamb should be perpendicular to the opening. Then you can put the slab back in place.

Once you hang the door, you can adjust the top jamb and the striker plate jamb (the side of the frame containing the metal piece the door latch fits into) so you've got an even gap all the way around. The door itself needs to be absolutely level, of course—it has to swing evenly in the frame—but you can be a little more flexible with the trim. Sometimes you have to throw away your level and eyeball it to make it look right in older homes.

If the door doesn't fit because it's too tall for the opening, always trim the door from the *bottom*. A big mistake people make with a pre-hung door is cutting it from the top. But cutting from the top changes the height where the door hits the striker plate (the metal plate that catches the door latch): the two won't connect, which means the door won't close properly.

After you get the door hung, all the finishing work still needs to be done: drywall, painting and trim, plus siding and insulation if it's an exterior door.

MISTAKE #69:
NOT KNOWING WHEN TO PASS ON A PRE-HUNG DOOR

Now, when would you want a **slab door** instead of a pre-hung door? If the jambs are still in good shape and the door operates well in the existing frame, there's no reason you can't pull out the door slab and swap it for a new one. Maybe you want an antique door or something else unique. A slab door is also a good option if you want to leave the trim in place because of the quality or type of wood used or because of the character it adds to your house. If you're leaving the trim up, it's easier to leave the jamb in place and just replace the door slab. However, if you're taking the trim off anyway, it's probably easiest to just pull out the jamb and install a pre-hung door. Slab doors are also cheaper than pre-hung: less material, less cost to ship.

You can also manufacture your own jambs using pine or MDF stock, but it takes some skill to assemble and machine everything correctly. There's another option: a **Fast-Fit door**. The kit includes all the components already machined and ready to go: door slab, frame, hinges, strikers, everything. The door is not yet hanging on the frame, but everything is there for you to assemble. You cut the jambs to the right height, pop them in, square the frame around the door, and you're done. The advantage here is that the frame is adjustable, so you can compensate for most irregularities in a door opening.

MISTAKE #70:
SCREWING UP ON SHIMS

Installing a door is not as easy as it may look, even if it arrives pre-hung in the frame. First, you need to make sure the rough opening for the door is larger than the door frame itself. I know that sounds obvious, but it's worth repeating since it's one of those things people underestimate. You need to minimize the structural pressure on doors (and windows)—if the door is installed too tightly against the framing, you're effectively making the door bear a load, which can cause problems with the way the door opens and closes. To prevent this, make sure the rough opening for the door is about an inch larger than the door jamb. This gap is essential to transfer loads around the door and to make small adjustments during installation that will help the

Use tapered wood shims to snug a door against the framing lumber. Cedar shims are easier than pine to trim.

door operate smoothly for a long time. Check the installation instructions: some suggest a $^3/_8$-inch gap on each side and at the top, while others recommend $^1/_2$ inch.

That's where shims come in. As mentioned, shims are thin strips of wood that taper at one end. The weight of the door will transfer to the frame at the shim points. The shims help you get the door to sit nice and snug against the framing lumber so it doesn't wiggle around. (If you have a choice of shims, go for cedar over pine. You can easily trim cedar with a knife; pine shims are way harder to trim.)

Start by working on the hinge side, inserting shims between the jamb and the door frame and lining them up with the hinges. Usually you shim in pairs: one goes in from one side of the jamb, and the next shim goes in from the other side. You're looking to make a solid connection without any gaps. Single shims may be needed if the lumber in the rough opening is warped, but otherwise you usually don't use too many single shims since a triangle of wood obviously isn't going to be stable in the long run.

While doing the shimming, use a 4- to 6-foot level to make sure the door stays plumb and level along all three planes: up and down, in and out and side to side. Check for level and plumb by placing the level horizontally at the top of the door and vertically along the door's face. Measure to make sure the door is centred: the whole frame must be square, or the door may not open and close properly.

Next, you have to nail or screw the jamb to the framing, ideally through the shims. Be careful: if you compress the shims too much, you'll wind up sucking the frame out of alignment and pulling the door out of square. And if you do that on each side, you'll end up with a door frame that has curves in it—and if it's an exterior door, the weather seal won't be as effective. To

Make sure the rough opening for a pre-hung door is about an inch larger than the door jamb. Beside the hinges, insert shims between the jamb and door opening. Make sure the door stays plumb and level from top to bottom, in and out, and side to side. For an interior door, I nail blocks on one side so they sit flush on the drywall. I can push the jamb against the blocks, and they'll hold the jamb in place.

avoid compressing the shims, put the screw in and over-tighten it a bit, then back it off—it should be tight enough to stay in place, but not so tight that it's putting strain on the frame.

Here's one trick you can try: if I'm installing an interior door frame, I'll nail blocks on the other side so they sit flush on the drywall. That way I can push the jamb against the blocks, and they'll hold the jamb in place so I don't have to constantly move the jamb in and out.

Mistake #71:
NOT LEAVING ENOUGH ROOM FOR INSULATION

In a lot of older homes, you can feel the cold air coming in around the perimeter of the entry door. If you remove the trim, you'll usually see pink fibreglass insulation stuffed into that gap. Fibreglass is good at preventing heat transfer, but not if there's air flowing through it. Take out the fibreglass and fill the gap with low-expansion spray foam, which you can buy at the hardware store (this is a simple job any home-owner can handle; this isn't the same spray foam that requires professional installers). To use, shake the can for a good minute to mix it well; then insert the straw applicator that comes with the can. When you put the applicator into the gap and spray, the product will instantly foam up and begin to harden. Work quickly and move to the next spot, filling each cavity about halfway. You can always backfill areas that don't get enough foam on the first pass. If the gap is overfilled, trim back the excess with a utility knife once it's cured. Spray foam is a much better choice around exterior doors and windows because it prevents heat transfer and airflow.

One of the most common mistakes I see homeown-

Fibreglass alone isn't enough to seal and insulate around windows and doors. For that, you need low-expansion spray foam.

ers making is not leaving enough space around windows or entry doors for that foam insulation. Make sure you leave at least ½ inch around the frame to insert your foam, or you're going to end up sending heat right out the window or door. Remember that the house expands and contracts, too. If the house contracts and squeezes that door frame because there wasn't a gap, the door may not open or shut smoothly.

If you're hiring a window company to put in custom windows, the installers need the true dimen-

sions of the rough opening, not the dimensions of the glass. You won't know the size of that opening until you take the trim off, and this isn't something you want to eyeball. Once you measure the rough opening, always make sure the window frame is at least an inch smaller than the rough opening (closer to 2 inches is standard for rough openings in new construction).

Once the new window is in place, get the right kind of expanding foam. High-expansion foam is no good in this case because it can squeeze the window to the point where the frame buckles and the window sticks. Use low-expansion foam for doors and windows since it doesn't put pressure on the frames.

One other tip: take the screens out of the windows when you're installing everything. If you get foam on the screen, it's a nightmare to get off!

Mistake #72:
NOT SEALING AROUND AN EXTERIOR DOOR

I've heard people complain, "Our door doesn't close properly—you really have to put your shoulder into it." That's actually what you want—the weatherstripping provides the seal. Think of your entry doors as airlocks that keep the outdoor air and weather sealed out. (The

Polyurethane spray foam requires a professional, but any homeowner can insulate around windows with a can of low-expansion foam.

key is to have that tight seal when the door is closed but the door opening without a fight.)

When you think you're done installing an exterior door, give it a slam. Does it shut all the way? If you've done your job right, and it's a good-quality door with proper weatherstripping, it shouldn't slam shut without some effort. You're supposed to have to give the door a good push into the weatherstripping to compress it, which allows the latch to hook into the striker plate to help the door stay shut. Compressing the weatherstripping is the key to stopping heat from leaking through the front door.

Occasionally, a door won't be perfectly square. The weatherstripping will deal with that to a degree, but then you need a very tight-fitting door. To get that tighter fit, you can move the striker plate so that when you close the door, it hooks and latches properly.

MISTAKE #73:
USING THE WRONG CAULKING

Windows and exterior doors need to be caulked on the outside so air, water and snow don't make their way into your home. The problem is, the sealant section of the building centre is like the candy rack at the convenience store—you'll be standing there staring at dozens of options.

Pay attention to labels to pick up the right one for this job. Paintable latex caulking designed for indoor use isn't going to cut it. You need flexible caulking designed specifically for exterior jobs. If it's not flexible, the caulk will crack as the temperature changes and the space you're trying to seal starts to expand and contract.

Before you jump in there with your tube of sealant, take the time to clean the area first. If you skip this step and apply caulking on a brick ledge with dust and grit all over it, then the sealant will stick to the dirt and not

the window. Finally, make sure you apply the sealant on a day when it will have time to dry: it needs to fully cure (which takes two to four hours) before it can be exposed to moisture.

MISTAKE #74:
BLOCKING A WINDOW'S WEEP HOLE

If your home has a brick exterior, you may have noticed that along one of the bottom rows of brick, there are gaps where the mortar would normally be. The bricklayer wasn't being sloppy: those gaps are there for an important reason. They're called weep holes, and they provide ventilation for the home's internal walls, as well as an outlet for moisture to escape.

Many storm windows have similar weep holes along the bottom of the frame to prevent water from accumulating along the sill. Make sure you don't plug those holes when you're caulking around a window. And if you notice the weep holes are clogged with dirt, clean them out to allow for proper airflow and drainage.

MISTAKE #75:
NEGLECTING TO CHANGE WEATHERSTRIPPING

Weatherstripping is usually included on new exterior doors. If you're repairing an older door, you can rip off all the weatherstripping and replace it. Over time it will start to leak air, and you'll feel drafts or notice light creeping in through cracks. Updating the weatherstripping is a simple thing you can do to reduce your energy costs and get rid of those cold spots.

There are a few kinds of weatherstripping available. Vinyl bulb weatherstripping comes on a track. You measure it, cut it and screw it on the exterior jambs against the door. Some doors have a groove for weatherstripping, and you can replace the original

Replacing old weatherstripping around exterior doors helps plug air leaks and reduce energy costs.

material when it wears out. Tension seal weatherstripping is a durable strip of metal or plastic folded into a V shape that can be installed with its own adhesive strip or with finishing nails along the sides and top of a door. Smaller gaps between the door and the jamb can often be plugged with simple, pliable strips of adhesive-backed weatherstripping. The best kind of weatherstripping has a compression memory: the material compresses and seals when the door is closed, then springs back when the door is opened. Small gaps may not need as much reinforcement as some of the heftier weatherstripping options provide. In fact, you might not be able to close your door if you over-weatherstrip! Before heading to the weatherstripping aisle, take a look at the cracks around your door to get a feel for how wide the gaps are.

Whatever type you use, make sure the surface is clean before applying. If you're working with dirty surfaces, your brand new weatherstripping is not going to adhere properly, and you'll end up with gaps.

Most weatherstripping breaks down after a winter or two, so put this on the fall checklist around the time you call for your annual furnace maintenance.

Mistake #76:
Coming Unhinged

One of the things I've seen go wrong in older homes is the door hinges starting to loosen and pull away from the jamb. If the original hinge was installed with a 1-inch screw, which is too short, this will happen over time.

Typically, an interior door will have ½-inch screws in the jamb, while the jamb itself is nailed to the framing through the shim. If the framing is perfectly plumb, you can nail your inside jamb directly to the framing and shim the other side, because you don't need to leave a gap for insulation like you do with an exterior door. But if the hinge is coming loose, I recommend putting in a longer screw that goes through the jamb and into the framing.

Once you get into the framing, keep in mind you're at risk of pulling that whole section out of alignment. That's why you need shims behind the jambs—that way, when you drive in those screws, they don't drag the whole frame out. It helps to have a level handy to make sure at every stage that your frame is sitting straight, plumb, level and square.

Mistake #77:
Overestimating the Skill Needed to Fix a Sticky or Misaligned Door

Houses settle over time, which can have a surprisingly big effect on doors and windows. If your floor is slanted or sinking, you may end up with a door that's out of square, with a gap at the top or along one of the sides. Adjusting an exterior door that is really out of square is pretty finicky—fitting it back in the frame properly isn't easy. A better long-term solution is to have a professional repair whatever structural problems caused the door to go off-kilter in the first place. Then I'd pull out the door and install a new one. Usually older doors and jambs have been beaten up to such an extent that removing everything is the best way to go.

If you have a gap because your door is hanging on an angle, don't just cut the door to fit the opening. You might be able to camouflage the problem by attaching trim around the door frame in a way that masks how skewed it is. This is when you throw away your square and your level and just do your best to make everything look good. In any case, the operation of a door counts more than aesthetics. If a door that's angled isn't rubbing or sticking, then just make sure it fits well in the frame and do what you can to level out the reveal (that's the horizontal gap between the top jamb and the door).

There are a couple of tricks you can try if your door is sticking. If it's a solid wood door, which is rare these days, you can plane the part that's making contact with the jamb. Most, though, are hollow-core paper-filled doors, and they'll fall apart if you start planing them too much. If you've got a hollow door that's sticking, you may need to remove the trim and adjust the shims, or cut the screws or nails (since the fastener heads will be covered by the casing) and remove the shims completely. Then you can adjust the jamb by knocking it in or out a bit before replacing the shims. Occasionally, you can make minor adjustments without removing trim by using a rubber mallet or a framing hammer with a tapping block, but this takes a bit of finesse.

I'm warning you, though, that fixing a problem door is not easy—it's better for a finish carpenter to do than someone with only basic DIY skills. If you don't know what you're doing, you might end up making it worse!

MISTAKE #78:
INSTALLING A WINDOW OUT OF SQUARE

I don't consider installing windows a job for the average homeowner. It's a pretty tedious process to get the window to sit perfectly square and then to air-seal it properly with foam. Plus, windows aren't cheap or light to work with, so a mistake could be especially costly. But I know my warning is not going to stop some of you! In that case, make sure you take some time to learn how to do it properly. One of the most common issues is installing the window out of square.

Normally the rough opening will be about an inch larger than the window. One installation technique is to place strips of ½-inch plywood along the bottom of the rough opening. Then place the window on top of those strips and make sure it's level. To square up the window, use shims on the sides. The shims should fit in snugly, but never force anything so you're bending the frame. If that happens, the window may not open without effort, or you might have problems closing it tightly because the frame will have shifted to accommodate the shims. Keep checking with your level and your carpenter's square to make sure everything is still aligned.

Don't forget that when you're shimming, you still need to leave room for low-expansion foam insulation (see Mistake #71, page 146). The idea is to have a continuous line of foam around the window so you've got a solid air barrier. If your window isn't perfectly square, but it operates smoothly, don't panic. Occasionally, you'll get a frame that's slightly out of square from the manufacturer, but they normally operate fine.

the inside of the jamb. When you measure a window, measure from inside edge to inside edge along the sides, top and bottom. Sometimes the easiest way to mark for length is to take your piece of trim and stand it up beside the door and then mark the start of your cut with a pencil. Just make sure that if you are marking on the short end, you make the 45-degree cut in the right direction. (I cover more detail on cutting in Mistake #80, below.)

Then add ¼ inch to your measurement: this allows you to leave a ⅛-inch "reveal" along the edge between the casing (trim) and the door or window frame (jamb). If you bring the trim right to the edge of the casing and it's even or "underlapping" just a bit, it looks terrible. But if you've got that ⅛-inch reveal, you will get a nice, clean look. Don't try to line up the trim with the frame—you're never going to get it perfect.

It's important to measure and install the trim pieces in the right order. When you're doing door trim, start on one side (doesn't matter which), then do the top, then finish with the other side. If you do the top piece last, one of the vertical pieces may end up slightly longer than the other, and the seams won't be as tight. At first, just pin the pieces lightly with one nail so you can adjust them slightly, and only fasten them securely after you've got all three pieces fitting snugly.

When you're trimming a window, tack the bottom piece in first. Then do one side, the other side, and finish with the top piece. When you start with the bottom piece first, you can rest the other pieces on top.

MISTAKE #79:
MEASURING THE TRIM WRONG

Trim is not particularly difficult to install around doors and windows, but you need to be precise for the seams to look good. If any of the pieces are cut wrong, the flaws will be noticeable. Experience definitely helps, because there are a few tricks that make the job easier.

Many first-timers take their measurements wrong. When you are measuring a piece of trim that will be mitred (cut on a 45-degree angle), remember to always take the *inside* measurement. For trim around a door, measure the vertical pieces from the floor to the top of

MISTAKE #80:
MAKING SLOPPY MITRE JOINTS

If you want your trim to look good, your mitre joints need to be clean. Trim really is the finishing touch, and nothing is going to cover it up besides caulking and

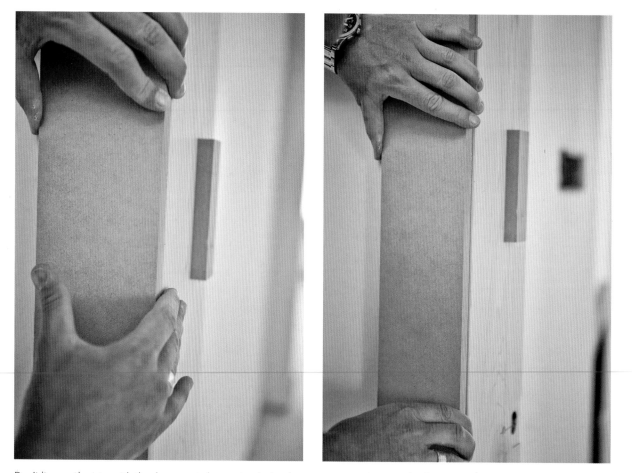

Don't line up the trim with the door or window casing. Instead, create a more attractive finish with an ⅛-inch "reveal" along the edge.

paint, so precision matters. You really need to use a mitre saw, because a handsaw or a framing saw won't give you that precise edge. Borrow or rent one for the afternoon if you're doing a small project like the trim around one window.

When you cut on a 45-degree angle, there are two possible measurements: the short or the long end of the piece of trim. You always use the short end: that's why we measured the inside edges of the door or window. (Remember to add that extra ¼ or ⅛ inch to allow for the reveal.) Mark the shorter dimension with a pencil and position the saw so the

45-degree cut will be in the right direction (when you make the cut, the outside edge of the trim will be longer than the inside edge; the top piece is also longest on the outside edge and shortest on the inside edge). Don't forget to allow for the width of the saw blade. If you're unsure the first couple of times, don't be afraid to cut the piece a bit too long at first, especially if it's a piece of vertical trim for a door. You can always bring it back to the saw and cut a bit off the floor end (but first change the mitre saw setting so you don't have the angle!). Stretching the trim isn't an option, trust me.

Any time you put trim around a doorway or window, use full pieces (window and door mouldings are typically available in 8- to 16-foot lengths). If joints appear anywhere other than the corners, it really doesn't look good. (Seams may be unavoidable if you're installing baseboards in a large room, but it's usually no problem on door and window trim.) If you do need to use more than one length of trim, cut each piece on a 45-degree angle rather than just butting the two pieces together.

MISTAKE #81:
IMPROPERLY SECURING THE TRIM

The best way to attach trim is with a pneumatic gun and brad nails. Cordless brad guns are really popular now, too. Brads don't have a large head like a standard nail, so they disappear right under the surface of the wood. Cover the hole with a dab of caulking or wood filler before you paint, and it becomes invisible.

For windows and doors, the standard nail is 1½ inches, which will go through trim and the drywall. For thicker trim designs, you need a 2-inch nail. The important thing is that the brad penetrates into the framing—the trim won't stay in place if you just tack it to the drywall. With a window, there should be solid wood about an inch behind the frame. (Typically, you'll find about a ½-inch gap between the rough frame and the actual window to allow for insulation.) With a door, there should be studs on both sides of the casing, and a sill above.

Holding the trim in place, angle the nail gun away from the window or door and fire a nail into the inside edge, about ¼ inch from the edge to prevent splitting—the goal here is to attach the trim to the frame. Then add another nail at the outer edge of the window or door—this locks the frame into place. Place the

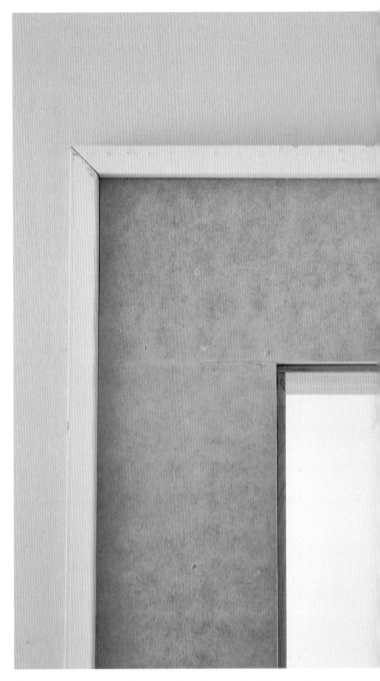

With most trim designs, all corners should have mitred joints, cut on a 45-degree angle (*top*). Only if the trim has no profile can you use butt joints.

nails so you have two nails, about 12 to 16 inches apart, all the way around. (If the wall is wonky, you may have to use more nails.)

With thicker kinds of trim, I use some glue in the mitre joints and then put a nail through the side of the trim so it goes into the perpendicular piece. That seems to keep the trim flush all around (just take care not to split the wood). Sometimes you will need to slide shims behind the mitre joint, to make sure the corners are both 90 degrees and flush front to back. When the glue sets, cut off the shim and put some caulking across the top. You can also use a bit of caulking to fill in the joints. Use a wet sponge to wipe the trim clean before you paint.

Brad nails have smaller heads than standard nails do, so they disappear right under the surface of wood trim. If you use a pneumatic gun to install brads, fill the hole with caulking or wood filler before you paint.

With thicker trim, I use some glue in the mitre joints and then fire a nail through the side of the trim so it goes into the perpendicular piece. To install trim, angle the gun away from the window or door and fire a nail into the inside edge. Then add another nail at the outer edge. Sometimes you'll need to slide shims behind the joint to make sure the corners are both 90 degrees and flush front to back (*bottom right*).

CHAPTER SEVEN

PAINTING

PAINT IS OFTEN THE FIRST THING YOU SEE WHEN YOU WALK INTO A HOUSE. EVEN WITHOUT REALIZING IT, YOU NOTICE THE COLOUR AND FOCUS ON HOW SHARP THE LINES ARE. THEN YOU CHECK OUT THE QUALITY OF THE DRYWALL FINISH, TRIM WORK AND TILES—OR AT LEAST I DO—BUT PAINT IS DEFINITELY THE FIRST IMPRESSION.

It's a good idea to update your paint every few years, once the colours start to fade and walls get dinged and need patching. Nothing makes a house look cleaner than a fresh coat of paint. Actually, make that two coats. That's usually enough if it's properly applied.

The number-one mistake people make when it comes to painting is underestimating the value of a professional. A good painter uses a lot of skill and patience to get a beautiful finish—it's not just a matter of opening a can and throwing paint on the wall. But for some reason, people think painting is something absolutely everybody can do. And I guess it is, technically. But few homeowners paint so well that you don't notice the flaws.

Maybe people think they should save a few bucks on painting because they have no choice but to pay licensed pros to do the electrical and plumbing. The stakes are obviously not as high with a painting mistake. But compared with the hourly rates of one of the licensed trades, the cost of painters is relatively affordable. In fact, hiring a painter is one of the most cost-effective and least invasive things you can do to completely change the look of your home in a day or two. A professional painter also doesn't just paint: a big part of the job is prepping and repairing blemishes on the walls and trim to ensure a better finish. Another nice thing about a pro: they know how to work efficiently and can have the house done in way less time, which means your household won't be disrupted as much as it would if you took on the job yourself.

If you do decide to tackle a paint job on your own, this chapter has some advice for avoiding the biggest mistakes.

PAINT BASICS

DIFFICULTY: 6 OUT OF 10

Paint is like chemistry in a can—different formulas are designed for different conditions. For example, exterior paint is formulated to stand up to Mother Nature, while interior paints are designed to be washable. Primer is the undercoat used to prepare unfinished drywall for paint, to transition from an old paint colour to a new one or to help water-based latex paint stick to a surface previously coated with oil-based paint (or vice versa). When you're painting a room, you prime first, then paint the trim and baseboards and then finish with the walls. Walls should be coated one at a time starting with corners and edges, then finishing with the wall surfaces themselves.

CHOOSING PAINT

- **Buy good primer.** This undercoat helps your finish colour adhere, so you'll get a better-looking paint job. If you buy good primer, one coat should be enough.

- **Choose water or oil.** Water-based paint has the advantage of being safer and easier to work with because it generally contains fewer VOCs (volatile organic compounds) and can be washed up with water. Oil-based paint (also known as alkyd) is good at preventing show-through of rust, sap or stains, but you need solvents for the cleanup.

- **Consider finish.** The finish refers to the way paint absorbs or reflects light. Low-sheen finishes (flat/matte) are good at hiding wall imperfections, but they're harder to clean; save these for low-traffic areas. Mid-sheen finishes (satin, eggshell) are easy to wipe clean in busy rooms. High sheens (satin, semigloss, gloss) are easy to clean and great at highlighting trim and mouldings.

- **Make it green.** If you're concerned about the health of your family and the planet, choose no- or low-VOC finishes. They give off fewer chemical fumes and protect the air quality inside your home. Lighter colours and flatter sheens also require less pigment, which means they contain fewer VOCs than darker shades and high-gloss finishes.

TOOLS AND MATERIALS YOU'LL NEED

- paint
- primer
- paintbrushes
- roller and roller covers
- extension pole with threading to attach to roller
- paint tray and inserts
- drop cloth or tarp to protect furniture, floors
- painter's tape
- premixed compound for repairing holes and scratches
- 3-inch putty knife
- 120-grit sanding sponge
- screwdriver/drill to remove switch covers
- stepladder
- damp rags

MISTAKE #82:
OVERLOOKING NO-VOC AND LOW-VOC PAINT

Remember the old days when you'd paint the house and nobody could breathe for a week? You could smell the paint for months. That was all the volatile organic compounds (VOCs) coming out of the paint and off-gassing fumes into your home.

VOCs are gases, some of which have been linked to health problems, emitted from certain solids and liquids. These chemicals aren't just in paint; they're in thousands of items, including air fresheners, cleaning products, pesticides, building materials, furniture, carpets, glues and even permanent markers. When using these products, some people might notice their eyes, nose or throat feels irritated, or they might get headaches. Some organic chemicals have no known health effects, while others are so toxic they're known or suspected to cause cancer (though at concentrations way above what's found in the average home). Because so many of us use these products, in houses that may not have great ventilation, the air inside is often more polluted than the air outdoors. There's not a lot of evidence directly linking VOCs in homes to health problems, but the concern is that the effects add up over time.

If you want to play it safe, check out the low-VOC or no-VOC paints on the shelf. They used to be harder to find, but most of the major paint brands offer this option now. Prices for healthier paints range from the same to about $10 more per gallon from the big brands. Regulations require that low-VOC paint contain less than 50 grams of volatile organic compounds per litre before tinting; zero-VOC paint must have less than 5 grams per litre.

It's also worth mentioning that those figures are for the untinted white base, and some paint stores tint with colourants that are full of VOCs—sometimes containing hundreds of grams per litre. Your preferred colour and sheen might be adding VOCs without your realizing it. The darker the paint colour, the greater amount of VOCs in the tint because these hues require more pigment. Same with finish: the glossier the sheen, the more VOCs the paint will contain. To keep the VOCs in your paint low, choose lighter colours, ask the store to use a low-/no-VOC tint, and lean toward flat or mid-sheen finishes.

MISTAKE #83:
PLAYING IT SAFE WITH COLOURS

We've all seen this before: a couple walks into the home-improvement store because they know they've got to paint, but their hearts aren't in it. They're not really thinking much about the colours; they're saying, "Let's just pick something and get it done." As a result, they play it too safe.

Paint is pretty inexpensive, so you don't have to be conservative and stay with the muted colours everybody uses. You can afford to have some fun and take a few risks. If you paint an accent wall a bold colour and decide it doesn't work, you can just paint over it. It's not like removing the wall or re-tiling a floor. But people find it difficult to take the leap.

To me, there's nothing worse than painting the whole house and standing back and thinking, "*Meh*. Sure it's a different colour, but it still looks plain." Paint has the ability to transform a home, but only if you're willing to move away from boring and predictable colours.

MISTAKE #84:
CHOOSING YOUR OWN PAINT COLOURS

If you're having a problem choosing paint, or if you always seem to be repainting because you regret your choices, ask for some help. It might be worth getting a designer or decorator to pull together a palette or suggest some ideas you may not think of on your own.

Getting an outside perspective is really useful if you're planning a major paint job. It's tough to see the potential in our homes because we're in them every day. Ask a friend (or decorator) for advice—someone with fresh eyes who doesn't see the house the way you do could make suggestions that will surprise you.

Most of our clients tell us they never would have thought of this or that on their own. We get it all the time on *Leave It to Bryan*, especially since we choose projects and we're bringing in finishes. Halfway through the project, the owners are skeptical: "Oh, I don't know how that's going to turn out." At the end they admit it's better than they could have imagined— now they love it. I think having an outside eye helps. As a homeowner, you see your home every day to the point that you almost become blind to it—it can be hard to imagine it looking different. It also helps to have a professional eye. Designers and decorators choose colours all the time. They know how to pull together combinations and patterns that work together as a whole, even if their individual choices push you outside your usual safe zone.

So if you're going to spend the money to repaint the entire house, for a relatively affordable extra cost you can bring in somebody to suggest eye-popping accent walls or other paint tricks you probably wouldn't have considered. In the end, it's cheaper to hire some-one to help with paint colours than it is to buy all kinds of throw pillows or other accents to spice up a room that's painted a muted neutral colour!

You don't have to be afraid that a designer will only suggest the season's trend colours, which you'll tire of in six months. Usually they will create computer images or paper drawings of your space reimagined with new paint and fabric swatches, and maybe a few different palettes to give you an idea of what the colours will look like. Then you should take a little time to think about it—print off the sheet of possibilities and leave them on the kitchen counter during what I like to call a cooling-off period. We do that with the blue-prints every time we do a house. We've pored over the plans hundreds of times before we get to the finishing stages, and there comes a point when we just need to live with them for a while without having to make deci-sions. Don't rush your decision—make sure you'll still love the colours in a week or two. And if you do choose a colour that you end up getting tired of, it's easy to fix. Or I guess you could always pass it off as art.

MISTAKE #85:
JUDGING A COLOUR BY ITS PAINT CHIP ALONE

It's not easy to pick paint colours. Sometimes it's hard to imagine what a colour will look like when it's up on the wall. Those paint chips mean well, but they can be a real pain. The swatches are typically so small that it's hard to even see what the colour looks like. As well, what looks great in the store can look like a whole new colour once you take it home and put it on the walls under totally different conditions.

Remember that when you're in the paint depart-ment, you're looking at the chip in an area of the store that's well lit. There's always light focused on the swatches so the colour looks ideal. Does your house look like a retail store? Mine doesn't. When you're look-ing at the swatch, see if you can pull out anything other than the obvious colour. For example, some taupes have a pink undertone you may not readily notice in the small chip. You might not want the pinkish tone, or you might think it's perfectly fine—taste is personal. We all have our preferences. That doesn't mean that taupe is a *mistake*, but it may not be right for everyone. I tend to just get a gut feeling about colours—I know what I like, and I go with it.

Fortunately, many paint brands have smartened up and enlarged their paint swatches. Samples used to be the size of a postage stamp, but now you can borrow swatches that are 6 × 6 inches, or even 12 × 12. You can take them home and tape them on the wall to get a better feel for what the colour will look like. If you're still not sure, some paint stores will sell you a mini tub—even smaller than a quart—for a few bucks. Brush a coat or two onto a patch of your walls, let it dry, and check it out during different times of the day to see if you still like the colour. You might change your mind, or you might like it even better. Or paint a sheet of bristol board instead so you can move it around to see how the colour looks on different walls, where the lighting can affect its appearance.

Those tiny paint chips don't cut it: paint or tape a large swatch on the wall to get a better idea of the colour.

Do your research if you have no idea where to start. Get some reno magazines, look online and read about basic design. There are some general rules to keep in mind when you're deciding. Using darker colours in a room with little light, for example, will make the room appear smaller. That kind of colour scheme might give the space a cave-like feeling, but then again dark colours can also add drama to a room. I've seen houses where the ceiling's painted really dark on purpose to make the room feel more intimate. It all depends on what look you're going for. That's where a designer can help. Decorating specialists can zero in on what kind of colours you like and what effect you want the colours to have, and they can help you make it happen through colour choices.

MISTAKE #86: CHOOSING THE WRONG PAINT SHEEN

Selecting the right level of sheen for each room is almost as important as choosing the colour. Sheen determines whether the paint will have a shiny or matte look once it dries, and also how it will perform. The options—from shiniest to least shiny—are gloss, semigloss, satin, eggshell (sometimes called low-lustre) and flat/matte. The glossier the paint, the better it stands up to abuse and the easier it is to clean.

Use gloss or semigloss paint on trim, moulding, doors and cabinets—spots that see a lot of scuffs that need to be scrubbed clean. Some people also use semigloss in bathrooms and on kitchen ceilings because it will stand up to lots of cleaning.

You'll usually see satin and eggshell on walls in living spaces like the dining room, hallway, family room or a kid's bedroom or playroom. A satin finish looks a little more understated, so it's versatile in rooms that

Use a semigloss or high-gloss paint in areas prone to abuse: they're more durable and make it easier to clean scuffs like these.

see lots of action. You can wipe it clean, but you won't be able to scrub it like semigloss or gloss.

Flat or matte sheens look really smooth and subtle in a living room, dining room or bedroom. Flat sheens are great at camouflaging flaws (unlike gloss paint, which shines a spotlight on any imperfections), but they really hold on to dirt. You might wreck the finish if you rub the walls too hard or use a strong cleaning product.

Mistake #87:
OBSESSING OVER BRANDS

There are so many paint brand choices out there, but if you have selected the right colour and sheen, any of the major brands will do the job just fine. Different painters have their favourites—they like the way a certain paint feels coming off the brush or how it appears on the wall—but they're all good products. In most cases, as far as the quality of the big brands

goes, we're not comparing an entry-level Hyundai with a Ferrari—it's more like a Chevy versus a Buick.

That said, there's affordable paint, and then there's stupid cheap paint. If the paint is a fraction of the cost of the brand names, just avoid it. It will likely be as thin as skim milk, and you'll have to put up too many coats to get that nice saturated colour. I've heard of paint that's so poorly made that when you try to clean the walls, the paint wipes away along with the dirt. You're better off spending a few bucks more to get something that will cover the walls in two coats.

If you like a colour in one brand but you prefer the quality of another brand, you can have the store colour-match for you if you have a paint chip—any paint manufacturer will reproduce any other brand's colours. They use colour codes that provide a recipe for any paint chip. Same goes for pretty much any colour you want to re-create, whether it's on a pillow you like or in a painting you've got hanging up at home. Whatever it is, bring a sample to the store for them to colour-match, and they'll pump out the colour using a custom mix done by computer.

Mistake #88:
USING THE WRONG PAINT ON THE CEILING

If you're painting a room, it's a good idea to do the ceiling, too—and to paint it before you do the walls. We tend to ignore ceilings, but if you shine some light up there, you'll see how ugly they can be and how difficult they can be to work on. Drywall tends to look worse on ceilings because it's difficult to mud a horizontal surface, and it's harder to get your paint lines straight, too. You'll need a long extension pole that screws into your roller and maybe some goggles to avoid getting a drip in the eye. Oh, and Advil for your neck would be a good idea.

Ceiling paint is different from the kind used for walls. Traditional ceiling paint is very chalky and flat. But don't worry about the washability of a low-sheen in high-traffic rooms: you're typically not wiping sticky finger smudges off the ceiling. Ceiling paint typically comes in a "Don't pay attention to me" shade of white that hides a lot of flaws. Now you can get varieties that look pink when you roll them on and then dry to pure white. They're easier to apply because you can see where you've painted, whereas it's hard to tell the difference between white primer and white ceiling paint. Ceiling paint is also specially made to reduce drips—you'll enjoy this feature when you're painting above your head and you don't want to get splattered.

If you don't use the pink-to-white stuff, make sure you have a really bright light to work with. Point it at the ceiling so you can instantly see where you've rolled and where it looks wet. Without good lighting, it can be tough to see the difference between painted and unpainted ceiling, and you might leave bare patches that will then be visible in certain lights. Be extra careful about roller lines because they're hard to get out of a ceiling.

Don't be afraid to use colour on the ceiling instead of white. Painting a ceiling with a deep colour and leaving the walls light is not my favourite choice—this combination makes the room feel heavy and brings the ceiling down. But I've seen other ceilings painted a very light colour that look great. The light colour makes it feel like the ceiling's not there, like there's a sky above and it's a cloudy day and the ceiling is floating—that's kind of cool.

MISTAKE #89:
ASSUMING YOU NEED TO USE OIL-BASED PAINT OUTDOORS

Some painters swear by the ultra-smooth finish of oil-based paint. For many years, that's what we used to paint exteriors like brick. Alkyd, which is another word for oil-based paint, penetrates the surface better and is more durable, especially against the elements. Oil paints adhere and block stains better, making them good for soiled surfaces, metals that rust and woods that leach out sap or tannin. One of the problems with oil-based paints, though, is they take forever to dry—anywhere from 8 to 24 hours—whereas water-based latex paint dries in 1 to 6 hours. They're also not as eco-friendly: you need to use solvents to clean your hands and brushes, and they contain way more volatile organic compounds (see Mistake #82, page 162).

It used to be that the chemical makeup of water-based latex meant it wouldn't stand up as well against Mother Nature. However, paint technology is improving, and we can now safely use water-based latex outdoors. That's what we sprayed on most of our cottage. Water-based paints are flexible, so they'll expand and shrink with the seasons as your siding changes. They're also breathable, so they won't trap moisture and crack or peel. And as I said earlier, they dry way faster. If you're using latex outside, just make sure you buy a paint that's rated for outdoor use—it'll say "exterior" right on the label. Exterior latex paints typically come in semigloss or satin sheens.

If you're repainting something outdoors, it's even more important to prepare well if you want long-lasting results. If you drive through subdivisions that are 10, 15, 20 years old—even new ones, where a surface hasn't been cleaned or primed well enough before painting—you'll see a lot of peeling paint. Don't just paint over the old surface: first, use a paint scraper to remove the loose flaky bits. Then remove the existing caulking (use a caulk remover tool for this). If it's outdoor caulk, it's probably silicone, and you can't paint

Prepping is everything in painting, especially outdoors. Remove all loose paint flakes and dried-up caulking before you repaint.

over that—the paint won't adhere. If you want to paint over the caulk after you redo it, look for a paintable latex caulk rated for outdoor use. Then coat it with a very high-quality primer before painting it.

There's no magical solution for painting outdoors: it's just hard work. Pick a few days when the weather is going to be nice and dry so the paint will have time to cure. Warmer temperatures are better. Most brands will tell you to wait until the weather is above 10 degrees Celsius, so make sure you check your favourite weather app before setting out your drop sheets.

One more thing about exterior paint: exterior paints are specially formulated to stand up to sun, wind, water and mildew on stucco, masonry and other surfaces, while interior paints are designed to be washable (depending on the sheen level). Because of its stronger formulation, you might be tempted to use exterior paint indoors. I wouldn't. That strength comes with more harmful VOCs (volatile organic compounds), which are released as the paint dries

and aren't healthy to breathe in. Interior paints give off fewer fumes, so they're safer to use indoors.

MISTAKE #90:
BEING CHEAP WITH PRIMER

In general, if you're using a dark latex paint over a lighter shade of latex, you probably don't need to prime. But when the wall is navy blue or bloodred and you want to switch it to light pink or beige, using a nice thick primer will help you avoid doing six coats of your new colour.

A really thick primer with a high volume of solids will mask (to some extent) any imperfections in the wall. Look for cans of primer labelled as high-build, high-solids or high-volume. A cheaper primer will have a skim-milk quality: it doesn't give good coverage, and you end up having to do three coats instead of the standard one.

A quality primer is especially important when you're working with new drywall. As you roll cheaper primer on, it sucks the dust out of the little imperfections and holes, so you start to see pinholes and little flaws like that. It's even worse when you're trying to cover fibreglass-faced drywall, which is more resistant to mould but has a rougher texture. You can't use regular primer on that, or the walls will look terrible.

MISTAKE #91:
USING WHITE PRIMER ON UNFINISHED DRYWALL

Whenever possible, I use tinted primer. Coating fresh drywall with primer reveals any spots where the drywall needs touch-ups. But if you prime bare walls with white and then go back and do your touch-ups with white drywall compound, you can't see where you've fixed because everything is white on white. This is a problem because when you go to paint, you'll probably find you missed some spots that need to be sanded again. It slows you down. (It's also next to impossible to sand compound after you've painted it.) Also, if you patch imperfections in the drywall and don't prime over the patch before rolling on your finish coat, those spots will look darker.

The best thing is to get the primer tinted to the same colour as your new walls will be. That way, when you prime the room, you'll get a preview of the final colour. While you're finishing the reno or the rest of the build, you're living with that colour and getting to know it. And then when you actually paint, you may get away with only one coat.

And here's a little tip if you do use white primer: if you are patching holes, add a little powdered chalk—blue, red, black, it doesn't matter—into your drywall compound before you do your touch-ups. When everything dries, the repairs will be easy to see because of the colour, so you'll know where you need to sand.

Mistake #92:
NOT PRIMING OIL-BASED PAINT BEFORE SWITCHING TO LATEX

This is a mistake a lot of people make. They pick up a can of latex paint and brush it on baseboards or roll it on walls, and a few weeks later, the paint starts to peel off. Or it comes off when they peel back the painter's tape. Odds are they've rolled latex paint over oil-based paint—that's a no-no.

It's important to prep and prime a surface that's been coated with oil paint so your latex will adhere to it. The primer helps seal the original coating and prepares it to bond to the latex paint. If you're not sure whether the old paint is oil (there's no surefire way to tell by looking), take a cotton ball and some rubbing alcohol or acetone, and rub the wall firmly several

times: if the paint is latex, it will come off and the wall will feel sticky; if it's oil, nothing will happen. If the paint on your walls is oil, get a primer that's specifically designed to prepare oil-based paint to be covered with latex.

Use acetone to test whether a surface is painted with latex or oil-based paint: if it's latex, the paint will come off.

If you're doing the reverse—painting oil over latex—you'll need to prime the surface with an acrylic primer first.

MISTAKE #93:
CHEAPING OUT ON PAINTING SUPPLIES

People who buy cheap supplies and throw them out after one job drive me nuts. I think every homeowner should invest in a good painting kit.

Spend some money on a high-quality angle-cut brush with a wooden handle. Forget the cheap ones with the plastic bristles that fall out or point in all directions. Take a longer view—if you buy one or two brushes for $20 or $30 each, and you clean and take care of them, you can use them for years. Or you can spend hundreds of dollars on disposable brushes over a lifetime and spend half of your painting time picking stray bristles off the wall. You tell me what's the better deal.

Buy a good metal paint tray, too. You can get a tray liner for a buck to make cleaning up easier, but spend a little extra to get a solid tray. And use a quality roller handle, not a 99-cent wobbly one. Look for one with a good sturdy metal arm that won't bend.

Consider a couple of features when you choose roller covers: the material and the nap length. Nap is the depth of the material on a roller cover; the shorter the nap, the smoother the finish you'll get when you paint. You'll need a 10-millimetre nap for flat walls or a 15-millimetre to fill in rough surfaces like stucco, concrete or brick. Synthetic fabric covers work best for water-based paints. Foam is great for oil or glossy paints, and it gives an extra smooth finish. Wool covers hold the most paint, so they're especially effective when you're painting with oil on semi-smooth or rough surfaces. Like cheap brushes, cheap roller covers

are a waste of money: they don't hold paint well, they splatter and they create more work for you.

If you have to stop a paint job before it's complete, there are some tricks to save you the task of washing your brushes and roller covers: put them in an airtight plastic bag, or wrap them with plastic wrap. It prevents the paint from drying, and you can use them the next day without having to clean them. Storing them wrapped like that in the fridge or freezer will usually keep them viable for weeks or even months!

There's also a lot of stuff you *don't* need. You don't need 50 rolls of expensive painter's tape, although it does have its place if you're doing decorative painting. And take a pass on those gimmicky things with the wheels that promise to help you cut in along the ceiling. The problem is the paint gets on the wheels and then they roll paint on your ceiling. I'm a pretty good painter, and I've tried to use those things—it's just a nightmare.

Cutting in is the term for using a brush to paint neat edges in corners or along trim, baseboards and ceilings. There really are no gadgets to make this easier—patience is what you need. (If you're tempted to tape all the edges and corners, see Mistake #96, page 172.) Just get a good-quality, angled, 3-inch brush and take your time. Hold the brush with the long bristles along the edge you're trying to fill in, and grip it loosely near the bristles, not the handle, for better control. As you move the bristles along the line you're painting, let them fan out a little—you only really care about the outermost long bristles since they're the ones drawing the line. Remember, the drywall in the corners between the wall and the ceiling has been mudded by hand—they're not perfect, machined corners—so you need to make adjustments with a brush as you go. Sure, with a film crew and editors and 50 takes, it's possible to do

Don't waste time and money with cheap painting materials. Buy good-quality brushes and rollers and make them last by wrapping them in plastic between coats.

one quick coat and make it look perfect, but not in real life. In real life you need good tools and patience.

MISTAKE #94:
OVERESTIMATING HOW MUCH PAINT AND PRIMER YOU'LL NEED

When it comes to figuring out how much paint I need, I can usually eyeball the job and get pretty close. But most people buy way too much. I don't know anyone who doesn't have a pile of paint cans in their basement from years gone by. To be safe, measure your room and plug those dimensions into an online paint calculator. Pretty much every building supply store and paint manufacturer has these tools on their websites. You can do the same for primer; budget enough for one coat if you're using a good-quality primer (see Mistake #90, page 167).

Usually you can't return tinted paint for a refund if you don't use it, but some stores do take it back and will recycle it, which is a great idea. Ask at the paint department if the store offers that service. It's a good way to clear out all those cans in the garage.

Whatever you do, save some of your leftover paint. The more paint in the can, the longer it will last, assuming the can is well sealed—it should be fine for a couple of years at least. Label each can so you know what room you used it for, and make sure you don't paint over the colour code. At some point you might damage a wall and need to do some touch-ups.

If you don't have any leftover paint, at least save the paint chip or the name of the colour so you can get a new can. A lot of paint shops now will save a record of all the paint you've bought, so that helps, too, if you shop at the same one all the time. And even though the brands bring out a new colour collection each year, they should still have the formulas to make colours from past collections.

MISTAKE #95:
FAILING TO PREP THE WALLS

Doing the preparation work before painting is just as important as preparing the subfloor for tiling or hardwood. If you don't prep walls properly, you may see little pinholes all over the paint. That's a sign that you've made a big mistake. I guess people see a big paint job and just want to "get 'er done." But they usually end up regretting a rushed job because the finish is rough.

Start by moving everything away from the walls— preferably right out of the room. Then take the cover plates off electrical outlets and switches, tape up chandeliers so they're out of the way, get some drop cloths down on the floor. Using a putty knife, remove any loose paint that might be peeling away, and then sand with 150-grit sandpaper to smooth out the remaining paint. If you don't sand, you'll notice the edges of the paint once the wall is re-coated.

With a mild detergent or household cleaner, wash any soiled walls, trim or doors, especially if the area may be coated with oily cooking residue. Paint won't adhere properly to a dirty surface. Make sure you wipe away the soap with a damp cloth and then let everything dry.

Next, get out your drywall compound or your spackle repair to fix any irregularities and fill any holes in the walls. We've all seen old houses where you go in and think, "Look, a freshly painted crappy wall." Taking the time to do the prep work gives the look of a brand new wall, not of the old crummy wall that's just been painted over. Look for nail holes, cracks or other imperfections. If you have plaster walls and notice cracks, rake out any loose particles with a putty knife. Fill the crevices and holes in drywall or plaster with spackling compound, pressing it into place and smoothing it away until the compound is flush with the surface. If mitred joints on your trim have opened up or come away from the wall, press the compound into the crevices and smooth it out with your finger. Let the compound dry and then lightly sand with 150-grit sandpaper. The compound usually shrinks as it dries, so you might need to apply a second coat, then proceed with smoothing, drying and sanding again before you prime and paint.

MISTAKE #96:
GOING OVERBOARD WITH PAINTER'S TAPE

Personally, I'm not a big tape guy when I paint. Too many people rely on tape as a crutch, and they use it everywhere. The best way to paint along a ceiling or trim is just to work really slowly and use two hands if you need to: one on the brush and one on the wall to steady your hand with the brush. (I've found sticking out my tongue really helps my concentration, too, so I can paint within the lines.)

For some specific jobs, tape is necessary. Maybe you want to do a feature wall with stripes or a pattern, and you want to tape off the different sections to get clean, crisp lines between colours. The first trick is to push the tape onto the wall tightly. Run your finger or a putty knife along the tape to ensure a good seal. But even if you do that, some paint will still bleed underneath the tape. So the second trick is to put very little paint on the brush when you're working along the tape. If paint drips off the brush, it will seep under the tape. The idea is to get a thin layer of paint on the edge of the tape so it seals any little gaps, let that light layer dry for a few minutes and then go back and paint a heavier coat. That's how to get a crisp line.

Cutting in takes patience and practice. Use an angled brush and grip it loosely near the bristles for better control. Let the bristles fan out a little as you move along the line.

MISTAKE #97:
MESSING AROUND WITH LEAD PAINT

If you live in an older home, there's a chance you've got lead paint on the walls. Homes that went up or were renovated before 1960 likely contain lead-based paint; even homes constructed between 1960 and 1990 probably have lead paint in them, though the lead content may be smaller. Manufacturers stopped adding lead to most paint around 1991. Exterior paints used to contain the highest amounts of lead.

We've known for years that lead exposure can be dangerous. According to Health Canada, it can cause anemia or damage to the brain and nervous system, which can lead to learning disabilities. Children are most at risk: even small amounts of dust containing lead are dangerous to kids. If a pregnant woman is exposed to lead, it can affect her as well as the baby.

If you've got lead paint in your home, it may be buried beneath layers and layers. If that's the case, and the paint isn't chipping or within reach of children who might chew on it, you're wise to leave the surface alone rather than trying to remove the paint. I often see lead paint in exterior buildings and old garages, and I've seen people scrape down old window frames or baseboards without even knowing whether they're dealing with lead paint. If you start scraping, sanding and creating dust, then it's an issue—you and your family could be breathing in lead. If you don't mess with it, you're fine. It's only an issue once the particles are airborne. So you can prime and paint over it.

The best way to find out if you've got lead paint—before you start chipping everything off—is to send a paint chip sample to a lab (find one through the Standards Council of Canada at scc.ca). Just make sure you check with the lab first to get directions for gathering and sending the sample. I wouldn't necessarily trust those DIY lead-test kits. Sure, they're less than $30, and you don't have to wait long for results, but they're not as accurate. It's possible to get a false positive. Plus, you have to reveal every layer of paint, and darker paints make it tough to read the test results.

If you discover there is lead, it's often best to bring in the pros to work with it. They will seal the area off completely using heavy plastic sheets, remove every single item from the room (or cover it all with two sheets of plastic so no lead dust gets into a toy that your baby is then going to chew on). They will all show up looking like they're working on the space shuttle with the full coveralls, hair coverings, goggles and approved respirators to protect themselves from lead dust and fumes. They'll also clean up carefully afterward, and they won't be eating or drinking on the job. This is one of those times when I might be asking myself if those baseboards are really worth all the work and the danger. Sometimes it's better just to remove and replace them.

MISTAKE #98:
UNDERESTIMATING THE WORK INVOLVED IN STRIPPING OLD FINISHES

I won't lie to you: stripping old paint or stain is a real pain in the butt. If we're talking about a deck or a fence, let's be honest: it's not worth the trouble. But if you're restoring an old home and you want to bring back the original trim, it may be worth the effort to retain that heritage value. You may not want to rip it out and start fresh if the trim is solid poplar or oak and 8 or 10 inches high—you just don't get baseboards like that anymore. When you've got real character like that, you may want to strip the wood.

When painting features, make a good seal with the tape so the paint doesn't bleed underneath, and don't overload your brush. Apply a thin layer of paint at the edge of the tape and let it dry for a few minutes before applying a heavier coat. Remove the tape carefully before the paint is completely dry.

Before you start, make sure you assess the paint—is it possible that you're dealing with lead paint? (See Mistake #97, page 173.) Next, make sure you have the patience to see the job through. Stripping the wood is not simply a matter of removing the trim, applying a chemical stripper and wiping the paint away. You put the stripper on the wood and let it bubble, and then you scrape it, remove it and repeat the process a few times, because you never know what you'll find underneath the layers. These solvents are pretty nasty. As you're watching the paint peel and bubble, you might be thinking, "This can't be healthy." (Fortunately, you can get less-toxic alternatives. I've seen an organic orange peel stripper and some made from soy. I haven't used them, so I'm not sure how well they work, but you can look into them if you want something that's not as harsh as the traditional stuff.)

As an alternative, use a heat gun to strip the wood. This basically melts the paint, and then you use a scraper to remove it. The problem is you're breathing in all those fumes from the melting paint. And this work is pretty painstaking.

If the paint you're stripping is from your grandparents' era, then it probably contains lead, and you don't want to disturb it, especially if you've got children or if someone in the home is pregnant (see Mistake #97, page 173, for the risks and protocol for working with lead paint).

Mistake #99:
SLOPPY ROLLING TECHNIQUE

You can borrow a few tricks from the pros if you want to improve the quality of your painting. First, do your prep (see Mistake #95, page 171). The pros start by using a brush to apply paint around the trim and baseboards, in corners and across the top edge of a wall where it meets the ceiling. If you cut in around these edges first, you can roll your paint on pretty fast because you don't need to worry about smudging the wall colour on the trim or the ceiling. I like to cut in once, then roll on a coat of colour over the rest of the wall. If the edges look streaky, I cut in a second time, but this isn't always necessary. I finish by rolling on a second coat. Paint one wall at a time so that the brushed edges and rolled paint blends together. Otherwise, you'll get lap marks, the darker colour that you see when you roll over dried cut-in paint.

Experienced painters have their favourite routines for rolling paint, but most use a technique called the W. First, load up your roller until it's pretty heavy with paint but not so saturated that it's dripping, and roll along the top two-thirds of the tray insert to spread the paint out evenly on the roller. Then apply it to the wall by making a quick W-shape. Then you use the remaining paint on the roller to fill in the areas around the W. The key is not to push your roller and squeeze globs of colour onto the wall, or the paint won't spread out evenly, and it will look terrible when it dries. We've all done that—tried to squeak a little more paint out by leaning on the roller. To avoid this, never fully empty a roller-load of paint before you refill it: try to keep enough on the roller that the colour always applies easily without having to roll over the same spot 10 times.

Plan to tackle a wall in 16-square-foot sections, which is about a 4 × 4 square at a time. I like to start at the top left of a wall. I roll on my W, fill in that square, then move down below and repeat. I end up covering the wall by moving from top to bottom, then left to right, just like you read a book. With every roller-load, I can usually cover 16 to 20 square feet. You may not have room to paint tight areas above windows and doors with a standard roller. You can either use a mini foam roller or, if this strip is really narrow, a brush.

You'll notice that the side of the roller where the arm sits will leave paint lines because that's where you put the most pressure. To make the lines less obvious, roll toward the arm of the roller. So if you're holding the tool with the roller arm on the left, you'll need to roll to the left. (When you go back over that spot, flip your roller over so the arm sits on the right.) As you move across the wall, you're applying a lot of paint on the leading edge of the roller, so this technique helps you feather out that line with the soft, trailing edge.

If you end up covered in dots, looking like you've got the paint measles, then you're rolling too fast and flinging paint around. Just slow down a little, and you

The most popular roller technique is to work in a W pattern, being careful not to squeeze too much paint onto the wall. To keep your lines smooth, reload the roller before it's completely empty.

You'll naturally apply more paint on the leading edge of the roller, because that's where there's the most pressure. Move toward the arm of the roller to compensate.

won't have that problem. Rolling should be nice and even and gentle.

MISTAKE #100:
PAINTING TRIM AND DOORS IN THE WRONG ORDER

The architectural highlights of a room are often the baseboards, trim and doors, so you'll want to highlight these with a fresh coat of paint before you coat the walls. Semigloss and gloss finishes are the most wash-able, so I'd recommend these higher-sheen finishes for woodwork since it always seems to look grubby from handprints or boot splatters by the front door.

Start by cleaning grimy surfaces with a household cleaner or mild detergent. Whether it's bare wood or painted, lightly sand the flat surfaces of woodwork and doors with 120-grit sandpaper, which will allow paint to adhere better. I hold the sandpaper in my hand so I can get into any depressions in the wood. For trim with contours, it's better to use a soft sanding block or sanding sponge (get these at the hardware store), which hugs the contours of the wood. Steer clear of glass when you're sanding windows or doors, or you'll scratch the glass. Sweep away the dust or remove it with a shop vacuum, then wipe everything clean.

Use a 2.5- or 3-inch angled brush when priming and painting trim and doors. Start by priming any bare wood. If you're using the same type of paint (e.g., latex over latex or oil over oil), you won't need to prime a previously painted surface as long as the paint is in decent shape. (See Mistake #92, page 168, for the right way to paint oil over latex or paint latex over oil.) Let the primer dry. Sand lightly with fine-grit sandpaper such as 220-grit. Again, remove the dust.

Fill any cracks or nail holes on woodwork with a water-based wood filler. Let it dry, then sand again. Use a caulking gun and paintable caulk to fill any gaps between the baseboard and the wall (both should be primed before you do this step). Smooth out the bead of caulk with your wet finger; you'll paint over the caulking so it's the same colour as the wall later. (Generally the white painter's caulk matches common white trim and baseboards.) Apply a first coat of the finish colour for trim and baseboards using the tips in Mistake #93, page 169. You'll end up reloading the brush about every 12 inches or so. Once it's dry, sand

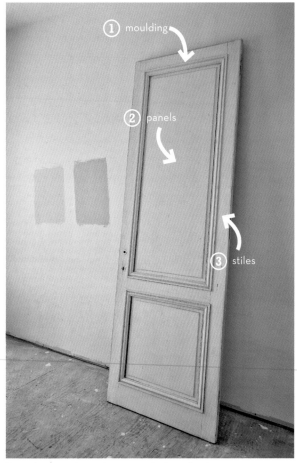

Paint doors in this order to get the best finish.

together), and then the top and sides. If you end up smudging paint on the glass, let it dry completely; then spray with window cleaner and remove the paint with a window scraper or straight razor blade—it'll come off without a fight.

MISTAKE #101:
USING TOO MUCH PAINT

As I said off the top, two coats of paint is usually enough if they're properly applied. Don't make the mistake of thinking that three or four coats is going to look even better. The paint will be thicker, but you won't get better coverage. If you have to put on more than two coats, there's something wrong with your paint—or your painting skills.

Three (or more) coats used to be necessary for deep colours. With new paint technology, you should be good to go after two coats even if the colour is dark. But that depends on the original colour of the wall. Trying to paint white over a black wall could be a little more challenging. In that case, I'd suggest you use a nice thick primer instead of applying more paint.

Another thing people do wrong is dip the brush too far into the paint can. Before you know it, there's paint on the brush handle and the metal band around the bristles and then everywhere. You really just need to apply paint to the first inch or inch and a half of a paintbrush. Don't load paint up to the metal.

Laziness is the biggest mistake in any job, and I'm not above it. I have been the victim of my own laziness multiple times, so believe me, you just end up creating more work for yourself in the long run if you take shortcuts. I've seen people load so much paint onto the brush that it's dripping down the handle and onto their hands. They're in such a rush that they try to cut in the entire height of a wall from top to bottom without

the paint lightly and clean up the dust. When you apply your final finish coat, you'll have a nice smooth finish.

If you're painting an interior door, set it up on a sawhorse or table so you won't end up with paint drips. Start at the centre of the door and work toward the outside. Paint moulding first, then the recessed panels. While these parts are drying, you move outward to the sides. Then paint the four edges.

When you're painting a window, follow a similar formula. Paint the bars of the window first (muntins are the separation pieces on a single window; mullions are the bars that connect multiple windows hung reloading paint. You're better off dipping the tip of the brush, painting 12 to 16 inches, loading up the brush again, cutting in another 12 to 16 inches and so on. Most professional painters don't have paint streaks on their brush handles. Only the cheap, fast ones have brushes covered in paint. A good painter can do the job while wearing a suit.

MISTAKE #102:
MIXING PAINT AND LADDERS

When cutting in along the ceiling, you can get sick of going up and down the ladder 10 times, and so you may decide to put the paint can on the ladder. Bad idea. What if you knock that whole thing over? One of the best tips for cutting in is to pour some paint into a family-size yogurt or sour cream container. Or use a disposable coffee cup—it's big enough to fit your brush, yet it's light and comfortable in your hand.

Another tip: avoid those A-frame ladders with the flap that holds the paint can. They're garbage. Get a three-step ladder with the handle over the front. They're easy to move around, plus they've got a nice big platform to stand on. You can easily reach up to

8 feet with them because they raise you up 2½ to 3 feet, which is a comfortable height for painting.

MISTAKE #103:
RECKLESS CORNERING

Let's say you want to paint adjacent walls two different colours. They're going to be side-by-side on an internal corner, and it's tough to get them lined up without smudging one onto the other.

Here's what you do: paint the lighter wall first. Once that's done and dry, move on to your accent colour. Load up an angled brush and start painting a few inches away from the corner; then work your way in slowly until the bristles find the groove. You'll get a feel for that perfect angle, where just a few hairs are in the corner creating a crisp line. If you instead put the brush right in the corner, you'll end up with a big gob of paint running down the wall and probably some colour on the adjacent wall, as well. It's always easier to start with a lot of paint well outside the corner and then gradually push it in.

An external corner is a different challenge. Let's say your living room opens into the hallway, and there's

Why lug around a heavy paint can when you can fill a coffee cup or yogurt container that fits comfortably in one hand?

Don't overload your brush! You need only 1 to 1 ¹/₂ inches of paint on the bristles.

When painting inside corners—including the line along the ceiling—use an angled brush and start painting a few inches away from the corner. Then work your way in slowly until the bristles find the groove. That's the secret to getting a nice, crisp line.

no trim on the doorway. If you're rolling the paint on those corners, some might wrap around the corner and onto the wrong wall. You *can* do this properly with a roller, but only if you adjust the amount of paint so the roller's not sopping wet. Have just enough on your roller to apply a light coat of paint without being forced to press down on the roller. The secret for success is having patience and taking your time. It also doesn't hurt to have a wet rag handy, so when you do make a mistake, it's easy to wipe it off.

MISTAKE #104:
RUSHING THE SECOND COAT

There's another reason not to hurry when you're painting. The paint may feel dry on the surface, but if it hasn't cured completely and you go back and do the second coat right after you finish the first coat, the first coat will peel off in places where the paint is still tacky. The first coat needs to set—it will be ruined if the second coat goes on too soon. A lot of factors determine how quickly paint dries—humidity, temperature, the size of the room, the thickness of each coat—and, unfortunately, it's impossible to know if the paint is dry just by touching it. You can speed up the drying process, though, by running a fan to move the air around. Never apply more paint unless you know the wall is completely wet or completely dry.

It sounds obvious, but the most important thing you can do for any job is to read the instructions. The paint label will say how long to wait before applying the second coat. I bet most people have never taken the time to read the side of the paint can. You should. All paints are different. The manufacturers of that product have spent a lot of money and time in labs and warehouses testing their paint so they can instruct you on how to get the best results. The last thing they want is you ripping the first coat of paint off by painting a second coat at the wrong time and then phoning to complain to them—and everyone you know—that their paint is crap.

MISTAKE #105:
CAULKING OVER YOUR PAINT JOB

I'm not sure why, but some people assume you caulk *after* you finish painting walls and trim. It's important to do it first. Before you paint, fill holes in drywall with compound, and fill nail holes in baseboards with caulk. (If you decide to paint first and caulk second, you have to wait for the paint to cure.)

Make sure you get the right caulking. There are a million different kinds in the store: some for exteriors, others for bathrooms, and the like. For trim and baseboards, use a latex caulk that's designed to be paintable. Run the caulking gun (or a product that's squeezable and doesn't require a gun) along the trim to fill any gaps. Then wet your finger and use it to wipe the caulk right into the corner. With a damp sponge, wipe back and forth to take all the caulking off the wall, leaving just enough to seal that gap where the baseboard or trim meets the wall. If you're sloppy about it, you're going to see the caulk smudged on the wall.

Whatever you do, don't use silicone to seal walls and trim because you can't paint it. It bubbles up when you roll over it with latex paint, and it won't hold the paint colour. All you'll see is that thumbprint of silicone on the wall. (See more instructions for caulking in Mistake #16, page 41.)

Use caulking before you paint, not after. After applying a thin layer, use a wet finger to smooth it out and make sure the gaps are filled.

Filling in any nail heads and cracks is crucial prep work for a perfect paint finish. Save yourself years of staring at the little hole and just fill it in now.

CHAPTER

EIGHT

BASEMENTS

OUR EXPECTATIONS FOR BASEMENTS HAVE REALLY CHANGED OVER THE YEARS. NOW A LOT OF PEOPLE WANT A BATHROOM IN THE BASEMENT OR A MAN CAVE WITH HIGH-END ELECTRONICS. WE PUT IN A MINI HOCKEY RINK FOR ONE FAMILY. THERE WAS NO ICE, BUT THEY HAD THE BOARDS AND THE PAINTED LINES AND EVERYTHING.

Nowadays, we are finishing basements to gain more space. Families want to stretch out and use the basement for everything from storage for wine and ski equipment to hanging out to a fully furnished granny flat. What people may not realize is that the basement may be secondary when it comes to living space, but it's the most crucial part of the house because that's where all your mechanicals live. Everyone says the kitchen is the heart of the home, but your electrical panel is the heart of your plumbing, electrical and HVAC system—everything is down there in the basement. Those controls are in the most vulnerable position: the basement is surrounded by foundation walls, and the whole house sits on top of them. So it really is a very important area of the house, even if people tend to marginalize it and think they can just slap up some drywall, throw down some carpet and treat it as a secondary living space.

BASEMENT BASICS
DIFFICULTY: 6 TO 9 OUT OF 10

Renovating a basement involves a combination of skills, many of which are discussed elsewhere in this book, including framing, drywalling, flooring, HVAC and insulation. But there are a couple of unique considerations that make building underground different from remodelling rooms that sit above grade:

- **Keep it dry.** Most foundations are built from concrete, which is porous enough to allow moisture to seep in through the walls and slab floor. Deal with dampness and leaks before finishing a basement to protect new flooring, furniture and drywall from potential water or mould damage. Waterproofing is most effective (and expensive) if done from the outside.

- **Keep it warm.** An uninsulated basement wastes energy. Remember to insulate the walls and floor to conserve heat and make the finished basement more comfortable. (See Mistake #14, page 39, for the best ways to insulate basement walls.) Heating and cooling systems may need reconfiguring by an HVAC specialist to provide even heating in the new finished space and the rest of the home.

TOOLS AND MATERIALS YOU'LL NEED
Depends on the specific job

CROSS-SECTION OF A TYPICAL EXTERIOR WALL AND ASSEMBLY

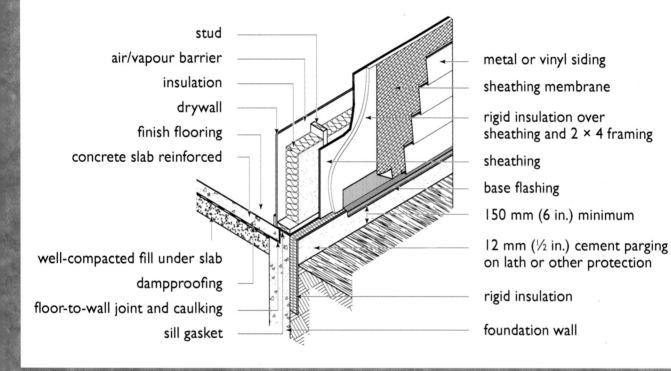

stud

air/vapour barrier

insulation

drywall

finish flooring

concrete slab reinforced

well-compacted fill under slab

dampproofing

floor-to-wall joint and caulking

sill gasket

metal or vinyl siding

sheathing membrane

rigid insulation over sheathing and 2 × 4 framing

sheathing

base flashing

150 mm (6 in.) minimum

12 mm (½ in.) cement parging on lath or other protection

rigid insulation

foundation wall

MISTAKE #106:
VALUING ALL THE WRONG THINGS IN A FINISHED BASEMENT

When you're in the market for a house and the real estate agent says the basement is finished, chances are you look at that as a plus. Thanks to that finished basement, the agent tells you the home is worth an extra $50,000 or so. Here's what I'll tell you: if a basement was finished by a homeowner without permits, I see that as a potential $50,000 liability, because I know if somebody finished the basement without pulling permits, they probably didn't make sure the waterproofing and framing were done properly. Chances are

there isn't a proper subfloor, either. And if the electrical was done without permits, you've got a fire risk. All of that *lowers* the value of the home. Plus, now I have to tear out the basement and redo it the way it should have been done in the first place. So not only do I have to spend $10,000 to $15,000 removing it, I need to get all the required permits to put it back together properly.

I think a lot of people walk into a basement and focus on the wrong things. They'll look at the nice cabinets and fall in love with the wall colour and notice the pot lights. But if the lights were cheap and likely to overheat, or if there are 30 of them on a single circuit and the breaker is going to blow all the time, or the

All the things you should value in a basement—dry, safe, permit-inspected—are nearly invisible. Notice I didn't say "flat screen" anywhere in there.

electrical mistakes present a fire hazard, the basement isn't adding value to the home. Cheap finishes may make a basement room show well at the open house, but in the long run, they're a waste of money. If a basement has been finished professionally and the owners can confirm the details—it was properly waterproofed by a reputable company, they put in the right subfloor and insulated properly, they pulled electrical and plumbing permits and had the wiring and pipes properly inspected—then I know the basement is an asset that will increase the value of the home. If you're having doubts, it doesn't hurt to ask to see copies of the renovation receipts and permits.

MISTAKE #107:
FINISHING A BASEMENT THAT WILL BE BARELY USABLE

Basements weren't originally intended as living spaces. Back in the day, they were where we stored root vegetables, coal and food for the horses. So before obsessing over paint chips and floor samples for a basement reno, ask yourself, "Should I be finishing this basement?"

Some houses are built on pressure-treated wood foundations (you can see the wood above grade, the same way you can see some of a concrete foundation). I know these have been code-approved in Canada and the U.S. for at least four decades, but if you encapsulate that wood and start covering it up with drywall and insulation, you're asking for trouble. It's not going to have a chance to breathe or dry if you have a flood or a serious leak, and it's pretty much guaranteed to rot. Why would you finish a basement in a house like that?

Consider the ceiling height. If your current basement is barely a crawl space—let's say 5 or even 6 feet high—you need to ask yourself whether it is going to be usable living space. Even a basic finish, such as putting in a laminate floor, insulation and drywall, a ceiling and some pot lights, is probably going to cost you about $35 a square foot. If you're putting in a bathroom or kitchen, then you're probably looking at $50 to $70 per square foot. If you're also adding bedrooms, you can be spending upwards of $90 to $100 a square foot. And you'll lose at least a couple of inches finishing the ceiling—so you might find yourself stooping in the world's most expensive cave.

Remember, too, that the contractor who says he can come in and finish your basement for $10,000 is just going to bang up a couple of 2 × 4s and drywall. He doesn't care about making it waterproof. Your new rec room might look good for a while, but that won't last, and you'll end up unhappy.

If you're going to put a bedroom down there and use it as a rental unit, you need to ensure the finished basement meets the requirements for a legal basement apartment. Building code varies by province: in Ontario, the finished ceiling height has to be at least 6 feet, 5 inches. Each bedroom you build in the basement also needs egress windows, which need to open large enough to be used as an escape route in the event of an emergency, such as a fire. (See more on this in Mistake #110, page 193.)

MISTAKE #108:
MISUNDERSTANDING UNDERPINNING AND BENCH PINNING

If you don't have enough ceiling height, consider digging out the basement. There are two ways of doing that: underpinning and bench pinning.

Underpinning involves slowly and methodically digging around the perimeter of your basement wall

below the foundation, removing 4 feet at a time, and pouring a new foundation and footing wall beneath. It's got to be done right: this is the foundation of your whole house, so the structural load has to be carefully supported. The advantage of underpinning is the new interior walls will be flush from top to bottom. Since it requires more engineering and labour and nets you more space, underpinning is also more expensive and time-consuming.

If the budget won't allow for underpinning, and you don't mind sacrificing some square footage, there's another way to dig out a basement—bench pinning. This involves digging down and pouring a big "bench" around the exterior walls of the basement to prevent the existing footing from slipping in. The disadvantage of a bench footing is you lose some of the existing floor space—you'll end up with a ledge all the way around the perimeter of the interior walls (the deeper you dig, the wider the bench needs to be). The benefit is bench pinning is cheaper than underpinning. But really, both of these options are expensive: expect bench pinning to start at about $150 per linear foot, and underpinning to cost about $300 per linear foot and up. In both cases you have to break up the concrete floor, and you have to haul all of that concrete under the house, which usually means setting up a conveyor belt and taking it up through a window. If there's no room, your contractor will be hauling out buckets of concrete.

Bench pinning is about half the cost of underpinning, but you will lose some square footage along the perimeter.

Mistake #109:
REMOVING OR MOVING A SUPPORT POST

This seems like such a silly, obvious mistake, but I see it all the time. The posts and beams in your basement are not there to look good but to hold up the rest of your house. That means you should never remove any of those members unless you're working with a structural engineer and have proper permits. If there is a support post in a really awkward spot and you want to remove it or relocate it, it might be possible to compensate by reinforcing the beam above it. Even so, this is not a do-it-yourself job. Some people think you can just move the post to a different location along the same beam, but it's not that simple. That post is sitting on a footing in the ground below your basement slab, which you can't see. Moving that post a couple of feet away means it's going to be sitting just on the concrete slab, which isn't strong enough—the post could crack the concrete and compromise the structural integrity of your house.

If you've got a post in the basement that you can't move for structural reasons, you have a couple of options: you can frame and drywall around it so it becomes a square column, or you can build it into a wall. This is something to be aware of if you are buying a new house from the building plans. In most cases, it's cheaper to have smaller beams and more posts, compared with stronger beams and fewer posts, so many builders plan basements with a lot of posts and tiny steel beams to save money. If you're planning on finishing the basement, look at the basement drawings and, before construction, ask the builder to upgrade the beams and reduce the number of posts. Consider also asking the builder to dig down an extra foot to give you a basement with 9-foot ceilings.

A jack post like this can temporarily support a beam, but remember that you can't remove a post in your basement without consulting a structural engineer.

Mistake #110:
INSTALLING THE WRONG WINDOWS

A lot of houses, even newer ones, have those tiny steel windows in the basement. And for some reason, builders jam them at the very top of the wall, right against the ceiling. If you drop the window down a little bit, it looks much better, but you might need to add a window well outside for drainage. That increases the cost, which is why builders don't do it, but I recommend it if you want a little more light in the basement. I admit window wells don't provide the most attractive view, but you can use dry stacked stone or other materials to make them look decent.

The most important thing to remember if you're putting a bedroom in a basement is it must have an egress window—that means an operable window that meets certain criteria so it can be used as an escape hatch in the event of an emergency. Check the building code in your area, but typically the window has to have a minimum area of 4 square feet and an opening that measures at least 15 inches vertically and horizontally. The window well has to be a minimum size so someone could safely crawl out through that window if they had to.

Window wells don't just give you light below grade; they can also provide an escape route in case of a fire—or can be a wrestling belt in a pinch.

Some people, when they are drawing up plans and applying for permits, will get sneaky and call their planned bedroom a storage room to get around that requirement. Don't ever do that. If you ever have a fire and someone is using that bedroom, you'd have a catastrophe. Yes, it might cost $1,000 or $1,500 to put a proper egress window in, but it's something you have to do for safety.

MISTAKE #111:
FINISHING A WET OR LEAKY BASEMENT

Before you start choosing a sofa and buying a big new TV, you need to take a serious look at your foundation. If your basement smells musty, if the walls, floor or carpet feel damp, or you see efflorescence (whitish powder) on the walls, you've got moisture coming in. It makes no sense to finish a basement with a leaky foundation. Any area that combines moisture and organic material (such as wood or the paper covering on drywall) has the perfect conditions for mould. And when you put a bunch of dry building materials into that wet area, you're setting yourself up for rot. It's like leaving a pile of fresh food on the counter: it's only a matter of time before it gets mouldy. (Even in an unfinished basement, I wouldn't want to see signs of moisture: too much will weaken a concrete foundation over time.)

How does water end up inside in the first place? Sometimes it's a natural condition known as hydrostatic pressure. As the earth around your home collects groundwater, the soil expands. This extra weight builds up and presses against the foundation walls and up against the foundation floor. As the pressure builds, water can come through cracks in the walls and floor of the foundation or through the pores of the foundation itself.

You don't need hydrostatic pressure to have a wet basement. Storm water and even a garden hose could be part of the problem. Most often, though, water vapour is the culprit. Moisture circulates around the house as vapour, which is created by activities such as breathing, cooking, doing laundry and showering. When warm, moist air cools, some of the moisture evaporates. That's what's happening when warm air hits a cold window, for example—the glass becomes coated on the inside with a layer of condensation. Even without any windows in a basement, moisture can condense on cool surfaces such as the concrete floor under carpeting or the brick or concrete block behind exterior basement walls. These damp conditions are perfect for uninvited visitors like mould, which can destroy the structural integrity of the foundation itself.

Moisture can also be caused by a problem with the weeping tile. *Weeping tile* is a bit of a misnomer. These are perforated tubes that slope away from a home's foundation, right down by the footings. Any groundwater that seeps down from the surface or percolates up from below gets led away from the foundation by gravity and the weeping tile. If water is no longer draining properly, those tubes could have become damaged or separated. Blame tree roots, soil movement, freezing and thawing or age. In older homes, weeping tile is made of clay, which doesn't last forever (these days, we use weeping tile made of plastic). A waterproofing pro can inspect the condition of the weeping tile, and you may be able to have it patched, if you're lucky. If it's in really bad condition, it might need to be replaced. That's a big, expensive job (see more on waterproofing in Mistake #112, next).

Let's say your foundation is made of stone rubble (we see these in older parts of Toronto and other cities across the country). These are loose and crumbly, and when you mess with them, you get all kinds of sand coming out of the joints. The foundations look heavy and solid, but they are very porous, which means water passes right through them, and you're going to need to waterproof before you do any finishing of the space. Even if your house has a block or concrete foundation, you should have it inspected before you start any basement renovations.

MISTAKE #112:
WATERPROOFING A BASEMENT FROM THE INSIDE

Think of the hull of a ship. If it's leaking, do you want to patch the ship from the inside or the outside? Obviously you want to patch the outside so the pressure from the water can work in your favour and hold that patch in place. It's the same with your basement.

That said, digging up the entire exterior of your home isn't always feasible. In these situations, water coming through the foundation can be directed toward an interior weeping tile into a sump pit and then pumped clear of the house. But this method has limitations and challenges when it comes to basement finishing.

I'm going to warn you, exterior waterproofing is no fun. It's expensive and messy work, but if you are investing in a finished basement, you need to protect that investment. If you have a moisture issue, you need to solve it before you start finishing. It's tempting to want to patch a leaky basement from the inside, because it's so much less work and less expensive. But if you have a choice, I'd recommend an exterior job.

If your weeping tile needs to be replaced or there are cracks in the foundation, be prepared to have about 24 inches around the perimeter of your house excavated. Yes, that means tearing up garden beds,

Perforated plastic weeping tile directs water away from the foundation while keeping out soil and silt.

A dimpled plastic membrane can be placed between the foundation wall and the soil.

the driveway, the lawn, and so on. Old clay weeping tile will be dug up and replaced by perforated plastic hoses that let water in while keeping out soil and silt (which could eventually block the tube). While the foundation is exposed, you can have it inspected. Now's the time to repair and patch any cracks.

Then you'd have waterproofing material applied to the foundation. That will be either a liquid membrane applied by trowelling, spraying or rolling on, or a dimpled plastic membrane wrapped around the foundation. If any water gets through the membrane, the airspace created by the dimples help direct moisture down into the weeping tile. Groundwater won't have a chance to push up against the foundation once you've set it up properly for drainage.

Unfortunately, some homes are built practically right on top of each other, so there's not enough room to excavate properly around the foundation on the outside. In that case, you can add an interior weeping system. For interior waterproofing, the basement floor needs to be dug up. A weeping system is created in a trench along the footing, and the walls are wrapped in a waterproof membrane. If water gets in, the system lets it run down the inside of the walls into a bilge,

which then gets pumped out. There's a weeper along the footing, but there's also a membrane on the wall. Anything that comes through the foundation goes down that membrane into the weeper and into a sump pit.

This basement wall has been excavated and is ready for weeping tile.

Waterproofing properly means excavating a couple of feet around the foundation, applying a membrane and then adding gravel for proper drainage. It's a big job, but it's worth it to prevent leaky basements.

MISTAKE #113:
USING MOULD-RESISTANT MATERIALS INSTEAD OF WATERPROOFING

The industry has come up with all kinds of products aimed at minimizing mould, which is a huge fear homeowners have, and I've tried a lot of them. The latest thing is mould-resistant lumber. The wood looks pink or blue because it's been treated with a coating to resist moisture absorption and protect against mould, wood rot and wood-eating insects such as termites. There may be situations where the extra cost and carbon footprint are warranted, but honestly, if you build a house or finish a basement properly, you don't need chemically treated lumber. We rip apart 100-year-old homes all the time, and they're usually not rotting or infested with mould or insects. Why not just build houses and finish basements properly so we don't have moisture problems in the first place, and keep all of those chemicals out of our homes? That just makes more sense to me.

There is also moisture-resistant drywall, with gypsum faced with fibreglass. The lack of organic material (paper) inhibits the growth of mould. These products are a good choice in a bathroom because you're throwing water vapour at the walls with every bath and shower. It's also great for basements, but again, it shouldn't be the only line of defence. I would rather control the moisture content in the air with proper ventilation than rely on the materials to hold their own in a hostile environment. You might end up getting some moisture in the basement despite your best efforts, but many of these products are overkill.

The way I see it, you've got two choices. You can finish a wet basement using chemically treated lumber, mould-resistant drywall and laminate floor that has

Lumber and drywall are available in moisture-resistant varieties, but these have limited value. A better solution is to prevent moisture issues from occurring in the first place.

no organics and hope your materials will stand up to the environment. Or you could spend the time and money to fix the basement so it's not leaking and full of moisture, and then use more natural, environmentally responsible products to finish it. I know which one I'd choose.

MISTAKE #114:
OVERLOOKING PROBLEMS CAUSED BY GRADING AND DOWNSPOUTS

Before spending a fortune on weeping tiles and waterproofing, go outside and make sure your property isn't causing your water problems. A well-graded landscape will be sloped so water can easily drain away from the house and the foundation. If you're experiencing new water in your basement, think about what has changed. Have you recently done any landscaping, such as installing a patio, pathway or driveway? Have you dug new flowerbeds next to the house? Did you make sure the soil was graded properly before the stones were laid and the shrubs planted, or are you now irrigating your foundation every time you water that new tree? Don't underestimate the power—for good and evil—of grading. See Mistake #188, page 293.

Eavestroughs and downspouts are crucial to keeping the basement dry. Your gutters are supposed to collect all the rain or snow that lands on your roof. If they're set up properly, the downspouts should carry the water far away from the house. I've seen houses, though, where the downspouts are directed right into the ground. Again, if you're watering your foundation, you're asking for trouble. Make sure downspouts are set up to drain at least 8 to 10 feet away from the house. Clean out your gutters—or get someone to do it for you—twice a year. If leaves or sticks get in there, they can create blockages that cause your eavestroughs to overflow and dump water beside the foundation instead of carrying it away to a safe spot where it can drain away from the house. Concentrated water will slowly percolate into the soil and spread outward, so you want that water far enough away from the house that by the time it starts sinking and spreading out, it's not near your foundation walls.

An improperly positioned downspout (*above*) is inviting trouble. Use one that is long enough to keep rainwater well away from your foundation.

MISTAKE #115:
SCREWING UP IN-FLOOR PLUMBING

A lot of new homes come with a rough-in for a bathroom in the basement. The rough-in usually includes a 3-inch pipe poking up from the floor where you can put a toilet, a 2-inch drain for a shower or bathtub and a third pipe protruding from the wall for a sink. The builder just wants to bang them in there so they can say the basement has rough-ins, but the plumbing won't necessarily be in an ideal location for your basement finishing plans. Getting roughed-in plumbing moved to a better spot may sound like a simple request, but it requires breaking up the concrete floor. I haven't worked on many basements where we didn't have to open up the floor at some point. Smashing concrete, digging out some ground and putting in new plumbing is not something the average homeowner should be messing around with: hire a licensed plumber.

Tearing up the foundation floor to have plumbing installed or moved can easily add $3,000 to $5,000 to the tab. In some cases, you can help with some of the demolition—breaking up concrete and hauling it out—to reduce the cost, but you need to be careful about where you dig. Talk to the plumber before you pick up a sledgehammer and start flailing away, or you could damage essential drainage pipes.

If the rough-in location will work for you, or if your budget is limited, plan to build a bathroom using the existing rough-ins. The toilet might not end up in an ideal spot, but you need to ask yourself whether moving it is worth $5,000.

It's especially important to involve a plumber if you want to add plumbing to an old basement in which the plumbing might be made of clay. If you're chipping away at the concrete around your home's main plumbing stack, be very careful not to break that pipe, which empties into the sewer. Clay pipe is actually not that fragile—it's strong, but it's brittle. Don't expect to be able to cut it cleanly yourself. Again, for that, you'll need a plumber with the right tools. If the stack is cast-iron, the plumber will use a giant snap cutter, which is a little like a chainsaw, but instead of teeth, it has carbide wheels and it's inside out. The plumber puts that around the pipe and works it to a point where the pipe just snaps.

Another problem comes up if the in-floor plumbing is below the level of the sewer or septic system. This doesn't happen very often in new subdivisions, because the sewer pipes are buried pretty deep, but it can easily happen in an older home if you're digging out the floor to gain extra ceiling height. (If you're not sure whether your basement bathroom is going to be below the sewer, you may need to check your survey. The elevation of the sewer pipe should be marked on there.) In that situation you have to put in a sewage ejection pump so everything from the toilet runs into what is basically a sealed sump pit. There's a macerator inside that pit, and that chews up everything and then pumps it up and out to the sewer—and produces even more expense and more maintenance. And at some point in the future, that pump is going to fail and you're going to need to replace it.

By the way, if your basement is below sewer level and there's a sewer backup, you'll be the first to know about it. Crap flows downhill, as they say.

MISTAKE #116:
NOT VENTING THE PLUMBING PROPERLY

If it takes forever for a sink to drain, or if water burps out of the tub or shower, the plumbing may not have been vented correctly. Think about a can of beer: if you open it and turn it upside down quickly, the beer trickles out pretty slowly, but if you punch a hole in the bottom of the can, the beer shoots out. That's the idea behind your plumbing stack, the giant vent pipe that goes up through the roof. It vents sewer gases and allows air into the drains to prevent the formation of a vacuum behind the moving water. That vent is like the hole in the bottom of the can that allows the air to flow out and the water to flow quickly and smoothly.

Venting isn't important just in the basement: you need to make sure every sink, toilet and faucet in the house has proper airflow. There are a ton of rules and local codes around venting, which is why I suggest you hire a licensed plumber instead of trying to figure this stuff out yourself.

MISTAKE #117:
NOT PUTTING THE VENTILATION FAN ON A TIMER

Speaking of ventilation, make sure you've got an exhaust fan in a basement bathroom (and every bathroom that doesn't have a window). I don't recommend hooking it up to the same switch as a light because you don't want to shut down the fan every time you switch off the light. It's better to put the fan on a timer and, after every shower, run it for a good 20 to 30 minutes to suck out all that humidity. If you don't, the moist air could create mould problems. Make sure the fan vents outdoors, not in behind drywall or into joist cavities.

MISTAKE #118:
IMPROPER HEATING

Because the basement is at the lowest point in a house, and because warm air rises, the basement is naturally

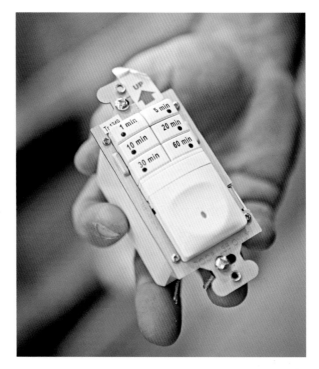

A ventilation fan can solve a lot of moisture problems in a bathroom. Install it with a timer so you can let it run for 20 minutes or so after your shower.

going to be the coldest place. On the bright side, the furnace is down there, so the basement rooms are typically the first ones to get heat.

When your basement is unfinished, it's often just one big room. But once you start putting up partition walls, you need to plan for those smaller rooms to get hot air. What you typically see in a basement are a couple of heat registers in the ceiling. But in some municipalities, code now says that if you finish your basement, you have to bring those registers down and install them in the wall about 12 inches from the floor. You would run a duct down the wall, and then frame out a box for it. And that's another mistake people make: they don't frame that box. They just run the duct down the side of the wall and drywall around it without insulating the duct. The problem is now the duct is right up against a cold exterior wall. Running warm air through a cold duct reduces the efficiency of the furnace.

The other thing people don't even think about when they start finishing a basement with separate rooms is the need for cold-air return ducts. Those air intake vents—which are covered with a grille, similar to your heat registers—draw air, filter it and feed it to the furnace so it can be heated and sent back out to warm up your home. A proper HVAC set-up requires a balanced system of heat vents and cold-air return vents to keep the furnace running efficiently. In fact, a system has to inhale the same amount of air as it exhales. If cold-air returns aren't bringing new air to the basement, the furnace won't be able to pump new hot air into the house. You may end up with some rooms that are stuffy and others that are cool, which can lead to unbalanced air pressure and high energy bills. Just make sure you don't cover up any vents or returns with furniture. Let them breathe so your furnace can work properly.

Finishing a basement places extra demands on a furnace to heat more square footage than before, when no one spent time in the unfinished basement. For the whole house to be comfortable, the heating system needs to be re-engineered to account for the new finished space. Designing heating systems is not a DIY job. Hire an energy auditor or HVAC professional to do specialized heat-loss calculations for the house with the new basement taken into account. They will also make sure the system provides sufficient airflow.

If you don't want a forced-air gas furnace, you could look at a boiler system. If you're already breaking up the concrete pad to move plumbing, you might install hydronic radiant heating. Here's how it works: an energy-efficient boiler provides domestic hot water for showers and whatnot, while spreading heated water throughout the basement via a network of tubes embedded in the floors. Water holds heat much more efficiently than air, which means you get even heat without ducts and vents or those annoying cold spots. One drawback of hydronic radiant heat is the price tag. It's three to four times the cost of a forced-air gas furnace, but it sure feels great on your feet. We have been in old houses where the basement slab is so thin you can break it with a regular hammer. In those cases

radiant heating isn't very difficult to install, and you are going to have to re-pour the slab anyway.

Depending on what kind of floor you're putting down, electric in-floor heating is also an option. Heating coils are embedded in a prefabricated mat that gets installed under tile, laminate or engineered woods. (Some electric floor heat systems are DIY-friendly, and some require a little more skill, so gauge your level of skill carefully before attempting your own install.) If you're using a floating floor, you can't nail it down. Electric in-floor heating is generally less efficient than hydronic, but you can usually run it on a programmable thermostat.

MISTAKE #119:
SUFFERING IN THE COLD BECAUSE OF A SHODDY SUBFLOOR

One of the best ways to keep your basement warm is to install a subfloor. That's considered standard nowadays, and it makes a huge difference if it's done right. The subfloor needs to go down early in the process, before you start any of the framing. One product we use is called DRIcore. These 2- × 2-foot tongue-and-groove panels are made of OSB (oriented strand board) with a moisture barrier—a thick plastic foundation-wrap material—on the bottom. They leave a gap so the concrete can breathe, reducing the potential for mould and protecting your furniture and electronics from moisture issues. Just by creating that thermal barrier, this material really warms up the basement and makes the floor a lot more comfortable to walk on. The underlayment for carpet, laminate or engineered hardwood can go right over the DRIcore. You can put tile on it, too, but in that case, you have to screw each panel to the concrete (using Tapcon screws) to hold it securely. There are many other methods to create and install a subfloor in a basement, but in my opinion, DRIcore is

DRIcore panels make an ideal subfloor in a basement. You can lay them on the concrete pad and then frame overtop.

by far the simplest to install and the most effective.

The nice thing about doing a subfloor with DRIcore is when you do your framing, you can attach the bottom plates of the framing to the DRIcore panels without having to secure the plates into the concrete. Just remember those panels are only about an inch thick, so you don't want to go any deeper than that, or you'll quickly hit the concrete. If you're using a nail gun, I suggest you drive the nails in at an angle—if the nail hits the concrete, it will bend. Don't worry that you're going only 1 inch into the floor, either. These interior walls are not structural. When you're anchoring them down, the idea is just to prevent the wall from moving side to side. Any subfloor will cost you a little ceiling height, so remember to account for that when planning.

If for some reason you have not put down a subfloor, remember that you can't put regular lumber right against concrete. You have to use some kind of barrier, such as a sill gasket, between the concrete and the framing wood. See Mistake #41, page 93, for more details.

MISTAKE #120:
USING THE WRONG FLOORING

Real ¾-inch **hardwood** doesn't normally belong in the

basement because wood doesn't do well in extreme temperatures and humid environments. It absorbs and sheds moisture, so it will continuously expand and contract in a basement, which is often the most humid spot in the summer and—thanks to the furnace—the first area to dry out in the winter. That said, there are some kinds of hardwood that are so well sealed they would perform okay in a basement. But generally, you're asking for trouble if you lay solid hardwood floors below grade.

Engineered hardwoods are much more stable. With engineered hardwood, you've got a thin veneer of real hardwood on top of an engineered base made from laminated layers of fibreboard or plywood. The lamination strengthens the material and makes it moisture-resistant, which is why you can use it below grade. I like these floors—they look and sound like hardwood, yet they're designed to resist expansion and contraction. They're not cheap, though: you'll pay close to or more than what you'd pay for solid hardwood. And although you can refinish them once, they won't last as long as true hardwood because that top veneer just isn't thick enough to stand up to repeated sanding.

Tile works well in a basement, especially if you end up with unexpected water problems (you'll have taken care of waterproofing already, though, right? See Mistake #111, page 194). If a drain backs up or a washing machine overflows, the flooding won't damage ceramic or porcelain tile like it could ruin hardwood. The problem with tile is it feels cold unless you warm it up with in-floor heating or lay down some thick area rugs. But you can't beat it if you need something affordable and low maintenance.

Laminate can work well in a dry basement because this flooring doesn't actually contain any solid

Don't lay carpet on hard, bare surfaces, such as a concrete pad—or the top of my head. If you're going to use carpet, opt for the tiles with adhesive backing. It's easier if you need to remove a small area because of moisture issues.

wood—the top layer is just a picture of hardwood. Its bottom layer is reinforced with melamine or MDF for stability and moisture resistance. Laminate is pretty easy for a DIYer to install because it's light and it floats, meaning that it clicks together on the subfloor without being nailed down. My problem with laminate is I don't like the way it sounds—hollow. I strongly caution against the cheap stuff (find out why in Mistake #29, page 82), and I suggest you use the best underlayment you can get.

Vinyl is waterproof, so you can get away with using it in basements and bathrooms. Look for vinyl plank flooring if you want something quiet and relatively warm that resembles hardwood but costs a lot less. Be warned, though: the subfloor must be completely flat or you'll notice every flaw. Also, a caution for those with health and respiratory sensitivities: vinyl (and the adhesives used to install it) is known to off-gas.

At the end of the day, many opt for **carpet** because it's comfortable to walk on and feels warm—warmer than concrete, anyway. I don't recommend the installation that most homeowners tend to opt for, which is laying underlayment right on top of concrete and then putting down carpet. The problem is that it feels really hard underfoot, and it can still be cold. It can also create problems with moisture if your basement floor isn't properly insulated and waterproofed since groundwater can penetrate concrete and vapour can get trapped. The right way to install carpet on concrete below grade is to separate the two with a proper subfloor (like DRIcore—see Mistake #119, page 203), topped by carpet pad and carpet.

I have one other suggestion, especially for the basement: install carpet tiles instead of wall-to-wall carpet. If there are any moisture issues, you can remove the affected square and mop up before mould sets in. Again, you'll want to look at other options if you're concerned about indoor air quality: the adhesives, fire retardants and underlayment of the average carpet can all off-gas fumes into your home.

MISTAKE #121:
DOING YOUR OWN ELECTRICAL

Where I live in Ontario, you're allowed to get a permit from the Electrical Safety Association to do your own electrical and have it inspected. (Electrical code varies by province, so check yours to find out the rules.) But I can't tell people enough: if you're going to do it yourself without a permit and inspection, you *might* be fine. But you're literally playing with fire. If faulty wiring burns down the house or kills somebody, you're criminally liable. You just screwed your life up to save some money.

For a typical basement renovation, it's going to cost a couple thousand dollars for the electrical. Even if there is electrical in place already, you don't know what kind of condition it's in. Especially if you have an older home, it's worth hiring an electrician who can spot potential problems from previous installations. When Adam did his basement, he removed the drop ceiling and found all kinds of problems: wires crossed, junctions made with tape, you name it. There are codes you have to follow regarding how many items can be on a breaker, the correct height for switches and receptacles, and things like that.

So unless you are really experienced with electrical and you're willing to take the time to do it properly—and I'd say that applies to one in a few thousand people—it's just not something you should do yourself. If you insist, get a permit and have it inspected properly.

Some people want to install the fixtures and run the wires themselves and then call in an electrician to tie everything into the panel and do the inspection. Most electricians won't allow that—they want to do the work themselves to make sure it's done safely and properly. Otherwise, they could find themselves legally responsible for your mistakes.

MISTAKE #122:
CHEAPING OUT ON POT LIGHTS

Installing pot lights isn't a particularly difficult job. But my rule of thumb is to be smart and hire a professional any time you're uncertain about whether you can complete a project that includes a lot of electrical work. It's all about protecting the most important thing in your house—your family.

I'd recommend talking to an electrician even before you go out to buy your pot lights because there are a lot of cheap ones out there that are absolute garbage. A good-quality pot light costs at least $20, but if you buy them through your electrician, you may be able to get a deal on a better-quality light.

Consider installing newer energy-efficient lights like LEDs. They use a fraction of the electricity of halogen and incandescent bulbs (which are being phased out in Canada). You can screw an LED bulb into many pot lights, but the dedicated LED boxes will make the bulbs last longer so you get your money's worth. Some of these bulbs last up to 50,000 hours. You can screw in an LED when you bring your baby home and not change it until she's off to university!

Product info is another benefit of calling an electrician. Pros can explain the benefits and drawbacks of different lighting options and recommend the ones that make the most sense for your project.

MISTAKE #123:
SKIPPING THE SMOKE DETECTORS

Current building code requires you to install smoke alarms in the basement, yet almost no one does it properly. The smoke detectors have to be hard-wired with a battery backup in case of power failures. Not only that, but all smoke detectors now have to be interconnected so that if one in the basement goes off, the alarms in the whole house go off. This is not a DIY project: hire a licensed electrician to make sure the work is done safely and up to code.

Don't underestimate how important it is to have proper smoke alarms on all levels of your house. People think they will have time to escape a fire, but they don't appreciate that our homes are full of so much stuff that releases toxic fumes as it burns. I've spoken to firefighters who've told me that a single gulp of smoke in a house fire can pretty much incapacitate you. Spend the money to get your smoke detectors properly installed, and buy your family time.

MISTAKE #124:
NOT CONSIDERING MODULAR BASEMENT SYSTEMS

The old-school way was to finish a basement by building from scratch: stud walls, vapour barrier, insulation, drywall, the works. A new alternative is to use an all-in-one modular system of moisture-resistant insulated panels for walls, ceilings and floors, plus lighting, trim and everything else. The panels click together with plastic connectors. The advantage is you're supplied with all the parts you need, and they go up pretty quickly. Most brands say you can finish a basement in 10 days or less. My only complaint is some of them make your basement look like an office cubicle.

We were involved in developing one of these products: Smartwall engineered panels, which are manufactured by DRIcore. The 2- × 8-foot tongue-and-groove panels are about 3 inches thick, with foam insulation on the back and drywall on the front. Each panel has built-in horizontal and vertical channels to run electrical. No studs are needed: each panel is screwed into a rail along the top and bottom of the walls. There's also no taping required. The vertical seam between each panel is mudded with a special polymer that's flexible and won't crack, and most panels require just two screws. I like how the system takes care of framing, insulation (it's R16), drywall and a vapour barrier all in one. I've seen another similar product out there, but you still need to frame normally and then slide the panel into your 16-inch opening. That means you can't run electrical or anything like that.

These systems work best on the exterior walls when you have a basic basement layout. (If you have an old house with no straight walls, low ceilings and a wonky concrete slab floor, then engineered panels probably aren't for you.) A little conventional framing here and there is always required, especially for ceiling details. The Smartwall system allows you to install a suspended ceiling or a conventionally framed drywall ceiling.

The only planning you really need to do, other than measuring to see how many panels you'll need, is figuring out where you want your outlets and light switches, because some of the panels come with precut holes. You fish your wires down from the ceiling and pull them to these cut-outs.

These systems really cut down on mess because they can be cut with a handsaw, which is cleaner and easier than cutting lumber. Even the polymer compound is heavier than normal drywall mud, so you don't have to do as much sanding, and the dust settles more quickly.

It's impressive how quickly a basement gets finished with these modular packages. We can take a 10-foot section of wall (about 7½ feet high) from unfinished to fully covered with Smartwall panels and the first coat of mud in just over 30 minutes. For us to do that with conventional drywall and insulation would probably take more than two hours. So if you're a DIYer, you can probably get 30 feet of wall done in one evening. Plus, the margin for error is much lower with this type of panel system because you don't have to worry about framing on 16-inch centres, insulating properly or making sure your vapour barrier is tied in. You screw in one panel, and all those steps are done. Once you're finished the installation and you paint the panels (you don't even need to prime them), the end product looks exactly like regular drywall. So if you're going to use drywall elsewhere in the basement, such as on the ceiling, you can tie it all in, and it looks great.

Obviously, any system has its limitations. It's great for perimeter walls in a fairly simple basement, but if the basement is complex, with rounded walls or lots of angles, or there is a lot of back-framing to be done (which involves blocking the walls by installing pieces of lumber to anchor TV brackets, shower doors and the ceiling), I wouldn't use a modular system. But it is ideal for the majority of simple, subdivision-type basements.

MISTAKE #125: FRAMING TOO CLOSE TO DUCTWORK

Framing too close to the ductwork isn't a serious problem, but it can be a nuisance, because you'll hear banging as the ducts expand and contract due to the heat and cool cycles of your furnace. If you are framing around ducts, be sure to leave at least an inch between the metal and the lumber. This will save you the headache of listening to that rattling sound every time the furnace runs. Also, be sure that plumbing drains have ample space to move—hot or cold water coming down the pipe creates movement, which translates into sound.

Smartwall panels are a great alternative to traditional framing and drywall. The panels have foam insulation on the back and drywall on the front and are easy to cut to size. The panels fit together with tongue and groove: no studs and no taping necessary.

MISTAKE #126:
PREMATURELY DRYWALLING THE CEILING

There's no question a drywall ceiling is the most attractive option. It makes the basement more polished, and it gives a few extra inches of headroom.

Drywall is also the most difficult ceiling to install because you're cutting, mudding, waiting for the compound to dry, sanding, priming and painting. I would recommend doing drywall on the ceiling only once you're certain you don't want to do any other renovations in the basement. It isn't an interim solution. If you ever have a water leak or you want to rewire or access the plumbing, you'll be looking at a messy repair job.

The problem is, putting drywall on the ceiling buries a lot of important stuff. Your basement ceiling is likely filled with ductwork, plumbing, electrical, gas, wiring for your cable TV, speaker wires and a host of other stuff. Drywall isn't permanent, but it's definitely not fun to tear part of it down (and then repair it) just to access plumbing or electrical.

If you're gutting or finishing a basement, plan ahead and try to anticipate what you might need in the future. If you're going to renovate the kitchen next year, don't drywall the ceiling in the basement, because you might need access to install new plumbing. If you have plans for future renovations, consider roughing in some of the installations before you finish the basement ceiling. For example, if you know you want to have a natural gas stove or dryer eventually, have that piping installed now. Or you can run electrical conduit—tubing for protecting and routing wires—so you can feed the wires through at a later time. It's all about planning ahead.

MISTAKE #127:
NOT CONSIDERING CEILING OPTIONS OTHER THAN DRYWALL

You've got three other options for finishing a basement ceiling:

Suspended or **drop ceilings** are easy to install. We can start one after breakfast and have it in before lunch. The panels go in fast because they're really light, and there's no mudding, drying or sanding. All you need are a few basic tools: a screw gun, tinsnips, a knife, a straight edge, a measuring tape and a laser level. What I like about these systems is that you've covered up the guts of your house, but everything is accessible. If you need to get in there for electrical, plumbing or ductwork, it's easy to just remove a panel or two. You don't have to rip out drywall for every little upgrade or repair.

A suspended ceiling has four parts. *Wall angles* are L-shaped brackets that you screw to the perimeter walls to help hold up the other pieces. *Main Ts* are the primary rails that support everything else. You install these, suspended by wires, running perpendicular to your ceiling joists and rest them on the wall angles. *Cross Ts* clip into the main Ts to form the grid pattern that becomes the frame for holding up your ceiling tiles. *Ceiling tiles* come in two sizes: 2 × 2 feet or 2 × 4 feet. Before you start hanging your rails, make sure you do the math to figure out the layout. It's the same as planning a tile floor: you want to centre the ceiling tiles and make sure you don't end up with less than half a tile at one edge. If you have (or can rent) a rotary laser level, use it to mark the locations for your wall angles, and even pre-bend your main T wire—it makes a simple job even simpler and faster.

People used to hate drop ceilings because they looked too industrial. But some of the ceiling tile designs available today look great. There are tons to choose from, and you can get tiles in just about every colour, and even some that look like stone. Or you can paint the rails and tiles any colour you want. They also work with any kind of lighting, including pot lights and pendants. You just need to support the lights with support bars designed to work with the system you're using or a piece of wood that fits between the main beams (ceiling tiles and rails alone aren't strong enough to hold up lighting). It's a pretty flexible system.

The drawback for some people is that a drop ceiling costs at least 4 inches of height. In a typical basement, the wall angles will have to be placed at least 4 inches below the joists to avoid the ceiling being too tight to the mechanicals. I've tried to max out the ceiling height by installing a drop ceiling 2 or 3 inches below the joists, but it doesn't always work. To fit them into the grid, you have to angle the panels slightly, so you need enough clearance between the rails and the ceiling above, or wires and ducts will get in the way as you try to slip the panels in place. Leaving yourself less than 4 inches is like trying to do a 10-point turn with a Mack truck.

Another option is a **plastic panel system**, which is similar to a suspended ceiling. You can install it quickly without a lot of tools, it's paintable, and it's easy to remove and replace panels if you need to access plumbing or electrical. You start by putting an E-shaped piece of trim around the perimeter of the room. Then insert your first panel (they come in 8- or 12-foot lengths), attach a rail to that first panel, secure that rail to the ceiling joists, and repeat by alternating panels with rails. I've never tried this system, but since it goes right into the joists, you end up with a few more inches

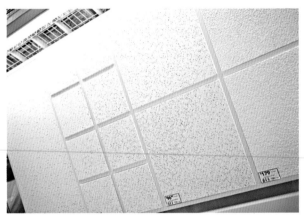

A drop ceiling isn't as attractive as finished drywall, but it sure makes things easier if you need to access electrical or plumbing.

of headroom. I can't say I'm a fan of the way it looks: almost like the ceiling of an RV. But it's an inexpensive alternative to drywall or a suspended ceiling.

There's one more option: forget the drywall and the drop ceiling and just **paint the unfinished ceiling white**. We were in one city basement with a 5-foot, 11-inch ceiling. We bagged all the electrical outlets, vacuumed out all the joists, cleaned everything out and used an HVLP (high-volume low-pressure) sprayer to cover the ceiling, ducts, wiring and pipes in white paint. If you do this, you need to clean the room thoroughly beforehand because if there's dust and dirt in the room, the sprayer creates a dust cloud, and the finish looks like crap. One drawback of leaving the ceiling unfinished is that without drywall or sound-reducing insulation, you'll get less noise reduction between the basement and the main floor. However, for a low ceiling in an older home, it doesn't make sense to lose even more ceiling height. Painting gives it that industrial look while brightening up the room and making the ceiling seem a little higher.

CHAPTER NINE

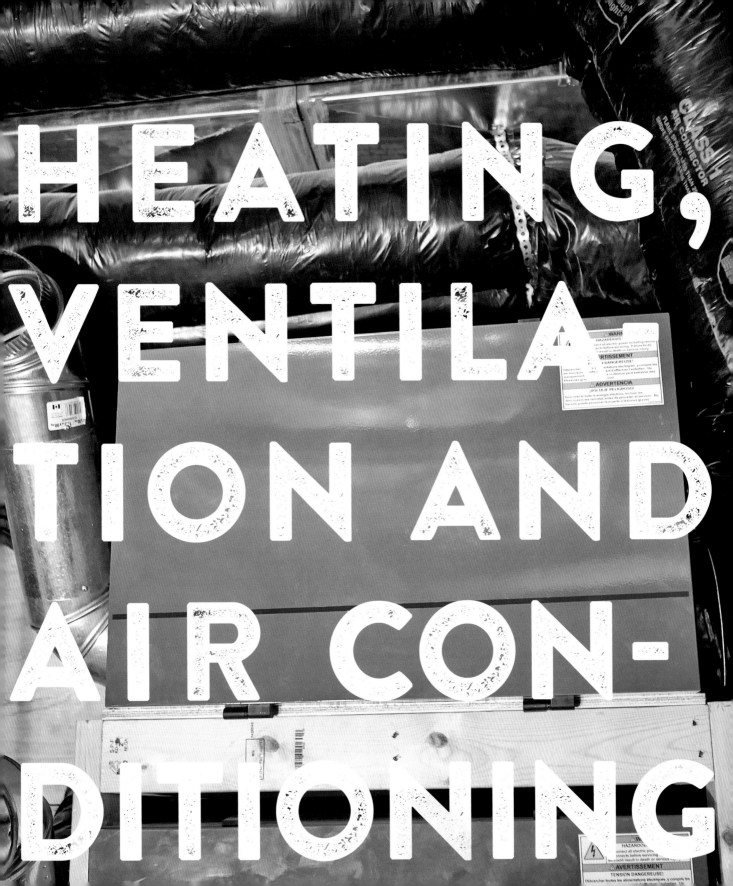

HEATING, VENTILA- TION AND AIR CON- DITIONING

YOU'VE PROBABLY HEARD ME SAY "HVAC" WHEN I'M TALKING ABOUT HEATING, VENTILATION AND AIR CONDITIONING. IT'S BECOME A MUCH MORE POPULAR TOPIC SINCE THE DAYS WHEN MOST HOMES WERE HEATED WITH RADIATORS AND *VENTILATION* MEANT CRACKING OPEN A WINDOW. TIMES HAVE CHANGED A LOT: AIRFLOW HAS BECOME AN IMPORTANT PART OF A HOME, NOT ONLY FOR COMFORT AND WARMTH BUT ALSO FOR HEALTH.

Our standards for energy efficiency and insulation used to be pretty low. In old homes you'd get fresh air coming in and stale air going out through every crack, crevice and poorly sealed door and window. It wasn't great for your heating bill, but at least you had a steady supply of fresh air. Then energy prices started to spike, and we tightened up homes so they'd be more efficient. The more airtight we build homes—more insulation, more air and vapour barriers—the better it is for energy conservation. Here's a perfect example: at my house we don't feel drafts. We've got 12 inches of concrete coated with 6 inches of spray foam insulation and triple-pane windows sealed with two layers of insulating gas. This house is comfortable and cheap to heat and cool.

While a well-sealed, well-insulated home is great for energy efficiency, it can be bad for air quality inside a house. Without proper air circulation, moisture can get sealed inside a home and cause problems with mould. Contaminants with health side effects, such as formaldehyde and volatile organic compounds (VOCs), end up trapped inside the house, where everyone breathes them in. Before, we'd crack open a window for natural ventilation. Now we use machines—a heat recovery ventilator (HRV) or an energy recovery ventilator (ERV)—to help feed fresh air into our homes and exhaust stale air. Just like people, houses need to breathe. I don't expect homeowners to be installing their own gas furnaces and ventilation systems, but it helps to understand how various components of a heating and cooling system work.

HVAC BASICS

DIFFICULTY: 10 OUT OF 10

Since heating, cooling and ventilation systems often involve electrical and plumbing and working with combustible fuels, this is one of those times that I absolutely recommend hiring a professional for just about everything except changing the furnace filter. That said, it helps to understand how various components of an HVAC system work.

• **Distribution** is a fancy term for the way the HVAC system delivers heating and cooling. A furnace and central air conditioning both supply conditioned air through a shared network of ducts. Boilers provide hot water or steam through pipes to baseboard radiators or radiant systems built into the floor. Electric heaters use wires.

• **Ventilation** supplies a house with outside air, exhausts stale indoor air and controls moisture (too much can cause mould and structural damage). **Natural ventilation** happens when air moves in and out of the cracks and crevices of an older home (these air leaks also waste heat and cooling). **Whole-house ventilation** is necessary in an airtight, energy-efficient home through the use of heat recovery or energy recovery ventilators, which are mechanical systems that pull in fresh air and vent stale air (learn more about HRVs and ERVs in Mistake #129, page 219).

COMMON TYPES OF HEATING

• **Furnaces** heat air by burning fuel such as natural gas or oil. About two-thirds of Canadian homes are heated by natural gas–burning furnaces. Furnaces are rated for efficiency by a measurement called AFUE (annual fuel utilization efficiency), or the heat output versus the amount of fossil fuel consumed by the system. A higher AFUE rating indicates a more efficient unit and lower monthly operating costs.

• **Electric heating**, the second most popular option, is generated in baseboard, wall-mounted or in-floor heaters.

• **Hydronic or boiler systems** heat a home using either hot water or steam. The system uses a boiler to heat the water.

COMMON TYPES OF COOLING

The most common systems are **window units**, which cool a room, and **central air conditioning units** (which cool a whole house). Central air units are rated like heating systems: the higher the AFUE, the less it costs to run. These units use electricity or natural gas to cool a refrigerant within the unit and send out cooled air.

TOOLS AND MATERIALS YOU'LL NEED

- furnace filters
- the number of a reliable HVAC pro

Mistake #128:
CHOKING YOUR FURNACE

It's a good idea to understand how your furnace works so you know how to take care of it. If you do, it should perform better, last longer and not poison your family (more on that later). So, here's a primer.

For a furnace to work properly, it needs a continuous supply of air. At the start of the heating cycle in a natural gas furnace, for example, a fan draws air into the unit. This is called combustion air, and it's required so the furnace can burn fuel to generate heat. The air comes from two places: from the basement (at least that's where most furnaces are installed) and from a vent that brings in fresh air from outdoors. Once there's enough combustion air, the gas valve opens and the gas is ignited. It will burn for a couple of minutes before the blower starts pushing air over the heat exchanger.

After a couple of minutes, a fan supplies heated air to the ducts first and then it flows out your heat registers. At the same time as warm air is pushed out, the furnace "inhales" cold air that sinks to the floor in rooms with air returns. That air travels back to the furnace through the ducts, where it is filtered, heated and sent back out again. An HVAC system runs most efficiently when cold air in equals warm air out—the system should be balanced. The furnace turns off once it warms up the house to whatever temperature is set on the thermostat.

When your furnace is working the way it should, you won't notice the other part of the heating process: venting exhaust. Burning fossil fuels produces waste gases—including poisonous carbon monoxide—that must be expelled outdoors, vented through either the roof or the side of the house.

If your furnace doesn't have a good supply of combustion air, it can run into problems. For starters,

Here's how air moves through your furnace in a heating cycle: air comes in the air return (1), moves through the air filter (2), then gets heated up in the furnace's heat exchanger (3) and pushed up through the trunk (4) above the furnace to be split into smaller ducts running to individual rooms.

the furnace will have to work harder and won't operate as efficiently. Not only that, but insufficient air can lead to incomplete combustion, which creates carbon monoxide (see Mistake #130, page 221). You might also run into a problem called downdrafting or backdrafting: the exhaust gases spilling into the house instead of outside. Backdrafting happens when your house is depressurized, meaning more air is moving out of the house (through exhaust fans, vented heating appliances and fireplaces) than into it. You always have to make sure that the air moving out of the house is replaced with air coming in.

People who live in airtight homes need an air exchanger to keep airflow in check. Some of these homes are so well sealed, there may not be enough combustion air to keep the furnace running at peak efficiency. So that's where an HRV or an ERV (see Mistake #129, next) takes over and feeds the furnace the air it needs.

Another way you might be sabotaging your furnace is by stuffing every inch of your basement with piles of stuff. I've been into lots of homes where the furnace room doubles as a junk locker: old paint cans, stinky hockey equipment, old camping gear, skis, you name it, all shoved in the corner all around the furnace. If you restrict airflow around the furnace, you'll cut off its combustion air supply. How can your heating system do its job when your furnace can hardly breathe? If you're guilty of this one, it's time to find another place to store all your junk.

The other mistake people make is permanently blocking vents. I've seen cold air returns plugged with a sweatshirt or a towel, or blocked by furniture. Some people presumably try to block the sound of the furnace turning on or just don't know enough to keep the air returns clear. I've also seen people build their furnace into a tiny utility room with a solid door that doesn't allow for adequate airflow. Bad ideas: again, your furnace needs air to operate, so make sure you give it a steady supply.

It's a good idea to periodically check the furnace exhaust vent to make sure it's kept clear of snow and leaves. If burnt gases can't exhaust outside, where do you think they'll end up? Inside your house. Not a good idea to fill your house with carbon monoxide. There are sensors on modern furnaces to ensure the exhaust fan is drawing correctly, but you're better safe than sorry.

MISTAKE #129:
NOT USING AN HRV OR ERV

As I said earlier, if you live in an airtight home, you need fresh air coming in and stale indoor air being exhausted out. One way to do this is with a heat recovery ventilator (HRV), which does exactly that. An HRV is an air exchanger—basically a pump—that can do another neat trick. The HRV reclaims most of the heat from the stale air with a heat exchanger and uses that energy to warm the cold air it pulls in from outdoors. Its use of waste heat to preheat fresh air will help you save on heating costs. HRVs are a good choice for people who live in cold climates, where the heat is on for a good part of the year.

I've heard of newly built homes that come with an HRV, with installation (about $1,000 and up) charged to the homeowner. Those in older homes can have an HRV retrofitted (expect to pay about $2,000 to $3,500 for an efficient unit certified by Energy Star). I don't consider this a do-it-yourself project. The intake and exhaust points outside the home have to be located a certain distance away from each other and from other gas-vented appliances vented out the same side of the house. Some of the HRV ducts must be connected to the furnace's ductwork and to plumbing so as to drain condensed water. A reputable HVAC specialist will make the installation safe, smart and up to building code.

If you're running an HRV in the winter, pay attention to relative humidity. These units typically reduce the humidity level inside your home, especially during really cold spells. Low relative humidity can dry out your skin, make your lips feel cracked and give you that scratchy feeling in your throat. It's not life-threatening, but it's uncomfortable. It can also affect the wood in a home: hardwood can develop gaps between boards that will disappear again in the spring.

You can reduce the effects of low humidity by running your HRV on a lower speed or intermittently (a good feature to look into when you're shopping for one). Or you can balance things out by using a humidifier. But this is one of those cases where it's possible

COMMON TYPES OF HEAT RECOVERY VENTILATORS (HRV)

Plate heat exchanger

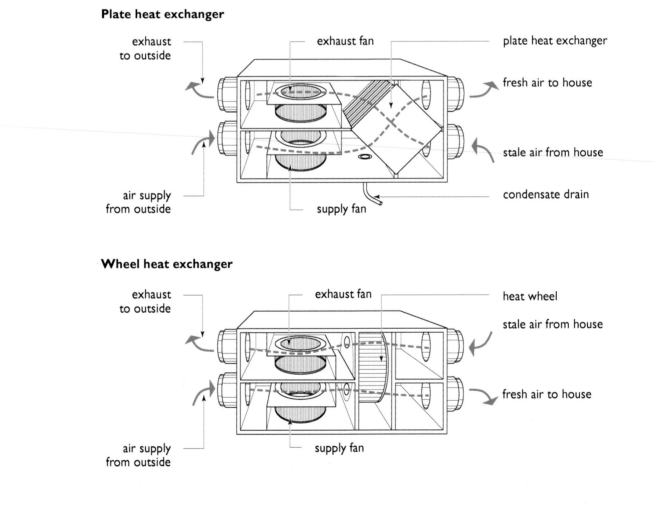

Wheel heat exchanger

to get too much of a good thing: too much humidity can promote mould (see Mistake #146, page 229).

An energy recovery ventilator (ERV) is very similar to an HRV. During the winter, an ERV gets heat from exhaust air and uses it to warm up cold, fresh air. But an ERV also recovers some of the moisture in the warm exhaust air and transfers it to the cold air supply coming into the house, which means the house will feel less dehumidified than it would with an HRV. This moisture recovery can help keep you and your floors from drying out during the heating season. When summer arrives and the air conditioning is running, the ERV does the same thing in reverse: pre-cools hot, humid air coming in from outdoors. It also captures moisture and returns it to the outside instead of making your home feel humid. These devices work in all climates. ERVs were once thought to be most effective in hot regions where the air conditioning is humming for most of the year, but recent field studies in Canada have found them to be more effective and efficient than HRVs, even in cold climates.

MISTAKE #130:
NOT HAVING A CARBON MONOXIDE (CO) DETECTOR

If you've got any appliances in your house that burn gas (that includes a fireplace, furnace, hot water heater, stove or dryer), you need a carbon monoxide detector. If any of those units malfunction and start leaking exhaust—that's CO—you and your family could be in real danger. CO is colourless and odourless—it's not like natural gas or propane because you won't smell the leak. You'll just fall asleep and may not wake up. It's serious stuff.

Let's talk about your furnace for a minute. One of the fans inside your heating system is responsible for

A carbon monoxide detector is a necessity if you use natural gas. They're about $50: a small price to protect your family.

blowing out all the exhaust, which is where the CO comes from. If that fan breaks down, there's another pressure switch that says, "Hey, we no longer have negative pressure in this hose, we're not sucking exhaust," which triggers the furnace to shut down. If that fan and pressure switch fail, you could theoretically get CO leaking. So it's a good idea to put a CO detector in the basement near the furnace, and on each level of the house, plus another near an attached garage. Choose models with UL certification, which means the alarm meets Underwriters Laboratories standards. CO alarms also lose their sensitivity over time (they typically last five to seven years), so buy units with a recent manufacturing date.

Just one warning for all of you with little kids: I wouldn't recommend testing the monitor if your CO detector is tied in to a central alarm system—at least not without warning everyone to plug their ears. I did that once without realizing it would set off every alarm in the house, and it scared the crap out of my son, Quintyn. I spent the next few hours trying to convince him the house wasn't on fire! (But the good news is that our CO detector worked fine.)

Mistake #131:
MAKING YOUR FURNACE
WORK OVERTIME

As I mentioned, your furnace takes some combustible air from the basement itself to heat your home. Let's say your basement is nice and warm: in that case, your furnace doesn't have to heat the air as much to spread warmth around to the rest of the house. On the other hand, if your basement is freezing, your heating system has to work a lot harder to warm up the cold air before sending it up two storeys to heat your bedroom to 20 degrees Celsius.

You can make your heating system burn more efficiently by insulating your basement. Put a subfloor over the concrete pad to warm it up, for example, and spray-foam the walls, which provides insulation as well as an air and vapour barrier (read more on spray-foam insulation in Mistake #11, page 34).

Mistake #132:
NOT CHANGING THE
FURNACE FILTER

Make sure you change the furnace filter at least four times a year, or according to the directions. A filter clogged with dust cuts down airflow into the heating system and the cold air returns (the grille-covered ducts that take in air and direct it back to the furnace). A clean filter will make your HVAC system run more efficiently.

First, buy a replacement filter that fits your unit (the dimensions are often printed on the filter's cardboard frame). Filters are inserted where the ductwork meets the furnace. Depending on the model, this might be directly adjacent to the furnace, near the bottom. It might be just visible inside a metal box it slides into, or it may be hidden behind a hinged door. Remove the old filter and place it in the trash. Slide the new filter in with the arrows pointing toward the furnace, which is the same direction as air flows through the furnace.

Replacing the furnace filter regularly is one of the easiest ways to improve the air quality in your home and keep your furnace running efficiently. But don't skimp by buying a cheap furnace filter. Look for one that that's thick enough to remove particles in the air—and hide Adam's face.

Mistake #133:
SLIDING A HEPA FILTER INTO AN OLD FURNACE

When you're buying a furnace filter, you need to balance two things: airflow versus the size of particles the filter will trap and keep out of your furnace. You want a filter that will capture the smallest particles but allow air to flow freely through it.

You've probably seen furnace filters marketed to people who suffer from allergies and asthma. They're called HEPA (high-efficiency particulate air) filters, and they promise to remove up to 99.999% of large and small particles floating around in the air. The idea is these filters will reduce allergens better than standard filters will, creating healthier indoor air for people who are susceptible to illness.

Some HVAC systems are designed to take HEPA filters, but others may not have a strong enough motor or fan to accommodate them. HEPA filters are thicker and may provide more flow resistance than the furnace and ductwork can handle. Check your manual to see if your unit can take a high-efficiency filter. You might need an HVAC specialist to modify the ductwork or install a more powerful fan to overcome the drop in pressure.

Mistake #134:
NOT UPGRADING TO A HIGH-EFFICIENCY FURNACE

I bet there are some people out there still using a furnace from the '60s. They're probably spending $500 a month to heat their home, but they think it's a good furnace because it's still working after all these years. I'm here to tell you it's not a good thing. That old clunker is sucking up a ton of energy, and you're paying for it. You'd be better off spending a few thousand bucks on a new furnace. Sure, it's a chunk of money now, but you'll get it back quickly in reduced energy bills, and you'll keep saving for the next 15 or 20 years.

We just put in a two-stage furnace that runs at a low rumble. Instead of waiting until the house gets cold, it runs gently most of the time, putting out steady heat. If I open all the windows, it'll run like hell to catch up fast, but overall, it simply maintains an even heat.

The question most people ask when they're thinking about upgrading is, Should I spend the extra money to get a high-efficiency furnace, or should I be content with mid-efficiency? You're making a trade-off between spending more once or spending more on every gas bill for the life of the furnace. It's pay now or pay later. How does this sound: if you're in a two-storey home in Toronto, upgrading to a high-efficiency furnace from a 20-year-old beast can save your family about $800 in gas and electricity every year.

I look at this the same way I look at a vehicle's fuel consumption. Do you buy the cheaper gasoline version of the pickup truck and then burn an extra couple thousand bucks a year in fuel, or do you buy the diesel that burns half as much but costs an extra $10,000? Over the life of the vehicle, the one that burns less fuel is likely to be cheaper.

Not only that, from an environmental standpoint, you're burning less fossil fuels. We all need to use less, and your furnace is a good place to start. I think it always pays to invest in the higher efficiency. The variable cost is a line on a spreadsheet as far as fuel and energy costs go for us. And they are saying that in the next 10 to 15 years that energy costs could double or triple.

We're always getting flyers in the mail from heating companies offering furnace deals. Before you buy, it pays to know what to look for in a high-efficiency heating system. Make sure you get one that's sized for your house. If it's too big for your square footage, it will keep blasting on and off, which wastes energy. It's like city driving. You want your furnace to run longer, which will get you better mileage, so to speak.

Furnaces are rated for efficiency. The term is AFUE, which stands for annual fuel utilization efficiency. This is the amount of fuel that's actually converted to heat—a certain amount gets wasted as exhaust. Furnaces manufactured since 2010 have to be minimum 90% AFUE. Higher AFUE means lower bills, so look for a furnace that's at least 95% or 96% AFUE.

Next, consider the burner. A one-stage burner is the least efficient because it can only run at full blast whenever it turns on. With a two-stage burner, the furnace can run at full capacity to warm up the house initially then downshift to working at 40% or 50% capacity—which requires less power—to keep it that way. A fully modulating burner can work anywhere between 30% and 100% capacity. Furnaces with a dual or fully modulating burner are the way to go: you can save 5% to 8% over a single-burner unit.

Finally, look at the motor. Furnace motors use a lot of electricity to keep the fan moving for airflow. There's a bit of lingo to learn here, but it's pretty straightforward. An AC (alternating current) motor is the least efficient: that would be like running an 800-watt light bulb every time the furnace powers up. A DC (direct current) motor or ECM (electronically commutated motor) is the better choice. It would be like running a 200-watt bulb.

MISTAKE #135:
NOT WEATHERPROOFING TO PREVENT AIR LEAKS AROUND YOUR HOME

If you don't like paying for heating that's going straight outside, you need to manage the airflow in your house.

The easiest way to stay warm is to control air loss. One simple thing you can do for less than $30 is to buy and use caulking. Caulk between your trim and the wall and around the casings on windows and doors. If you move your hand along the baseboard or the trim on an exterior wall, I bet you'll feel cold air coming in. Seal up those cracks and gaps, and your house will feel more comfortable, and you'll save on heating bills.

The next job is weatherstripping around exterior doors. I remember when I was a kid, our doors used to just glide closed without any effort. I didn't know it then, but a door that closes too easily is unlikely to be properly sealed around the edges. In most cases you should have to push firmly on the door to compress the weatherstripping around it so it maintains a tight seal. Take a look around the edges of the door when it's closed in the frame. If you can see light filtering in, it's not sealed. That means you're letting hot air (and money) go out the door.

Weatherstripping comes in a variety of styles and materials. The best choices are made of a material with compression memory so the stripping springs up when the door is opened and compresses to let the door close tightly. Look for silicone, EPDM rubber, neoprene, vinyl, wool and spring metal. Measure carefully to cover the full length of the door on both sides and along the top. Install a door sweep at the bottom.

After the weatherstripping, seal the windows. This is especially good with single-pane windows that leak a lot, but it will help make any home more comfortable in the winter even if you have double-pane windows. You can buy a kit at any hardware store and will have the option of plastic film or double-sided tape. Cut the film to fit, tape it up, then use a hair dryer to shrink the film over the window so it's taut. You can still see out the window, though, of course, you won't be able to open it, but that's not usually an issue in the winter. Little changes like this make a big difference—the plastic does a great job at stopping airflow through the windows and retaining heat. Glass is a terrible insulator, especially in old windows that aren't insulated or glazed. Many people don't like the way the plastic looks, but this really does make a big difference in how comfortable your house will feel in the winter.

MISTAKE #136:
WORKING OR LIVING WITHOUT AN AIR FILTER

When you're doing renovations or repairs in the basement, it's a smart idea to turn off the furnace. If you're cutting wood or drywall, or if you're sanding, your furnace filter is very quickly going to get jammed with all that stuff floating around in the air, and anything that doesn't get trapped is going to get distributed through the house. If you suspect your vents aren't blowing as much heat as they normally do, there's a good chance your filter is clogged with junk, so make sure you take a look at the filter and change it if necessary (learn how in Mistake #132, page 222). Otherwise, you'll be depositing dust all over the house as soon as you turn the furnace back on.

I also recommend running an air filter system for the whole house. Health Canada recommends keeping exposure to fine particulate—small particles in the air from smoking, cooking, cleaning, and so on—"as low as possible." When the guys were drywalling during one job in our home, we measured particulate matter at 100,000 parts per million—it was so dirty, it was off the scale. Within an hour of installing a hospital-grade air filter system on the furnace, we were down below 500 ppm. We had the same kind of system at our pre-

vious house, too. If you slammed a pillow, you wouldn't see that cloud of dust exploding in the sunlight in front of the window. The kids didn't get colds as often, and neither did I. Air filtration is key to having a healthy indoor environment.

MISTAKE #137:
PLAYING HVAC REPAIRMAN

When a furnace stops working, any number of things may be responsible. Most of the time, it's the brains of the system—the electronics. But there's also the chance you've got a problem with mechanical parts: fans, switches, heat exchangers. The furnace could be overheating if a fan isn't turning on properly.

If you're having issues with your furnace, bring in an HVAC specialist. You're dealing with combustible gas and electricity—this isn't like changing a light bulb. You never really want to do anything with HVAC besides change a filter or open and close your vents.

One of the biggest mistakes people make with their furnaces is opening the cover and trying to poke around. Don't. It's like trying to pop open your computer and mess around with the parts. When your hard drive is jammed, do you open up the panel and get in there with a pin to try to get it working? Your furnace is a complex and potentially dangerous unit, so leave the repairs to someone who's trained and experienced—it's just not worth the risk.

MISTAKE #138:
OVERHEATING ONE ROOM WHILE OTHER ROOMS FREEZE

If you live in a two-storey house, you might notice the upper levels feel cool in the winter and stuffy in the summer. Meanwhile, the basement is toasty in winter and cool in summer, but no one spends much time

A programmable thermostat allows you to dial back on the heating and air conditioning when everyone is sleeping or no one is home.

down there. It doesn't matter how old your furnace is: I've seen this happen in homes with both new systems and old ones.

Feel the register nearest the furnace room—I bet you it gets pretty solid airflow. Then feel the airflow in your bedroom—it probably won't be as strong. The air has to travel a long way to go from the basement through the floors and walls to the top floor. Every joint in the ductwork should have been taped to prevent air leaks when the system was installed, but that might not have happened—or the adhesive may have worn away over the years. (By the way, this was the *original* use for duct tape!)

If air is leaking out of those ducts into the joists and wall cavities all the way up, you'll have less air coming out of the heat register by the time it travels to those upstairs bedrooms. Imagine one of those long cardboard tubes of Christmas wrapping paper. If you punch holes in the tube and blow through it, the puff of air at the other end won't be as strong as if the tube had no holes along the way.

I don't know many people who are going to rip apart their walls and floors to tape up those ducts to reduce air leakage, but you can do one thing to try to regulate airflow: close the dampers on the heat

vents in the basement, which should force more air up through the vents on the main and upper floors. You might notice it gets a little cooler in the basement, but if you spend more time in your bedroom, that should be a good compromise.

MISTAKE #139:
INSTALLING A THERMOSTAT NEAR A HOT SPOT

We used to have a problem with uneven heating at the cottage. The hallways and main areas of the cottage have in-floor heating while the bedrooms are heated by the furnace. The bedrooms are exposed underneath: they're built on piers so there's no basement under them. We insulated the floor, but they were still freezing. The problem is the thermostat for the furnace was in the hall-way. With the in-floor heating on, the hallway would warm up, and the thermostat would believe the whole house was cozy—it would never signal the furnace to turn on.

The moral of the story is, Don't install a thermo-stat in the warmest room of your house. Avoid placing it in a wall that gets direct sunlight or in a room with a fireplace. Those things can inflate the temperature in that room while the rest of the house will be starved for heat. The opposite is also true: don't put your thermostat on an exterior wall, where the temperature can fluctuate.

Here's another tip: most HVAC systems can be set to run on different settings—heat, cool or fan (check your programmable thermostat to see the options). Running the fan without heating or cooling helps maintain a steady temperature throughout the house. When it's hot out, the fan will pull cool air from the basement and spread it to the rest of the house. When it's cold, the fan pulls warm air to the upper levels. The fan helps average everything out.

MISTAKE #140:
MOVING THE THERMOSTAT TEMPERATURE UP AND DOWN

Gotta love my dad. When it's cold, he'll set the thermostat to 30 degrees Celsius. Then when he feels too hot, he puts it back down. I know this is tempting, but remember, a thermostat isn't a throttle. It's better to just set it to a comfortable temperature and leave it there. That's why it helps to have a programmable thermostat.

With the most basic thermostats, you have to physically change the setting if you want to raise or lower the temperature when you're leaving the house or going to bed. The advantage of a programmable thermostat is you can set it to automatically lower the heat a few degrees at night after everyone's warm in bed and then raise it again before you wake up in the morning. You can also adjust for when everyone's at school and work, so you're not heating the house while no one's home. You can save about 20% on your annual heating and cooling bill if you do this. The latest thermostats can even be controlled remotely— if you forget to turn down the heat before you leave on vacation, you can lower it using your phone. Or you can pump up the heat at the cottage a few hours before you arrive so you don't have to sleep in frosty beds.

You can change a thermostat yourself, but take a picture of the wiring before you rip the old one out. The simplest systems have just two wires: one for heating, one for cooling. If you have an HRV you might end up with four to six wires. Read the instructions on the new thermostat, and it should be straightforward to determine which wire goes where. And don't worry, these are low-voltage wires, so you're not going to be electrocuted.

MISTAKE #141:
BUYING THE WRONG SIZE FURNACE

When it comes to HVAC, people sometimes go overboard and get a gigantic furnace or air conditioner. Or they get one that's too small to properly heat or cool the house.

There's one way to know you're getting a unit that's the right size for your house: call in an experienced HVAC specialist. These pros are trained in creating a healthy and comfortable indoor environment when it comes to heating, cooling, ventilation and humidity. The good ones take the time to do a heat-loss calculation. That involves measuring the proportion of your house that's covered with windows, how much air is leaking out through cracks and gaps, how much insulation you've got and so on. These calculations, plus the square footage of the house, help them figure out how much airflow you need. There's real science behind heating and cooling. You don't just look at an air conditioner and say, "That one's cute, I'll take it." You also shouldn't buy an oversized unit in anticipation of a renovation that may happen "someday." Until you actually expand a house, that furnace will use more energy than it needs to—which you'll pay for—every day it runs.

You definitely want to call in an HVAC pro when you're renovating. If you're building an addition off the back or adding another level, you need to make sure your heating and cooling system can handle the extra square footage. Again, the expert will run the numbers and can also make recommendations on running and insulating ducts and locating heat registers to keep the new space comfortable.

MISTAKE #142:
THINKING IT'S EASY TO MOVE A FURNACE

In a lot of new homes, you go down the stairs and walk straight into the furnace. It's right there in the middle of the room, which makes no sense to anyone but the crew who had to carry it down the stairs. If you're in this predicament, you have options—for the right money, anything can be disassembled—but I'm warning you, none of them are neat and tidy.

It's possible to move a furnace to a more convenient spot—we've done it. But you'll need to consult an HVAC specialist. The location of a furnace is important: often its position is determined based on well-thought-out calculations that take into account the size of the ducts, the volume of air in the ducts and how air travels around the house. So you may not be able to move that unit to the opposite side of the house without throwing off all those calculations.

If you move your furnace, you might need to follow that by moving or adding ducts. This, too, can be done, but think about it: ducts are tucked behind walls and between joists. To access them, you'll have to rip out walls and ceilings. If you're taking an old house on a boiler system and converting it to forced air, you're going to be making holes and building bulkheads to hide ducts. Again, just about anything *can* be done. The question is, Is it worth the money and the aggravation?

MISTAKE #143:
SKIPPING ANNUAL MAINTENANCE

You know those HVAC and utility companies that call asking if you want your furnace or central air conditioning inspected? They're not just trying to annoy you during dinner: an annual maintenance check is essential for both units. A furnace isn't a barrel with a fire

in it—it's a complex combustion system with sophisticated electronics inside. At an annual maintenance checkup, the technician will clean out the heating system and run diagnostics to spot small problems before they become big, expensive ones. Regular cleaning and maintenance should help keep your furnace and cooling systems running at maximum efficiency day to day and over the long haul.

It pays to plan ahead when doing preventive maintenance. I brought my lawn mower in to have it cleaned and sharpened one spring. The guy looked at me like I was crazy. "Why didn't you bring it in in the fall?" I told him I didn't think about it then. He replied, "Well, if you had, you'd be cutting the lawn by now." Turns out most people wait until the last minute!

Along these lines, it makes the most sense to schedule a furnace checkup in the fall, before you start to rely on the furnace. Even if the air conditioning conks out in the summer, you'll sweat a bit, but it's not a big deal if you have to wait a day or two for the repairman to arrive. It's a whole other story if the furnace dies in February, and you've got no heat for a few days. Consider this book a reminder to change your furnace filter immediately! (Some need to be changed once a season.)

If you've got a window air conditioner, you can do some of your own maintenance. Inspect the air filter once a month and change it whenever it looks dirty. Repair any cracked window seals and check the refrigerant gauge if there is one. A little routine maintenance can save on costly repairs.

MISTAKE #144:
NOT USING CEILING FANS WITH AIR CONDITIONING

Most people think that if they have air conditioning, they don't need ceiling fans, but the truth is these two systems work best as a team. A ceiling fan (or any fan, really) moves air around a room. If you're in a room where the air is moving, you'll feel cooler. This means you can raise the temperature setting of the air conditioner a few degrees and still feel just as comfortable. If your AC isn't running as high or as often, you'll create less wear and tear on the unit.

Using a fan has the potential to save on cooling costs. Think about it: a typical fan might use 15 to 100 watts depending on the setting. An in-window air conditioner might use about 1,000 watts; a central air system, up to 5,000 or more. To save energy, try raising the AC temperature by 2 degrees or so. If you don't adjust the thermostat, you're paying to have the fan and the AC at full blast.

What some people don't realize is that you have to be in the room while a ceiling fan is running to feel its cooling benefit. Fans don't lower the temperature in a room, they just create a sort of wind-chill effect that makes it feel cooler. If no one is in the room, shut the fan off. When you come home feeling overheated, crank up the fan instead of the air conditioning. You'll feel cooler much faster.

To maximize energy savings, look for a high-efficiency ceiling fan certified by Energy Star. Run it on the down flow setting during hot months to push air toward whoever is in the room. Some models can be reversed during winter to circulate warm air around a room more effectively. This can save on heating if you set your thermostat a degree or two lower. Keep a ceiling fan on low in winter so it doesn't create a cooling effect.

MISTAKE #145:
POSITIONING THE AC IN THE WRONG SPOT

Where you place your central air conditioning unit can affect its efficiency. For example, if it's in an exposed area on the west side of the house, where it will be blasted by the afternoon sun, the machine will have to work overtime. A better idea is to find a shady spot because the cooler it stays, the less power it needs to cool your home. Just remember not to crowd it with shrubs, branches and other obstructions. The unit may not look pretty, but to run efficiently, it needs air to circulate freely.

MISTAKE #146:
NOT CONTROLLING HUMIDITY IN YOUR HOME

The ideal relative humidity in most homes is about 30% to 50% year round. In the summertime, you get lots of moisture in the air, and that's when you might switch on a dehumidifier. In the winter, with the heating system blasting, it can get dry enough that you want some of that humidity back. When I've gone to Alberta in the winter, it's so dry that I start losing my voice in about 15 minutes if I don't keep hydrated!

You can watch for clues to tell you how you're doing at managing humidity. If your humidity is too high, you might notice your windows sweating in the winter or moisture running down the walls and along the ceilings. When humidity is high enough to produce this kind of dripping, you could end up noticing a musty smell. If the moisture hangs around long enough, you might end up with mould. You might not see it—it often hides behind walls, above ceilings and under floors—but it can cause ongoing problems ranging from eye, nose and throat irritation to coughing, asthma symptoms and allergic reactions.

If you don't have enough humidity indoors, you'll feel that, too. Your skin, lips and throat will feel dry, and you could notice more static electricity on your clothes or sparks when you're walking around on a carpet.

Over the long term, you might end up with damage to wood, which can dry out.

To know for sure whether you've got a problem, get a hygrometer, a sensor that measures the humidity in your house. Humidity can fluctuate from one room to another, so put the sensor in the room you're most concerned about or where your family hangs out the most. Once you know whether it's too high or low or just right, you can take action.

If the relative humidity is too high in your house, you can start by changing habits. Install bathroom fans if you don't have them already, and let them run for a good 20 to 30 minutes after showers and baths. Remember to turn on the vent hood over your stove while you cook to remove excess humidity from steam. You can also buy a stand-alone dehumidifier to strip out some of that moisture.

If you have a very dry house, you can benefit from sealing your home against air leaks. Use weatherstripping and caulking around windows, doors and spots where exterior walls are penetrated by openings for plumbing, ducts and ventilation. You can also use a stand-alone humidifier or install one on your furnace. Use it as directed, and maintain it properly by cleaning out the filter. If you don't, you could find yourself adding too much moisture and then dealing with mould.

Most homes don't need a humidifier because we create moisture through everyday activities such as showering, cooking, talking, perspiring, breathing, doing laundry and washing dishes. Even plants add humidity to the air. But every house is different. One that's airtight will have different needs than an old one with lots of small cracks and gaps. A well-sealed house with a heat recovery ventilator is actually losing moisture when that essential device is running, because HRVs act as dehumidifiers.

When you take possession of a new home, it's a good idea to see how the house responds to your routines. It's like a new instrument—you first have to figure out how to make it work. A previous house may have needed a humidifier based on air leakage, the condition of the windows and the number of people who lived and showered there every day. As your kids grow and start taking more showers or if they go off to college or if someone starts working out in the basement every morning, you might notice your humidity levels—and your humidification needs—change.

MISTAKE #147:
NOT CLEANING AIR DUCTS AT ALL— OR CLEANING THEM TOO OFTEN

We've all had a million calls from companies trying to sell us duct cleaning. They'll try to sell you on horror stories about the health hazards of dirty ducts. Don't panic quite yet. There are good times to have your ducts cleaned, but it's not as often as those calls would have you believe, and you need to be sure you're hiring a qualified company.

All components of the HVAC system—every vent and duct and right down to the drip trays—need to be properly cleaned to be effective. Duct-cleaning companies typically use a powerful truck-mounted HEPA-filter vacuum, remove the grate, connect to the main ductwork and suck everything out. Eventually, they work their way around to every heat register, return air vent and access ports in the main ductwork. Sometimes they need to cut holes in the ducts to insert vacuum hoses and mechanical brushes, but after the work is done, they patch the holes with plugs. Some companies send a camera in afterward to check the system and make sure they caught everything.

I think it's a great idea to clean your ducts once you finish building or renovating a house. It's a chance to remove all the construction dust, dirt and allergens from the guts of your heating system before you turn it on and breath it all in. You don't want to send that stuff blowing all over your furniture and into your lungs.

I've heard mixed opinions about the necessity of frequent duct cleaning. It makes sense if you have an issue with mould, a water leak in your ducts or a dusty renovation. Same thing if you have a lot of people living in the house, if it's an older home, if you smoke or if you have a lot of pets. But under normal circumstances, you probably don't need to worry about cleaning them more than once every 5 to 10 years. It's a better idea to have a regular inspection, which is something reputable companies will do.

MISTAKE #148:
CREATING POOR INDOOR AIR QUALITY WITHOUT KNOWING IT

Most people don't realize it, but the air inside our homes can be up to 10 times dirtier than the air outside. Sounds crazy, right? The truth is, we're bringing this stuff into our homes all the time. Household products and renovation materials—soaps, cleaners, paint, wallpaper, glues, plastic garbage pails, resins, mattresses, cabinets and carpet—can continue to emit fumes after you bring them home from the store. These gases are called volatile organic compounds (VOCs), and they're released into the air you breathe inside your home. You know that paint smell? That's what I'm talking about.

If you're not keen on adding those toxins to the air you breathe, and you don't have an air exchanger and hospital-grade air filtration system on your home, you've got choices. You can buy low- or no-VOC products. Pretty much every paint brand has healthier options, and building supply and specialty stores will now sell you things like grout, caulking and adhesives made without VOCs. You can order a new couch without the extra stain guarding, which adds more chemicals to the air. You can use area rugs instead of carpet. And you can make sure your home has a balanced supply of fresh air coming in and stale air being pumped out. It's important that your home be comfortable, but it's even more important that it's a healthy environment for you and your family.

CHAPTER TEN

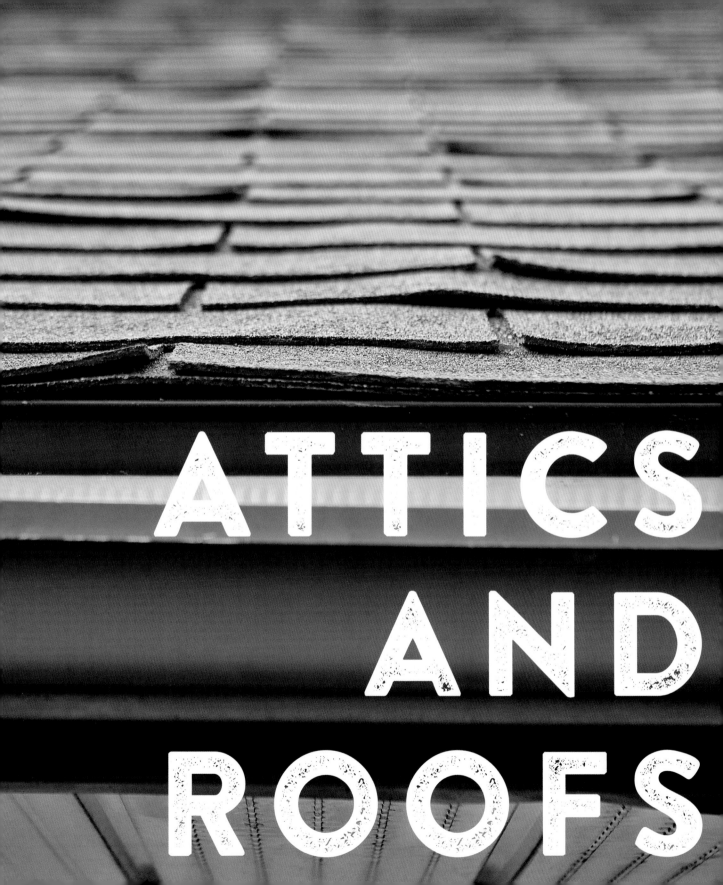

ATTICS
AND
ROOFS

IF YOU WANT TO TALK ABOUT A NEGLECTED PART OF THE HOUSE, STEP OUT TO THE CURB AND LOOK UP AT YOUR ROOF. I DON'T KNOW MANY PEOPLE WHO CRUISE BY A HOUSE AND SAY, "HEY, HONEY, LOOK AT THAT BEAUTIFUL ROOF." WE DON'T TAKE MUCH PRIDE IN A WELL-MAINTAINED ROOF—WE JUST TAKE FOR GRANTED THAT IT'S DOING ITS JOB UNTIL THERE'S A PROBLEM.

I think people need to give the roof a little more respect. Together with the foundation, it's the most important part of a house. If your roof is leaking, you're pooched—you're no longer in a shelter; you're in a dripping cave. The roof is largely out of sight and out of mind so doesn't get the maintenance it deserves. You'll notice a scratch on the hardwood, but it's harder to notice a hole in the roof because you're not up there every day.

Don't get me wrong: I'm not suggesting we all start climbing up extension ladders. I wouldn't recommend the average DIYer jump up on the roof and start poking around. Ladders can be pretty hazardous—even for roofers who climb them every day. What's going to happen if you walk on a loose shingle and it slides out? I once scrambled across cedar shakes covered in wet moss. Let me tell you, I almost went off the roof—that was pretty scary, even with a harness on. The roof is one of those areas where I recommend you learn about what might go wrong, prevent as much as you can and then call an experienced roofer when you need to.

ATTIC AND ROOF BASICS

DIFFICULTY: 7.5 OUT OF 10

Although I don't recommend the average homeowner make roofing and attic improvements, it helps to know the lingo so you can have an informed conversation when you're talking to potential contractors. Here's my blueprint for a healthy attic and roof. I go into much more detail about these concepts in this chapter, but here's a cheat sheet:

- **Ventilate** the attic. You need a series of vents in key spots, ideally along the top (high on the roof, or ridge) and bottom (in the soffits) of the roof, to allow fresh air to flow in and warm air to flow out. Like every other part of your home, you want to keep your attic dry; ventilation helps with that.

- **Insulate** the attic to R50 as a general rule. It's one of the easiest insulation retrofits you can do because you don't have to tear down walls, and insulating will lower your heating and cooling bills. I'm a big fan of closed-cell spray foam because it offers an air barrier and insulation in one product, but you could also use batt insulation or loose-fill.

- **Seal** the attic off from the conditioned living space of your home. Without some sort of barrier (whether spray foam or 6-mil polyethylene sheeting if you're using other insulation), you will get moisture and heat in the attic. Moisture can lead to mould.

- **Inspect** your roof for ice buildup in winter, which usually means there's a problem with heat escaping into the attic—another good reason to seal the attic off from the house. If you see ice buildup, it's time to make some improvements in the attic.

- **Maintain** your eavestroughs and downspouts. Clear them of leaves and debris in spring and fall so they can drain water away from the house instead of dumping it onto your foundation, where it could create moisture problems in the basement.

TOOLS AND MATERIALS YOU'LL NEED

- insulation
- 6-mil polyethylene for vapour barrier
- sheathing tape (Tuck Tape is a popular brand)
- mask and gloves
- long sleeves and long pants for working with fibreglass
- roofing vents (ridge vents, soffit vents, gable vents)
- extension ladder
- ice and water barrier for the roof
- roofing underlayment
- eavestroughs and downspouts

Mistake #149:
LETTING HEAT GET INTO YOUR ATTIC

If you've got snow melting on your roof, thick icicles along the roofline, steam rising off the roof or curling shingles, your attic may be overheating. Some people think of the attic as part of the house, but you actually need to think of it more as a covered outdoor space. An unfinished attic needs to stay cold in winter. If you were to check the temperature of the attic in January, you'd want to see it be within a couple degrees of the outside temperature, not within a couple degrees of the conditioned living space.

Keeping the attic cool and well ventilated helps protect your roof. Most of us like to forget our attics exist, but you should have a look inside every so often. If you take a look in the winter and see frost along the inside of the attic, that could mean warm air from the house is moving around up there, meeting the cold air from the exterior and causing condensation, which then freezes. If that condensation sticks

Uneven melting of snow on your roof may indicate that too much warm air has made its way into your attic.

around for the long term, it could lead to mould and rotted wood.

Heat in the attic can also be dangerous for shingles. Too much warm air from your house escaping into the attic can cause snow to melt and run down the roof toward the eavestrough. Then it can refreeze when it hits the edge of the roof above the soffit (which is just beyond the exterior wall of the house, so there's no living space below giving off heat). With the constant freeze–thaw cycle we get during winter, an ice dam can build up. Water rolls down off the roof and hits the ice dam, which gets bigger, potentially working its way beneath the shingles and damaging the roof. Eventually an ice dam can start leaking into your house along the exterior walls. You may not notice the water, but it could be wetting the insulation behind your drywall.

To help prevent these problems, you need to do two things: seal and insulate. You need to seal the attic against air leaks from the living space below it to keep the warm air in your house from reaching the attic. To seal against air movement, you'll need a membrane to act as a barrier—such as 6-mil poly sheeting—above the ceiling of the top floor. All of us generate vapour by doing everyday activities like talking, breathing, cooking, showering and laundry. The barrier helps prevent moisture from getting up there so the attic stays nice and dry and free of frost.

Next, you need to make sure you've got some insulation over that barrier, which I talked about in the insulation chapter. But again, you're not doing that to keep the attic warm; it's the opposite, in fact. You're doing it to keep the heat in your living space below the attic. The insulation belongs on the attic floor, where it insulates the top floor of your house. The most popular options are loose-fill insulation or fibreglass batts (more about insulation basics on page 30).

If you want to combine insulation with an air barrier, you can use polyurethane spray foam topped with batts or loose-fill insulation. As long as the layer of foam is at least an inch thick, it acts as a suitable vapour barrier, and the batts or loose-fill add additional R-value for less expense. Make sure you also insulate and seal the attic door—people tend to forget about that.

How much insulation do you need in the attic? New builds or retrofits require between R40 and R50, depending on where you live. Check with your local building office.

MISTAKE #150:
SKIMPING ON VENTILATION IN THE ATTIC

Okay, now that I've scared everyone about letting too much heat into the attic, I'm going to back up a little. The truth is, some heat is still going to find its way up there from your second floor, no matter how well you seal and insulate. Maybe your attic is sealed and insulated and you're *still* having problems that signal the presence of heat. You might not have enough insulation, or you might have blocked vents while insulating, trapping heat inside. So you also need to make sure that air has somewhere to go before it causes trouble.

That's why ventilation in the attic is crucial. If you live in a cold climate, you want to vent the attic to keep the roof cold so you don't get those ice dams I described earlier (see Mistake #149, page 238). If any heat or vapour enters the attic, you could end up with condensation or moisture, which reduces the effectiveness of fibreglass insulation and also creates conditions for mould. Even houses in warm climates need vents to allow hot air to escape from the attic, which reduces the strain on air conditioning. Plus, shingles break down faster if they get too hot. The general

Curling, crumbling shingles are another sign that your attic is overheating. It might be time to add more insulation.

rule for determining how much ventilation is needed is to make sure the total area of your vents is between 1/150 and 1/300 of the insulated ceiling area—it depends on the type of roof you've got. You can search online for roofing and ventilation calculators.

Letting your attic breathe starts with soffit vents. As you might expect from the name, these are installed in the soffit, which is the area under your eavestrough. They draw in cool, fresh air at the base of the roof (then the air flows out at the peak of the roof—more on that below). Some soffit vents are continuous, which means they run the entire length of the soffit. A do-it-yourselfer will probably prefer installing individual vents because they are smaller and easier to work with as you cut and fit them between soffit joists. Just remember, the more air flowing into your attic, the better, as long as it has somewhere to escape!

Most builders routinely install soffit vents in new homes. Older homes—well, you never know: some may not have any; others may not have enough. The

Box vents allow warm air to escape from the attic.

best way to see what you've got is to walk around the perimeter of your house and look under the eaves. If you see what look a little like heat-register covers, those are individual soffit vents. If you see thin narrow aluminum strips, you've got continuous soffit vents. If you don't have anything—or have ones that don't appear at pretty regular intervals—I suggest you get to work.

If you're steady on a ladder and you've got a well-stocked workroom, you might be able to put in some individual vents yourself. Plan to install them along the soffits, at evenly spaced intervals, on both sides of the house. Avoid placing them where you see nails and seams in the soffit since that's where framing is located in the attic, and you don't want vents to interfere with framing. Measure the size of the vents you want to install and then make a template out of paper or cardboard, but make sure the template is an inch smaller than the vent since that's the size of the part you'll insert into the hole you're about to cut. Once you've got the locations marked, drill into each one with a 1-inch drill bit and cut out the piece with a jig saw for rectangular vents, or use a hole saw for round vents. Install the vents in each hole with the fins pointing toward the

house. You can prime and paint the vents to match the colour of the soffit, but just make sure you don't clog the screen with paint. For aluminum or vinyl soffits, you may find it easier to use tinsnips to cut the holes, or you might just install new panels with integrated vents.

Then it's time to climb into the attic. Staple soffit insulation baffles into the spaces between rafters on the underside of the roof. This creates a channel for air to freely flow in through the vents past the insulation. If all this sounds like it's over your head—pardon the pun—leave it to the pros: call a roofing company to install soffit vents and baffles.

Soffit vents do a good job of bringing fresh air into the attic, but that's only half of the equation. You want half your venting to take place at the eaves and the other half at or near the ridge of the roof. This gives you continuous ventilation of the attic. The most efficient way to get circulation at the top of the roof is with a ridge vent, which runs all the way along the very peak of a sloped roof to allow plenty of airflow. Any warm attic air naturally rises to the highest point of the house, where it gets replaced by fresh, cool air coming through the perforations in the soffits. In the summer, this process is very similar—hot air escapes out the ridge vent and cooler air is drawn into the soffits. You may not notice ridge vents on some houses because they're often capped with shingles and blend in with the look of the roof.

One drawback of ridge vents is they're not cheap. Installing them requires a roofer to remove large sections of shingles and the supporting layers of the roof. There's also a risk of blowing snow getting inside a ridge vent, but most newer vents have angled channels to keep out driving rain and blowing snow. If you're redoing your roof, that's a good time to install new soffit vents to increase airflow up through the attic space and out the ridge.

Ridge vents allow warm air to escape though the peak of a sloped roof.

Box vents are an alternative to ridge vents. They look like they sound: vented boxes that sit on the roof and perform the same function as a ridge vent. They're cheap, but they stand out like a sore thumb on a roof. If your roof has lots of small peaks, though, this might be your best choice because a ridge vent may not work.

You sometimes see turbine vents installed on the upper part of a roof. These are also called whirlybirds because they have blades that draw air up from the roof space. However, they won't work well if there's insufficient air supply in the attic. In fact, if your soffits aren't properly vented, they may actually pull moisture into the attic from the living space, worsening your condensation problems.

MISTAKE #151: NOT TOPPING UP INSULATION

Standards for attic insulation levels have changed over the years. I remember when code specified R36 in the attic, which you could do with 12 inches of fibreglass. Now, depending on where you live, new homes require attic insulation up to R50. (Remember, the R-value of insulation tells you how well every inch of insulation resists heat transfer, so bigger numbers means better insulation.) Extra insulation can help you conserve energy when you're heating and cooling your home, which means you'll save money.

If you haven't taken a look around your attic lately, it might be a good time to do that. Insulation settles over time, which reduces the total R-value. Fibreglass batts that get wet and stay wet are less effective. Loose-fill can get packed down, especially if you're using your attic to store your old tuxedo or piles of boxes—it's a good idea to build a raised platform so your boxes don't compress the insulation on the floor up there. If you climb up into the attic hatch, you can take a look and see what you've got. (Any time you go into an insulated attic, you should wear a dust mask.) Are there signs of water damage, or is the insulation looking tired and saggy? If so, you can take out the old insulation and put in some new. If it's in good shape, you might want to just top up what you've got to bring it in line with new standards.

MISTAKE #152: BLOCKING SOFFIT VENTS WHEN INSULATING AN ATTIC

One of the most common mistakes people make when they're insulating is covering up their soffit vents. Remember, you need those vents to bring in fresh air to help you manage heat and moisture in the attic, so the last thing you want to do is block them. But that's what happens: a home handyman rents a chopper, throws up lots of insulation and plugs all the vents. Now you've got insulation, but you've blocked your airflow—you need both.

To prevent this you can install baffles—sometimes called venting chutes or rafter vents. These are sheets of foam designed to fit between the rafters in the attic. You install them around the perimeter of the attic to allow air from the soffit vents to travel up and over the insulation toward the ridge vent. The baffles let you blow in loose-fill insulation to cover the entire attic floor with a nice thick layer without the insulation dropping into the soffits, covering them up and choking your attic and roof of essential airflow.

MISTAKE #153: DISTURBING OLD VERMICULITE INSULATION

While you're up in the attic, take a look at the type of insulation you've got. Fibreglass batts are typically

Baffles like these fit between the rafters in your attic and prevent loose-fill insulation from blocking your soffit vents.

pink or yellow, mineral wool is generally green, and loose-fill cellulose looks like tufts of shredded cotton. I've seen white, grey, green—you name it. If you live in a house built before 1990 and you've got insulation of a sort you don't recognize, it might be vermiculite. These are shiny little chunks that look like rocks and feel like foam. In that case, you'll want to get out of the attic right away. Just kidding—sort of.

Vermiculite is a mineral that's fire-resistant and has good insulating properties, and it was used in lots of consumer products. Most of the world's supply came from a single mine in Montana that was found to contain asbestos. If your home was insulated with vermiculite (which was sold as Zonolite and other brands) any time from the 1920s to the late 1980s, it may contain some asbestos.

Asbestos is one of those materials many of us have in our homes but just don't know about—and dread finding. There's a good reason for that. There's a lot of evidence linking asbestos exposure to serious health issues, including lung disease and even cancer.

If you encounter vermiculite insulation, don't touch it. Disturbing it is what sends those fibres into the air and puts you at risk of inhaling them. If the fibres are contained in the attic and no one is jumping around up there and bringing them back down to the living space on clothing or boots, you should be fine. But if you're planning renovations or you want to upgrade your attic insulation, you've got to be careful.

If you're concerned, call in an asbestos remediation expert to test the insulation to see if it contains asbestos. If it doesn't, you're fine, and you can proceed with whatever you were planning. If it tests positive for asbestos, you'll need to have it safely removed by a professional abatement company. It won't be cheap: these guys have special training, and they wear all kinds of protective gear. But don't even think about fooling around with this stuff yourself. It's just not worth the risk.

Mistake #154:
VENTING A BATHROOM FAN INTO THE ATTIC

I see this one a lot: people venting their bathroom exhaust fan into the attic. Think about this for second. You want to take humid air from your bathroom and dump it in the attic? That makes no sense. You could end up with moisture condensing, leaking back into the house and causing water stains on the ceiling, not to mention mould on the underside of the plywood in the attic.

A better way to vent that fan is to send the air out through an exterior wall. Or, depending on the roof, you might be able to install a vent in a gable wall (gables

are the triangular sections in a sloped roof). Some people vent through the soffits, but I don't like that—hot moist air can be pulled back into the attic through the soffits themselves.

Your last choice would be to go through the roof itself. I don't like sending ducts up through the attic, because you'll end up with a bit of condensation in the attic, even if the duct is insulated and sealed the way it should be. I'd rather minimize penetrations into the attic to keep it sealed off against heat and vapour transfer. If you have no choice but to vent the exhaust through the roof, there are roofing "boots" made to fit around the roof exhaust vent. These are collars that circle the vent on the top of the roof; you shingle and add flashing over the boot to direct water away. Again, since this job involves going onto the roof, I'd suggest you call in a specialist.

Mistake #155:
IMPROPERLY INSTALLING POT LIGHTS ON YOUR TOP FLOOR

Everybody wants pot lights these days. The attraction is they're recessed, so they don't eat up any of your ceiling height like track lights or a flush-mount ceiling fixture does. The problem with incorrectly installing pot lights in a room under the attic is—you guessed it—air and heat.

To install pot lights, you have to punch a hole in the ceiling of the room, which is essentially the floor of the attic. Then you're adding heat to the attic every time you switch on the light in that room, and if the light isn't properly sealed, moist air and heat will escape from your house into the attic. That hot air rising into the attic could cause problems with ice dams, condensation and mould. Not only that, but a pot light needs space around it so it doesn't get too hot and potentially start a fire—and some people retrofitting them in an old home don't realize this danger. If you put a pot light in the attic and pile insulation right on top of it, the insulation and the light will both get very hot.

In newer homes, lights that back into the attic have to be installed to code, which means they need a metal box and a vapour barrier over the part of the fixture that pokes into the attic. Everything is sealed up to prevent heat and air transfer, and then insulation is put above and around it. The light is called an IC pot light, which means it's safe to come into contact with insulation. As a general rule, if you're not a licensed electrician or you have little experience, I don't recommend you install your own pot lights in the attic. Getting it wrong can be catastrophic. (The pot lights in your basement don't need that special treatment unless you're adding a sound barrier, in which case, they need space.

MISTAKE #156:
NOT SUPPORTING SKYLIGHTS PROPERLY

We once pulled down the drywall in a house with a huge tunnel skylight, a cylinder that stretched right up to the roof to bring in sunlight. Not only had the installers cut some rafters, they cut the collar ties, which are the horizontal framing members that connect opposing rafters. The ridge of the roof itself had sunk by about 2 inches because they had cut everything that was supporting it! We had to jack everything back up, support it properly and then replace the drywall.

I like skylights—we put a bunch of them in our house in Oakville—but you need to make sure they're given the right structural support. If you cut out part of a rafter to make room for a skylight, now an entire section of roof isn't supported. It's a Jenga puzzle, and you've just pulled out a piece that will weaken the

Collar ties are the horizontal framing members that connect opposing rafters. If you're making modifications in your attic, you can't cut these!

whole section. You have to double up the rafters on either side of the opening and add a header, just like you would when adding a window or a door. A header is a doubled-up framing member that helps split the load between the rafters; these pieces have to be doubled because they're now sharing more of the load than they were engineered to carry.

This is why installing a skylight isn't a DIY project for a novice. It's likely to involve structural changes to the roof, and structural changes should always be handled by a professional or someone with a fair amount of framing experience.

MISTAKE #157:
AVOIDING SKYLIGHTS BECAUSE OF A FEAR OF LEAKS

Some people are totally against skylights because they're convinced it's only a matter of time before they start to leak. The technology behind skylights these days is good. We've got eight Velux skylights in our house, and I'm not at all worried about them leaking. It's the roofing around the curb that's critical. Some people spend all this money on a skylight and then cheap out on the installation. Waterproofing a skylight properly requires an experienced roofer.

When you're shopping for a skylight, look for a model with several layers of waterproofing. The sky-

When you install a skylight, the framing members around the perimeter should be doubled up for additional strength. Don't cheap out on the installation: waterproofing a skylight properly is a job for a professional roofer.

light frame should have a gasket that seals it to the part of the roof curb where the roof membrane comes up and over. The skylight's flashing should extend down and around the curb. This combination is much more effective than older methods like caulking or roofing tar, which tend to break down over time.

Skylights also need to be sealed well from the inside to prevent indoor air from escaping. You'll get condensation and water damage if warm air finds a dew point. Although, as mentioned, most skylights come with a foam gasket that will seal the skylight

to the curb, I recommend also building an insulated curb—otherwise, you'll have a cold zone below the skylight inside the opening that can lead to condensation issues.

MISTAKE #158: CONVERTING YOUR ATTIC TO A LIVING SPACE

If your house was originally designed with stairs leading up to a loft, then your attic may be a legitimate living space. But if it's a place where you're liable to get a concussion when you walk around up there, be prepared to spend a lot of cash to reclaim the attic. It may not even be worth the time and money.

This is one of those decisions people make without really thinking it through. All they imagine is how they'll furnish their quaint new bedroom or office, but they don't consider that the attic was in no way designed to be a real room.

The attic and ceiling joists are designed to do nothing more than hold up drywall and insulation. Your ceiling joists are 2×6s, and if they span more than 10 feet, they aren't going to hold the weight of a floor with you and your family running around on it. So you'd have to convert the ceiling joists to floor joists to handle the extra load.

Ceiling joists can carry a "dead load," which is simply stuff sitting on them. Floor joists need to support a "live load," or things moving around. You might weigh 200 pounds, but if you jump off a chair, you might be hitting the floor with 400 pounds of force. Ceiling joists can take a moderate amount of weight, but they're not designed to hold up drywall, insulation, a bed, a desk and four people. Converting them to floor joists can be a big, expensive job.

The other thing to look at is the ceiling angle and height. Remember, an *unfinished* attic must be sealed off from the conditioned living space below and properly vented with fresh air. But if you're reclaiming the attic, that means you want it to be part of your living space, not sealed off from the rest of the house. So instead of insulating the attic floor, you need to insulate the roof to R40 or R50 (depending on where you live). By installing insulation between the rafters and the underside of the roof, you'll take away some ceiling height. Then you need to create airflow between the insulation and the roof deck—the wood just below the shingles. If you've considered all this and you have enough ceiling height to allow for living space up there, then go for it. If you're trying to save every inch of ceiling height, the best choice for insulation may be spray foam, since it gives you the most R-value per inch (about twice as much as batts). Again, though, spray foam isn't a DIY job, and it's not cheap. Consider all your options and the long-term costs before making a decision.

MISTAKE #159:
CHEAPING OUT ON ROOFING

No one wants to hear they need a new roof. It's a lot of cash to spend on something that doesn't really improve your quality of life the way a new kitchen or finished basement does. But your roof is your first line of defence against rain, wind, sleet, hail and snow, so you don't want to neglect it when your shingles start to crack, curl or fall off. What good are your granite counters and stainless steel appliances when your house is leaking? If you're due for a new roof, you've got some old and new options to consider. I've included some rough material costs to give you a general idea, though prices vary widely across the country.

Asphalt shingles have been the staple for years. Made of fibreglass covered in asphalt and ceramic granules, they're the most popular for a reason: cost. Asphalt is the cheapest option, and it comes in lots of colours and styles. Remember that asphalt is a non-renewable resource sometimes manufactured from crude petroleum (another non-renewable resource), so if sustainability is important to you, you may want to look at other options.

The other downside is they have a pretty short lifespan. Lots of people go for the cheap shingles that last 10 to 15 years, though I don't understand why anyone would buy a product they know will have to be replaced so soon. Some shingles claim they're good for 30 or more years, but that's probably under optimal conditions. Realistically, how many companies—or original owners—will be around in 30 years when you need to follow up on the warranty? (By the way, keep the package the shingles came in—that's your warranty.) For the shingles alone, expect to pay about $60 to $150 per square. A square is 10 × 10 feet (or 100 square feet), which is how roofers tend to quote, though their estimates will also factor in the cost of removal, disposal and labour.

I think more and more people are starting to become aware that we're not doing the world any favours if we think of everything as disposable. We're starting to have more of an appreciation for quality. Cheap ends up being expensive in the long run. It hits your wallet and it hits the environment. I'm pleased that we're slowly moving away from asphalt to more durable options.

Composite shingles look a lot like clay or slate, but they're made of composite plastic. They're lighter than the real thing, so you won't need to build up the strength of the roof structure like you would if you were putting in actual slate or clay tiles. Some of these composites come with a 50-year warranty and a price tag of about $400 per square.

People who want a natural look go for **cedar shingles or shakes**. A well-maintained cedar roof is pretty easy to repair and can last 30 to 40 years. One downside is it requires some skill to install, so not every roofer will be able to do this well—make sure you get someone with experience. It's also high-maintenance if you want to preserve the look of fresh cedar: you have to keep it free of debris (leaves, branches, etc.), or the

roof could stay wet and start to mildew and rot. That means clearing out the eavestroughs regularly. It also means cleaning the roof. There's some controversy on using a power washer to do this. A regular garden hose will help remove some debris, but a power washer could damage the wood if sprayed too closely or with too much pressure. You'll also need to apply a topical treatment designed specifically for cedar that repels water and guards against UV rays. In time, a cedar roof will turn grey. I know people call it silver, but it can look pretty tired and rundown. Cedar is also a fire hazard, whereas most other roofing is fire-resistant. It's environmentally friendly from the standpoint that you're using a renewable natural resource that's minimally processed. Expect to pay $100 to $165 per square.

There's also at least one company out there making **composite cedar shakes and shingles**. Actual wood fibres are used in the composition, and they've designed them to replicate the look of the real thing. The difference is the composite comes with a 50-year warranty: they're not supposed to crack or rot, and they resist mould and pests. At about $400 per square, they're not cheap, but over the lifetime of the roof, they cost less than the real thing.

If you get into the big money, you can look at **clay shingles, Spanish tile or slate tile**. They're fireproof, they're very low-maintenance and they've got a classic look that appeals to many people. Spanish tile is used in Europe a lot, where these roofs last for many decades. I've seen some out west and down south in North America, but I'm not sure how they'd fare in colder climates, as parts of Europe have milder winters than we do here in Ontario. From a longevity standpoint, clay shingles, Spanish tile or slate tile make a good choice for the environment: they last about 50 years, so you won't need to replace them as often as you would a cheap asphalt shingle. The downside is these materials are very heavy, so they require extra labour and materials to reinforce the roof to support the extra load. And, of course, they range from expensive to *very* expensive. Clay and Spanish tile cost $300 to $600 per square; slate rings in at about $450 to $1,500.

I really like **metal roofs**, because they can last a lifetime. You can get metal shingles or what's called a standing seam metal roof, which has panels that slightly overlap as they click into place. Both the shingles and the panels are light—they weigh less than asphalt—so they're easier to install than some of the other options. The material won't burn, and it does a good job of reflecting the sun's heat away in the summer to keep your home cooler. Yes, a metal roof costs $100 to $600+ per square, but you could replace an asphalt roof four or five times, or you could put in one metal roof.

MISTAKE #160:
OVERLOOKING THE BENEFITS OF A GREEN ROOF

If you want a great option for a flat roof, consider a green roof. We did one at the cottage: we covered the entire area with really hardy fire- and drought-resistant plants. I can see them sticking up when I'm on the ground. I keep thinking I should put a goat up there!

Whenever it rains, the plants hold about 90% of the water that hits the roof. It's great for the foundation because you don't get this flood of water pouring off. It also helps keep the sun off the roofing membrane—that's huge, because solar rays and heat are terrific at breaking down your roof. Putting in a green roof in the city eases the load on sewer infrastructure. We've also noticed that the green roof keeps our place cooler in the summer and warmer in the winter, so it's really great for conserving energy.

I realize, however, it's not an option for everyone. For starters, you need to have a flat roof or one with a very low slope. Then the structure needs to be engineered to manage the load. Between the 80,000 pounds of soil and the metre of snow we get up there in the winter, it has to support a lot of weight. And you need deep pockets: a green roof isn't cheap—typically about $15 to $20 per square foot.

MISTAKE #161:
INSTALLING NEW SHINGLES OVER OLD ONES

If you've ever watched a roof being replaced, you'll notice one of two scenarios. Some companies rip down every shingle and toss them in a dumpster, while others leave the old shingles and re-roof overtop. Which is better?

The roofing company may try to tell you it's fine to add another layer if nothing is leaking. What they're not telling you is it's better for *them*, because it lessens their labour and lowers their costs since they don't need to dispose of your old shingles at the dump. The truth is, it's always better to expose the roof deck—the wood underneath the shingles—before you re-roof. If you don't take off the old layer, you'll have no way of knowing if the roof deck is in good shape. Are there any cracks? Is the wood soft, wet or rotten or showing signs of mildew or rot? Yes, you can examine the wood from the inside to a degree, but ideally you should inspect the condition of the roof structure from both sides. This is also a chance for the roofers to check for missing nails in case the wood decking isn't firmly attached to the rafters below and to build up the roof properly to make it waterproof.

Next, the roof has to be prepared for shingles. The contractors will install a drip edge, which is a bent metal band that prevents moisture from getting underneath the edges of the roofing material. Then they should put up an ice and water shield. This waterproof membrane covers at least the bottom metre of the roof and anywhere you've got a chimney, pipe or vent penetrating through. Some pros will cover the whole roof with this membrane because it helps prevent leaks—not a bad idea if your budget can handle it. Alternatively, you can install a heavy-duty roofing felt or tarpaper, which prevents asphalt shingles from sticking to the wood and provides another layer of protection for your roof. Preparing the base properly like this is far better than just slapping a new layer of shingles over the old ones.

MISTAKE #162:
NOT READING INSTRUCTIONS WHEN INSTALLING SHINGLES

I know I said earlier that I don't suggest people start becoming their own roofers, but there are some small jobs you can do on your own. Maybe you've got an overhang above your front door or a shed that's low to the ground. It's only 50 shingles, so you figure you'll do it yourself instead of calling in a roofer. A handy homeowner can lay a few rows of shingles fairly easily, but there are some tricks to it, and those tricks are hidden in plain sight right on the package. But if there's one mistake everyone makes, it's not reading instructions.

APPLICATION OF ASPHALT SHINGLES

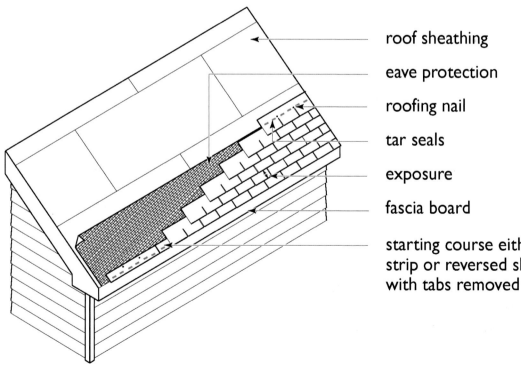

roof sheathing

eave protection

roofing nail

tar seals

exposure

fascia board

starting course either solid strip or reversed shingles with tabs removed

There are some tricks to installing shingles. The first row goes in upside down so the second layer has something solid under the notches. Be sure to fasten the shingles properly according to the manufacturer's directions, which are conveniently printed on the packaging for you—but of course you read them before starting, right?

How else would you know that the first layer of shingles are installed upside down? Shingles are notched. The first one goes in upside down so when you put the second one on top, you've got something solid under these notches to keep water off the roof. The idea is that every new shingle goes down and overlaps half of the previous one, so the water is draining onto a base that's solid instead of creeping in through the notch.

Some people nail the shingles in the middle instead of going in at the top of the gap, but a roofing nail should never be exposed—it should be covered by the next shingle. Another thing people get wrong is they don't overhang the shingles at the edge of the roof. If they don't, the water will run down, hook on the end of the shingle and fall into the fascia (the board that extends vertically under the roof edge). Fascia boards are typically made of wood, so you don't want to be throwing any extra water at it. If you extend the shingles past the fascia an inch or so, moisture should drip off the edge into the eavestrough, where it can be properly drained away from the house. The drip edge you installed earlier is another layer of protection.

MISTAKE #163:
OVERLOOKING THE IMPORTANCE— AND DIFFICULTY—OF ROOF FLASHING

Shingles aren't the only things that keep the weather off your roof. You also need flashing, the pieces of sheet metal that help prevent leaks on a shingled roof.

Every roof has various points that are especially vulnerable to wind, rain, ice and snow. These include junction points where the roof connects to things like the chimney, roof vents, plumbing pipes and so on. Flashing helps seal these points to make them water-tight and to deflect water away. A single roof might need several types of flashing. Valley flashing, for example, covers any joint where the roof changes pitch for architectural features, like at the base of a dormer. Then you'd need different flashing entirely around features like skylights, chimneys and vent pipes.

Each type of flashing requires a particular kind of installation, and doing it wrong could leave you vulnerable to leaks. The installation is a bit of a production, too. Sometimes you have to completely remove shingles or other roofing materials.

If you get water damage from your own shoddy or inexperienced work, will your insurance cover the damage? Will you offer the next homeowner a warranty on your work? Whether you need a patch around an old vent boot or a whole new roof, this is a good time to call in a pro.

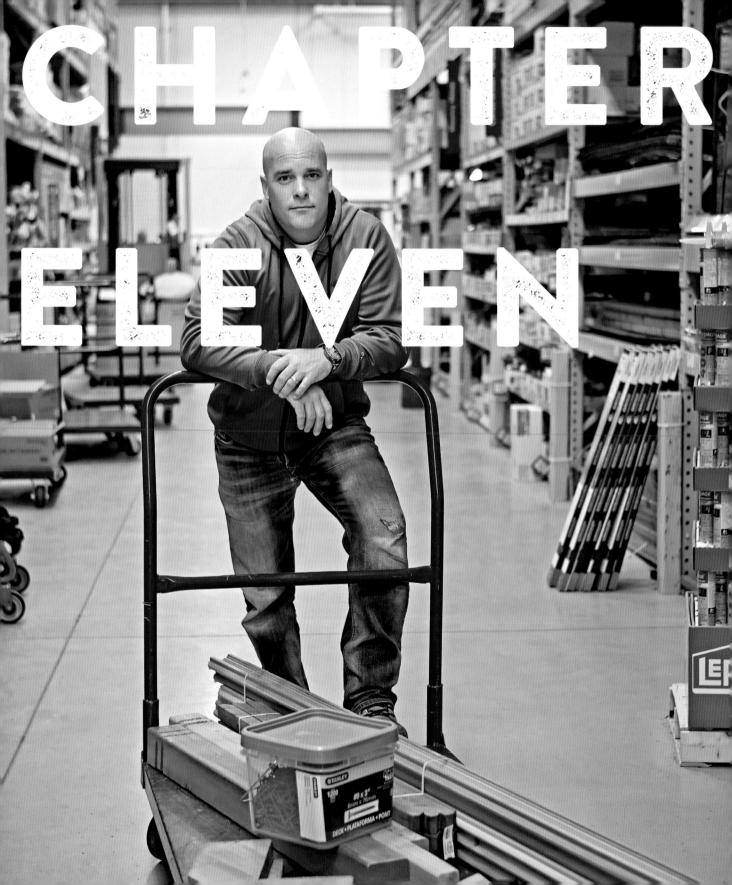

CHAPTER
ELEVEN

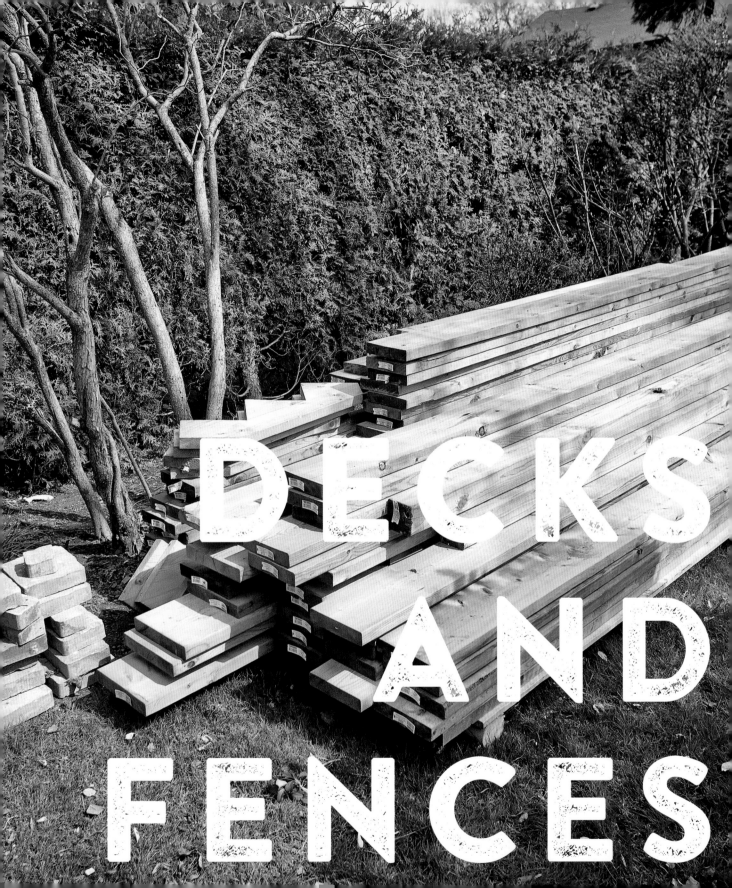

DECKS AND FENCES

JUST ABOUT EVERYONE LOVES HAVING A DECK IN THEIR YARD. WHETHER YOU ENJOY ENTERTAINING FRIENDS OR JUST HANGING OUT WITH A BEER AND A GOOD BOOK, A DECK MAKES YOUR HOME FEEL LIKE A COTTAGE, EVEN IF YOU'RE IN THE CITY OR THE SUBURBS. FENCES ARE A LITTLE MORE PRACTICAL, BUT THEY, TOO, CAN HELP YOU ENJOY YOUR BACKYARD AND ADD PRIVACY AND A BIT OF VISUAL INTEREST.

What's the biggest mistake people make when building a deck or a fence? Focusing only on the appearance. They put a lot of energy into mapping out the size of the deck or what the lattice will look like, but they're not really thinking about the structure—how to fasten the deck to the side of the house, how to properly secure the steps and railings or where the fence posts will go. As with any renovation project, it's worth spending the time to think it through.

If you're building a deck and don't have a lot of design experience, I recommend you check out some of the great tools available online to help with planning, such as Lowe's Deck Designer (lowes.ca). These planners will do everything for you: you start by creating the deck's footprint, and then the software walks you through all the important decisions about how to build it off the ground, where to place railings and stairs, how to lay out the deck boards and joists and posts, and which materials to use. Then it creates a 3D diagram, a list of tools and materials you'll need and instructions for the installation. The only thing it won't do is actually build the deck! If you think you're up for a challenging DIY project, grab your hammer and let's get building.

DECK AND FENCE BASICS

DIFFICULTY: 8 OUT OF 10 FOR DECKS; 6.5 OUT OF 10 FOR FENCES

A deck is typically supported by *posts* (usually 4 × 4 or 6 × 6) that rest on concrete tubes called *piers*. Running horizontally across the tops of these posts are a series of heavy framing members called *beams*, often made from two or even three 2 × 10s secured together. The *joists* run perpendicular to the beams and support the *decking* you walk on.

The stairs on your deck are built from horizontal **treads** (the part you step on) and vertical **risers** attached to notched boards called **stringers**, which are placed at both ends (and in the middle if necessary for added support).

Fences are built using many of the same techniques. The **posts** are typically 4 × 4, and they're set right in the concrete tubes rather than resting on top. The **rails** are the horizontal supports attached to the posts, and the **pickets** (or **fence boards**) are the individual vertical pieces attached to the rails.

CHOOSING DECKING AND FENCING MATERIAL

- **Pressure-treated (PT) lumber** is a popular choice because it stands up well to decay, and it's inexpensive. But it's vulnerable to warping and cracking, and it can be high-maintenance.

- **Cedar** looks good, has some natural resistance to rot and insects and tends not to warp or crack. However, it's rather soft and can quickly show signs of wear. It also needs routine maintenance to keep its colour if you want the natural look.

- **Composite decking** is made from wood and plastic or sometimes plastic only. It's extremely durable and doesn't need to be stained or painted, though it's not completely maintenance-free.

- **Exotic woods** like Ipê are beautiful and resilient, but they're also expensive and not as readily available.

TOOLS AND MATERIALS YOU'LL NEED

- measuring tape and pencil
- level
- string (for aligning adjacent posts)
- clamshell shovel or power auger
- framing saw or other circular saw (depending on the size of lumber you're cutting)
- framing hammer
- joist hangers
- galvanized nails or screws
- concrete forming tubes
- concrete

MISTAKE #164:
NOT GETTING THE RIGHT PERMITS

Whether you need a building permit for a deck depends on its size, height and location—and also where you live. Every municipality has specific bylaws above and beyond the building code, so your town might have slightly different deck construction rules than your brother's. In Kitchener, Ontario, for example, residents need a permit for any new or replacement deck that sits 24 inches or more above the ground, or for making structural changes to an existing deck. The code in Nanaimo, B.C., says the same thing but then adds a few circumstances outlining when you *don't* need a permit: if the deck is not part of your home's main entrance, not covered by a roof or not attached to your house, or if you're making minor repairs to a previously permitted deck.

Some bylaws also spell out maximum dimensions or the percentage of your lot you're allowed to cover with a deck. In some cases, you might need a site alteration permit instead of a building permit. It can get messy. Bottom line: before you head for the lumberyard, get the specifics from your municipality. You're responsible for making sure your building project complies with local bylaws. If you don't get a permit when you need one or if you break code as you're building, the inspector has the right to make you tear down all or part of your construction.

When you're planning your deck, don't just work on paper. Get outside and set up your laser level or string lines so you know exactly where each post will sit. Then call your utility company to locate the gas and electrical lines before you finalize the plan. If you find out there's a gas line right where you planned to put a pier, the deck footprint can stay the same; you just need to put that pier in a different place.

Typically you need to supply several documents as part of your application for a deck permit. They might include a site plan, a floor plan, an elevation view and a cross-section view. Some towns won't accept graph or lined paper and will specify the dimensions of the paper used for the plans—building departments are notoriously picky about these things. If anything about your application is wrong, you'll have to resubmit, delaying your permit. In some towns, the cost of the permit is determined by the value of the project you're building.

You probably think all of this sounds like a pain, and it's true, there can be some frustrating bureaucracy. But the permit process forces you to plan your deck carefully, and the inspection ensures you and your family that the completed work is safe.

MISTAKE #165:
NOT BUILDING A PROPER FOUNDATION

You can't have a usable deck without a solid foundation. The most stable foundations are concrete piers (pillars) resting on larger concrete bases called footings. But this technique involves some pretty serious

Start your planning with a scale drawing, but then get outside and mark each deck footing on the ground.

digging. You need an excavator, and it's not really a DIY job.

A much more common technique for deck foundations is building concrete piers to support wood posts. You still have to dig below the frost line to make sure the concrete won't move with the freezing and thawing of the soil around it, but the hole diameter is smaller, so you can use a post-hole digger, which is much easier to manage. This technique, if done properly, is plenty strong enough to support a residential deck.

Start by determining how deep you need to dig, which will vary with local building codes. In cold

(*Clockwise from top right*) Mark the location for each post hole using spray paint. You can dig the post hole by hand, but it's a lot of work! Make sure the concrete forms you use are wide enough to take the load.

(*Clockwise from top right*) In cold areas, post holes need to be at least 4 feet deep: don't stop at 3 feet, or your post will heave. If you're digging a lot of holes, or if the ground is hard and rocky, an auger definitely makes the job easier.

climates, you have to go down at least 4 feet. Don't skimp on this! Yes, it's deep, and it's a lot of work, so you might be tempted to stop digging after 3 feet, but you'll end up with a deck that heaves with the freeze–thaw cycle.

When you start digging, be prepared to find some rocks, roots or old bricks. Some people rent a two-man auger, which is operated by one person on each side. It's pretty easy to manage until you run into something solid. The problem is, there's no reverse on that equipment, so once you get locked into a root or rock, it can be difficult to get it out. You're sweating like a cow, and I've seen guys get locked in and take 20 minutes to get out. A rock bar is handy to have around if you have to break anything big and solid out of the hole. A power auger like a Dingo or Bobcat makes the job much easier if you have access to one. Or you can simply call someone else to do it: there are services that specialize in digging post holes. Because of this potential for barriers, you need to have some leeway with where your posts are going. Sometimes you'll run into problems you couldn't have foreseen, such as hitting a rock you can't get past. You have no choice but to change the structure slightly.

With the post-hole digger, go down a bit deeper than the minimum depth permitted in your area and add a 4-inch layer of stone at the bottom of the hole for drainage. (If rainwater and snow melt has nowhere to go, it's going to cause problems for your posts.)

A 4-inch layer of stone at the bottom of the post hole allows for drainage and can prevent heaving.

Then insert a cylindrical form, such as those made by Sonotube or Quikrete. These are sturdy cardboard-like tubes used to form concrete columns. You want the top of the tube to sit just above the level of the soil, or if you're handy with a laser level and string line, you can bring it all the way up to the level of the deck beams.

One problem I often see is people supporting a deck with posts or concrete piers that are too narrow. Think of it this way: if you're standing in deep snow

Use a level to make sure your concrete forms are plumb before you backfill the hole.

without snowshoes, you're going to sink. If you put a narrow footing in the ground and then place a bunch of weight on it, it's slowly going to sink in. A wider footing—such as a 6 × 6 set into a 12-inch Sonotube filled with concrete—will be able to carry the load better, like a bigger snowshoe. There are code requirements based on the height and size of your deck, but as a general rule, the bigger, the better.

Once your form is in place, mix your concrete according to the instructions on the bag and then shovel it in. When the tube is filled, smooth out the surface and carefully insert a saddle, which is a metal

To "wet-set" a metal saddle, fill the form with concrete and then scrape it smooth. Insert the saddle and make sure it's positioned in exactly the right spot: you won't be able to move it later!

bracket that holds the post. There are many designs, but they typically have a piece of rebar protruding from the bottom, and this gets set in the wet concrete. After the concrete cures, the wooden post is attached to the bracket. Inserting the saddle while the concrete is still wet is called wet-setting, and it takes a bit of skill because you don't have the luxury of being able to adjust it after the concrete dries. The position of the saddle has to be bang-on, so make your measurements carefully. If you don't want to wet-set, you can use a different type of saddle designed to be installed after the concrete dries. You then drill into the concrete and tack the saddle in place. These adjustable saddles are a lot more forgiving, but they aren't typically as strong.

With all the work that's required to drill and set footings, you might be tempted to use precast concrete blocks designed to support deck posts. These are pyramid-shaped blocks that just sit on the ground—no need to dig holes or pour concrete. They're intended for small ground-level decks or other small structures. The advantage is they go in fast, but they're not stable through freeze–thaw cycles, and I would never recommend them for any kind of large permanent structure, especially if it's attached to the house. (In most cases this won't pass inspection anyway.)

If you do want to avoid excavation and concrete, you can look at calling a pro to install a helical foundation system. These are steel piers with a giant screw blade on the end. Installers come in and drill them into the ground. The blade on the bottom (the screw head) sits at least 48 inches underground, and each post can take more than 50,000 pounds of load. Again, there's no digging or concrete: once they're in, you cut them off at the height you want and put the hanger on top.

Precast concrete blocks are the easiest footings to install, but they just aren't stable enough for any permanent structure.

MISTAKE #166:
SETTING FOOTINGS IN DISTURBED SOIL

When people move in to new subdivisions, they immediately start throwing up fences. Then a year or two later, the fences are falling over. That's because new subdivisions excavate massive holes, which then get backfilled. That backfill usually isn't compacted, and if you build a fence or a deck on top of that disturbed soil, it's going to move as the soil settles.

Deck and fence footings need to be on undisturbed soil because they must be able to bear weight. (A note about the jargon here: a footing is technically a large base underneath a pier, but informally both homeowners and pros often use the term *footing* when *pier* is probably more correct.) If you put a footing in an area that's been excavated, you have to dig all the way down to fully compacted soil, which can be much deeper than 4 feet. Otherwise, the earth is going to continue to sink, and so will your deck. If you move into a brand new subdivision, I suggest waiting at least one or two winters before you build a deck or fence. You can speed up the process by using a sprinkler to water the yard frequently in summer to help the ground settle and compact faster.

MISTAKE #167:
IGNORING CLEARANCES AND BLOCKING ACCESS

When you're planning a deck, you have to think about how it will affect the rest of your house. Keep in mind that adding or changing one design element can set off a chain of other decisions.

Even if you've planned things carefully on paper or online, remember to add some common sense.

Don't build a deck or fence too close to a tree. The tree might grow so large it will overtake the fence, and the roots can be strong enough to push up concrete footings. You also need to think about clearances. For example, you can't build a deck too close to your air conditioning unit or blocking your dryer vent. If your deck has stairs that pass by a window, code may say that window needs to be tempered glass. Or you might decide you don't mind if your deck blocks a basement window, so you'll have to close up that window and properly seal it before the deck goes up, because you won't be able to access it afterward. You can make any decision you want with your house—within the bounds of code, of course—but the key is that you want to be planning, not reacting.

MISTAKE #168:
FORGETTING ABOUT DRAINAGE

We worked on one house where the owners had landscaped the backyard with patio stones, and everything sloped toward the house. Every time it rained, the water would pool by their foundation, and eventually it leaked into the basement. I don't know if it was the owners who had graded the area, but it was like that for years. They ended up with black mould everywhere, and they had to rip everything out in the basement, get a mould remediation team to clean it and then refinish the entire basement after waterproofing the foundation and re-grading the patio to prevent the mould from returning. They spent thousands of dollars fixing a problem that could have easily been avoided by sloping the patio away from the house in the first place.

You can run into similar problems with a deck. Before you build a deck attached to the house, make sure your yard is graded *away* from the foundation: a

5% slope is ideal, which is 3 vertical inches for every 5 horizontal feet. At the same time, you need to make sure you don't cause drainage problems for your neighbours—call in the pros to make sure grading is done properly. Under the deck is another area where water can pool. One option is to put down a membrane that will channel the water away from the house. As a bonus, this will also help eliminate weeds growing up through your deck boards.

MISTAKE #169:
CHOOSING THE WRONG KIND OF WOOD

Okay, maybe *wrong* is a bit of an exaggeration. But the truth is there are all kinds of wood out there, and each one has pluses and minuses when it comes to appearance, maintenance, longevity and environmental issues. Here's how they rank in my books, from worst to best.

Pressure-treated (PT) lumber: I'd rate PT lumber as merely acceptable. It's treated with a chemical preservative that helps the boards resist decay from water and insects. It's the most affordable option, which explains its popularity, but it has its problems. Because the moisture content is usually high, the boards can shrink after they're installed, which causes gaps in your fence or your deck. The wood is prone to warping and splintering, and cracks can grow from year to year. PT also requires a bit of maintenance if you want to extend its life and keep it looking good: you need to apply a water-repellent coating every year or two once the wood has had a chance to cure, which can take a few months.

Regardless of your choice for deck boards, PT is almost always used to build the structure of the deck itself. In the past, it was recognizable by its signature green tint, but it's also now available in brown to more closely resemble the colour of cedar.

Cedar: There's no doubt cedar looks better than the old greenish PT lumber, and it stands up better than the new brown PT, but it's also substantially more expensive. I love the look and smell of cedar, and I also like that it's naturally resistant to rot and insects and that the boards tend to lie flat without cracking for at least a season or two. But cedar is relatively soft, so it can get banged up when you're moving furniture around or shovelling the deck in winter. Like PT, cedar needs routine maintenance with a water-repellent or semi-transparent stain to keep it looking fresh, or it will turn grey. Some people call that patina, but I think it just makes the deck look old and beaten up.

Wood alternatives: Composite decking is made from wood and plastic (sometimes recycled plastic and wood fibres) or from 100% plastic, either new or recycled. The boards won't splinter, warp or rot and never need to be sanded or refinished. Both composite and plastic decking are available in different colours and finishes, though the colours may fade slightly over time. Composite may need to be cleaned, as it contains wood that's susceptible to mildew—read the fine print on any product you're buying so you're aware of the necessary maintenance. The boards are heavy and can be hard to work with, and composite products cost more than cedar. The thing I don't like about some of these products is that all the boards tend to look the same—they don't have the natural variations you get with real wood. Plus, they also retain a lot of heat in the summer, which can mean burnt feet.

Exotic woods: I love the look and longevity of exotic decking, but for most people the expense (and lack of sustainable forestry practices in harvesting some of the more popular woods) just doesn't make sense. We found an amazing product made from acetylated southern pine: it was real wood, but modified to resist warping and cracking, so it was the best of both worlds. Sadly it's not being manufactured anymore. Until its return, you have to consider all of your options based on financial, moral and environmental factors. It's not easy, but only you can make the decision that's right for you.

MISTAKE #170:
NOT SEALING THE CUT ENDS OF PT LUMBER

When building a fence or a deck, you're going to be cutting a lot of wood. If you're using PT lumber, you need to replace the preservative on any cut surfaces. The manufacturer cannot get the preservative to penetrate the entire piece of wood, even under pressure, so any cuts will expose untreated fibres. If you don't seal these with some kind of preservative, moisture, fungus or insects will damage the wood as they would untreated lumber. So pick up a can of sealant specially designed for PT lumber and brush it on any cut boards before installing them.

MISTAKE #171:
USING THE WRONG FASTENERS

When you're putting up a deck, you can't just build it with whatever nails you dig out of the garage. Exterior projects are going to be exposed to the elements, so you need materials designed to withstand moisture. In

The end grain on PT lumber is treated with the same chemicals as the rest of the wood. If you make any cuts, you need to reseal those ends.

general, use galvanized or stainless steel for outdoor projects. Galvanized steel has been dipped in a molten zinc coating to resist corrosion.

That said, the fasteners also depend on the wood

you're using. I've seen homeowners bang up a beautiful new deck of pressure-treated lumber and then the next day find the wood is already stained with rust. Now that arsenic isn't used in PT lumber anymore, the wood contains a water-based preservative called ACQ (which stands for alkaline copper quaternary) that protects against rot and insects. What's not so good is the copper in ACQ is highly corrosive to common steel, which means you have to use the right kind of screws and brackets, or the chemicals in your wood will destroy your fasteners and it may not take long for your new deck to start falling apart.

If you're using PT wood, use double-galvanized or stainless steel fasteners. Look at the package: the label should tell you they're designed for pressure-treated or ACQ lumber. If you're building with cedar or tropical hardwoods, you will pay a little more—actually, a *lot* more, but it's probably worth it—for stainless steel to prevent staining around the screw heads.

Normally you should use nails to build the foundation and structural components of your deck. When you build the border and put in the joists, fasten everything with nails. That's code, unless you're using structurally rated screws. Regular deck screws aren't allowed because they don't have the same shear load rating as nails. What that means is that under intense pressure, a nail will only bend, but a screw could break. Use screws to install the deck boards, however, because nails have a habit of popping up over time. So, screws on the top, nails on the bottom.

MISTAKE #172:
INCORRECTLY ATTACHING THE DECK TO THE HOUSE

Do a Google search and you'll find all kinds of examples of what can happen if you don't attach your deck properly. If you do it wrong, the deck can collapse; it can even pull the entire veneer off the house—which is

DECK CONNECTION TO HOUSE

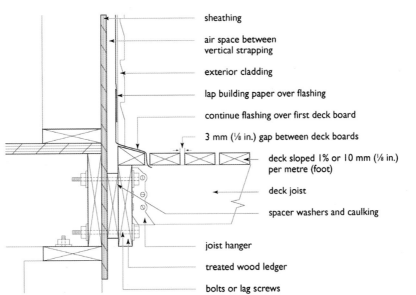

- sheathing
- air space between vertical strapping
- exterior cladding
- lap building paper over flashing
- continue flashing over first deck board
- 3 mm (⅛ in.) gap between deck boards
- deck sloped 1% or 10 mm (⅜ in.) per metre (foot)
- deck joist
- spacer washers and caulking
- joist hanger
- treated wood ledger
- bolts or lag screws

why almost every jurisdiction requires a permit for any deck that is attached to a house.

One of the most common techniques for securing a deck to a house is to use a ledger board. A ledger—which can be as small as a 2 × 6 or as large as a 2 × 12—is a long board bolted horizontally to the side of the house. The ledger needs to be tied into a structural part of your home, usually the rim joist (which rests on the foundation). You can't just attach the ledger to the siding. I've seen people anchor the ledger to the face of a brick house, which is

dangerous, because that brick veneer wasn't designed to take the weight of a deck. If you have no choice but to attach the ledger to the veneer, you'll need to support it properly so the structure of the deck will take the load, not the veneer.

Once your ledger is attached, use joist hangers—U-shaped mounting brackets—to fasten the joists to the ledger. The idea is to install the hangers so the top of the joist is flush with the top of the ledger. Then your deck boards sit on top of the joists.

A ledger board needs to be attached securely in order to support a deck. The proper technique is to use bolts that extend through the rim joist. Attach metal hangers to the ledger to support the individual joists. Each hanger should extend the full height of the joist—for example, don't use a 6-inch hanger with a 2 × 8.

Here's a trick the pros use when installing a series of joist hangers when the ledger is wider than the joist and the ledger is shorter than the joist. If you're using 2 × 8 joists, for example, cut a 2 × 8 block a few inches long to use as a guide. Rather than measuring the position of each joist hanger, just slip the small piece of lumber into the hanger, line up its top with the top of the ledger and tack the hanger to the ledger with a couple of nails. Then take the block away. This makes it easy to make everything flush. The other way is to tack the top of the joist into place with a deck screw, then install the joist hanger with proper nails—the screw just holds up the joist so you don't need a third hand while installing the hanger.

Make sure you use the right kind of hardware for this job. Nails designed specifically for joist hangers are double galvanized, and they're shorter, thicker and stronger so they'll resist bending. Fill all the holes within the hanger with these nails. Install the largest hanger to fit the lumber—if you're using 2 × 8 joists, never use a hanger designed for a 2 × 4; it won't be strong enough to support the weight.

Some decks aren't tied to the house at all. A deck that is low to the ground can simply be a freestanding platform. Depending on the rules in your municipality, this kind of deck, if under certain dimensions, may not require a building permit. The advantages of a low deck are you can put one anywhere and it's easy to build. The disadvantages are the frost can move them around and they're typically not as big, as high or as complex.

MISTAKE #173:
TOO MUCH SPACE BETWEEN JOISTS AND BEAMS

In order for a deck to be able to support the weight above it, the joists and beams need to be properly spaced. A standard deck board—the part you walk on—is called a 5/4 (five-quarter) board. They're really only ⅞ inch thick, but they're called 5/4 because before they're dried and milled, they're 1¼ inches thick. The standard width is 5½ inches. If you're using these boards and laying them perpendicular to the joists, you can space the joists with 16-inch centres (that is, 16 inches apart, measured from the centre of one edge to the centre of the next). If you're running the deck boards on a 45-degree angle, use 12-inch spacing for the joists, because each board will span a greater distance.

If you're laying 2 × 6 deck boards (which are really 5½ inches wide and 1½ inches thick), you can

Your joists must be close enough together to provide support. If the deck boards are laid diagonally, leave 12 inches between joists. If the boards are laid perpendicular to the joists, you can use 16-inch spacing.

get away with spacing the joists farther apart: 24 inches if you're laying the boards perpendicular, 16 inches for a 45-degree diagonal pattern.

The maximum length you can run a joist depends on a few factors, so check what's required by code. If you're building a huge deck, you can probably get away with using 16- or 20-foot lumber for the joists, but you'll need one or two beams to support it. The narrower the joist, the more support you're going to need—a 2 × 8 needs more support than a 2 × 12. Don't use anything smaller than a 2 × 8 joist.

If you opt for composite decking, it's important to follow the span limits specified by the manufacturer, because these may be different than they are for traditional lumber. Using 16-inch centres for your joists won't work for some composite products when you're installing the deck boards on an angle—you might need more joists. Stairs can pose another problem: you may require more stringers (the notched boards that support the treads and risers) if you're using composite boards. Some are limited to an 8-inch span when used as stair treads, which means you'd need four stringers on a 36-inch stairway (instead of the usual two for real wood). See Mistake #176, page 273, for more on stairs.

Read the instructions on composite boards and follow them carefully, or you could void the warranty. Online deck design software can also ensure you're not over-spanning, no matter what material you're using.

MISTAKE #174:
FAILING TO PROPERLY SUPPORT BEAMS

Remember, beams support the weight of the joists above them, so they need to be installed securely. Some people think they can sandwich a post with beams to carry the weight of the deck. The problem

Deck beams should be positioned on top of the posts, not attached to the sides.

with that is you're not only bearing on the beam, you're hanging off a bolt through the post. Most decks don't have many posts to begin with, so each one with beams connected to it is carrying a heavier load. You may not break your bolt with this set-up, but the wood around the bolt can be crushed, which will destroy that connection. You need to distribute the weight onto the beams, not onto the bolt.

Here's an example: if the deck plan calls for a 2-ply 2 × 10 beam, don't attach one on each side of the post. Instead, use a pair of 2 × 10s glued and nailed together to create one beam, and then sit it *on top* of the post.

The only time you should sandwich posts is if your deck is low to the ground, and you've sunk tons of foundation piers—not necessarily the best choice if you live in a region that sees a lot of frost, like I do.

MISTAKE #175:
INSTALLING RAILINGS INCORRECTLY

A lot of people will build a deck with a stairway and no handrail. They like the minimalist look, I guess. The thing is, code requires you to make your deck safe, and kids or older people will be in danger of falling if you don't include a railing. Any time you've got more than two steps, you need a handrail.

In my neck of the woods, if your deck is 24 to 60 inches off the ground, you need a 36-inch railing all the way around; any part of a deck that stands 60 inches or more above grade needs a 42-inch railing. That

WOOD DECK DETAIL

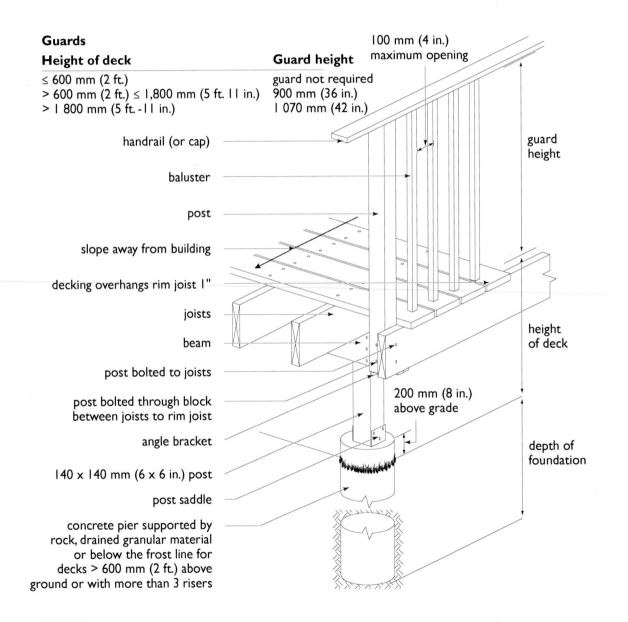

Guards

Height of deck	Guard height
≤ 600 mm (2 ft.)	guard not required
> 600 mm (2 ft.) ≤ 1,800 mm (5 ft. 11 in.)	900 mm (36 in.)
> 1 800 mm (5 ft. -11 in.)	1 070 mm (42 in.)

100 mm (4 in.) maximum opening

guard height

handrail (or cap)

baluster

post

slope away from building

decking overhangs rim joist 1"

joists

beam

post bolted to joists

post bolted through block between joists to rim joist

angle bracket

140 x 140 mm (6 x 6 in.) post

post saddle

concrete pier supported by rock, drained granular material or below the frost line for decks > 600 mm (2 ft.) above ground or with more than 3 risers

200 mm (8 in.) above grade

height of deck

depth of foundation

applies whether we're talking about stairs or the deck surface itself. These are local codes, so you've got to check with your city to find out the details there.

Handrail posts also need to be spaced properly. In most cases you need 4- × 4-inch posts spaced no more than 6 feet apart. Planning is your best friend when it comes to details like this. Don't think just about building the deck, and then tackle the railings on the fly. Plan how you're going to space out the railings so they meet code and are evenly spaced—obviously you don't want random posts all over the place.

One of the most dangerous mistakes is to improperly connect handrail posts to the deck. Wood screws aren't strong enough to take the weight if someone leans against the railing; if possible, use ½-inch carriage bolts that go right through the post and deck frame. In the same way, the most secure technique for fastening a post is to put blocking between the joists, put your post in and then block it again on the other side. Finally, put a couple of bolts all the way through the blocks, the joist and the post.

Don't forget to space the balusters properly. These are the decorative pillars or spindles that support the railing. They need to be close enough together to prevent an object that's 4 inches in diameter—the code makes it sound like some theoretical "spherical object," but really it's talking about a kid's head—from getting through or getting stuck. Since the space must be less than 4 inches, one easy technique to get it perfectly even is to use a 2 × 4 to measure and mark the space between each baluster. (Remember, a 2 × 4 is really 3½ inches wide.)

The average homeowner is going to install a wooden baluster, but there are lots of engineered railings out there: glass, wire, metal, just to name a few. If you're doing anything but wood, get a copy of the supplier's specs and submit these details to the city when you send in the permit application.

MISTAKE #176:
TRIPPING UP ON THE STAIRS

Stairs are tricky. Good planning can help determine the height of your deck, where you should place the stairs and how many steps you'll need. One basic rule is that the risers—the height between the surface of a step and the one above it—should be 7½ to 8 inches. If your riser is higher or lower, people will trip, because it's not what we're used to. (When you draw up your plan,

It's both cleaner and safer to use riser boards on your deck stairs rather than leaving them open.

you may have to adjust the height of the deck slightly to accommodate the number of stairs, because you can't end up with, say, four and a half steps.) Stair calculators are available online to help with the planning.

There are a few different stair techniques to choose from. You can build your own stringers using a 2 × 12, or you can buy them precut. Some people like the look of open risers, where the treads sit on the stringers and there's open space at the back of the tread instead of a vertical piece closing that gap. I'd recommend closing the risers so a child won't get caught in there and so you don't drop stuff under the deck where it could be hard to retrieve. When you're running up and down stairs during a summer barbecue, and maybe people are having a few drinks, it's just safer for that to be closed up with riser boards or a fascia board. It also gives the deck a nice, clean look.

You don't even need to use a stringer if you're building only a couple of stairs. You can build a box step: each step is essentially a small frame sitting on top of a larger frame. You might have to pour a concrete footing for a box step so it doesn't sink into the ground, but generally, for one or two steps, a bed of compacted gravel and screening will suffice.

MISTAKE #177:
MESSING UP ON MAINTENANCE

A lot of people build decks and fences using PT wood because it's more affordable. But they don't love the greenish look of the wood, so they try to cover it up with paint. I have to say I have an aversion to building a beautiful deck or fence out of wood and then painting it. Why would you cover up the natural material like that? I'm also not big on building something that's going to require a ton of maintenance. Once you paint a deck, you're committed to it for life. There are four

sides to every board that have to be coated. If you're building out of PT because it's cheap, you'll pay for it in labour if you decide to paint it.

If you are going to paint your PT deck, don't do it right away—that's a big mistake. You have to allow the wood to weather for a year before you apply a coating. Have you ever picked up a piece of PT and noticed it's heavier than it looks? That's because of the ACQ (alkaline copper quaternary) it's treated with. It starts out wet, so it needs time to cure, or the ACQ will leach out of the wood and push right through the paint. (Now you can get PT wood that's tinted brown instead of green, which is a better-looking alternative.)

Years ago, we did a show where we built a two-storey deck outside Toronto. The producer wanted us to paint it white even though we said it was too soon. They insisted, and the next morning it was mint green. *One day* and it was already ruined. We had to paint the wood again before we shot the reveal, and of course it was mint green again the next day.

Cedar has the opposite problem. You shouldn't let it weather before you finish it. People love the look of it, so they put up a deck and leave it untreated. Cedar contains natural tannins that preserve the wood, but what happens is it looks beautiful that first year, and after one winter, it shrinks and turns grey and suddenly doesn't look as good. Structurally, that cedar deck might be perfectly sound, but it can look like crap not protected.

I like some of the penetrating oils, like tung and linseed oil, though these can cause problems with mould. A water-repellent stain is the easiest to maintain, but it's also the most labour intensive since you might have to re-coat annually depending on how extreme the weather is in your region. The next easiest is a semi-transparent stain, which is good at helping the deck shed rainwater. Semi-transparent stains contain pigment that offers some colour and some protection from UV rays, so you get to see the wood through it.

That said, all decks and fences require some routine maintenance, even if they're treated. Make sure water drains from the deck and keep dirt, leaves and pine needles off it as much as possible. It's also a good idea to move around things like planters and benches to give the wood a chance to dry out and breathe.

MISTAKE #178:
BUILDING A POORLY ALIGNED FENCE

I go into some neighbourhoods, and the fences look like they've been to war and back. They're all falling down—it's like all the neighbours got together and picked the cheapest guy to build the fences. If you don't get the footings right, your fence is going to look awful in short order. And even if your fence is structurally sound, wood gets old and deteriorates over time. Fences take a beating: they're exposed to wind, rain and snow; the post footings can freeze and thaw; and there are roots growing underground. But if you do the job right, it will last longer than if you just bang it up and cut corners.

You can build a fence from scratch and design it to look however you want, buy pre-made fence panels, or get a kit with precut lumber. Whatever you do, make sure you start by building it straight. Measuring and positioning the posts will determine how strong your fence is structurally and how good—or crappy—it looks at the end. You don't want your fence to look like it came from Dr. Seuss.

First, you've got to space your fence posts 6 to 8 feet apart, depending on the terrain and the kind of fence you're building. Set your two end posts and then string a line from one to the other so you can line up all the posts in between. Bang in a stake at the point where you're going to dig each post hole.

The next step is to set the posts. As with deck piers, you need to dig below the frost line, which means 4 feet in most parts of Canada. Use a post-hole digger (rent one to save on labour), and don't skimp on the depth. You really need to get this right on corner posts, posts that will carry extra loads (like a gate) and posts that have to stand up to high winds.

Fence posts may not bear a ton of weight, but you still need to support them for a lot of lateral movement. For these, you don't want to use a saddle set into the concrete footing. The saddle will hold the post only at the bottom, and the post will flop around because it doesn't have any weight pushing down on it. Instead, put a few inches of gravel or stone in the bottom of the hole and, with the fence post, compact it. This will allow excess water to drain away from the post and will extend its life. Place your 4×4 post right into the hole and make sure it's plumb. Then fill the hole with concrete to hold the post in place.

Completely filling the hole around the post with concrete will give you the strongest post. (Some people use Sonotubes for fence footings, but they can lead to wobbly posts, because you're relying on uncompacted soil around the tubes to hold the posts in place.) The key is to be sure the posts are perfectly upright (plumb) before and after pouring the concrete. Use a level to check the position of each post. You should also eyeball them to see if they're straight: stand at one end of the row and look down toward the other end. Make any minor adjustments necessary, and then tamp down the dirt or concrete, sloping the surface away from the post to let water drain off. Brace

each post using stakes, and keep the stakes in place until the concrete has set.

It's a good idea to use posts that are longer than you need. Unless the ground is perfectly flat (and it never is), the posts are not all going to end up the same height. Once your panels are installed, you can go back and trim the posts as needed. Then you should cap them or round them to keep the water from settling and causing rot.

Once you've got the posts installed, the rails between each post go up next: one attached at the top and one at the bottom of each post. Or, if you're using pre-made panels—you've probably seen these at building supply centres—you attach the panel, level and plumb it and then pour in the concrete to complete the footing.

A big mistake is to set your bottom rail too low to the ground and then backfill soil against it. Maybe you

like the look of a fence as a backdrop for your garden, but you need a bit of space between the ground and your fence. If the fence gets water on it, that's fine, it will dry. But if the wood gets water and soil on it, and it stays wet because the soil holds the water, that's when the ACQ will be washed out of the lumber faster. There goes your wood preservative, which means it's going to start to rot sooner.

MISTAKE #179:
POORLY SPACING FENCE POSTS AND PANELS

Too many people don't take the time to plan before building a fence. If they're using 8-foot panels, they'll just start putting them up panel by panel until they end up in a corner and they're left with 1½ feet. So think about your spacing before you start digging your post holes.

Begin by measuring the total distance the fence will run. If you're using 8-foot panels, you divide by eight, round up, and that's how many sections you'll need. Unless the fence is very long, I don't usually account for the width of posts when I'm doing this calculation, but you can. (If you're doing a big, long fence, it may be wise to use 6 × 6 posts.) Let's say you end up with five 8-foot sections and one that's 6 feet. You could rework the panels so they're all about the same size—say, 7½ feet. Or you could space them out so the short section is the width of the gate.

Once you're done measuring, dig all your holes and set your posts in the gravel before you put in a single panel. You want each post to be anchored, or it will move around too much as you're working. If you're using pre-assembled panels, screw them to your posts on both sides, and then pour in the concrete. If you're building panels from scratch, you have to put the concrete in before adding the panels because you need the posts to be as strong as possible as you're building. When you're placing posts (or cutting top and bottom rails), be sure to take the measurement between the bottoms of the posts. Your 4 × 4s won't always be perfectly straight, and while it's easy to bend the top of the posts into position, the bottoms are locked into the footings and won't move!

Make sure you talk to your neighbour before you build a fence. If you build a fence so it sits entirely on your property, it's totally your responsibility, and you can do whatever you want as long as you're within height rules. (Many municipalities don't allow fences higher than 6 or 7 feet.) If you want to put it on your property line, then half of that fence is your neighbour's. They're financially responsible for half of it, unless they say they don't want a new fence—then it's up to you. But don't risk losing a good neighbour to a bad fence.

Mistake #180:
IMPROPERLY SUPPORTING A FENCE GATE

There's no such thing as a gate that doesn't sag. Over time, it's going to happen. But there are things you can do to build it stronger or fix it when it does start to slip.

Many people put a diagonal brace between the stringers (the top and bottom pieces that span horizontally and hold the pickets in place), but most put it in the wrong way. The diagonal piece should run from the bottom of the hinge side to the top of the latch side. That way the top won't sag, because it's pushing on the

brace, which is supported by the bottom stringer.

You can also get anti-sag kits for gates once they've started to lose their shape. The kit contains a couple of corner brackets to attach a steel cable and a turnbuckle. The cable should span diagonally in the opposite direction from the brace—from the top of the hinge side to the bottom of the latch side. If you've done it right, the wood brace and the wire cable will make an X. Use the turnbuckle on the cable to adjust the tension until it barely starts to lift the door, then back off a turn or two.

The diagonal brace on a gate should run from the bottom of the hinge side to the top of the latch side.

CHAPTER TWELVE

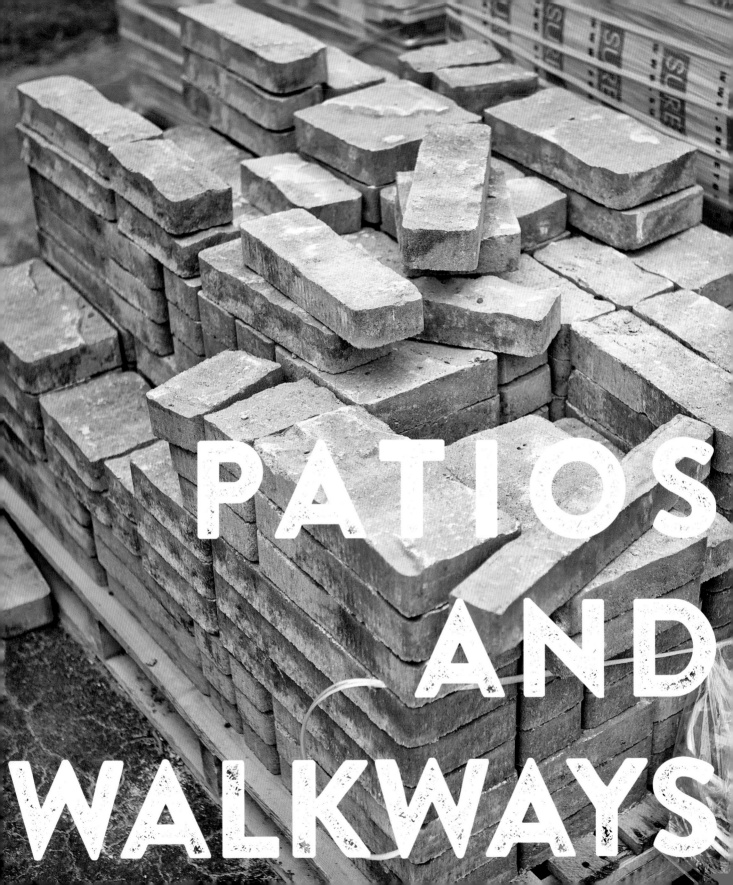

PATIOS
AND
WALKWAYS

BUILDING A WALKWAY OR PATIO CAN BE A SIMPLE DIY JOB IF THE PATH IS STRAIGHT AND THE BACKYARD IS FLAT AND LEVEL. BUT IT GETS TRICKY AS SOON AS YOU TRY TO COVER AN AREA LARGER THAN ABOUT 12 BY 12 FEET. IF YOU'RE THINKING ABOUT DOING YOUR DRIVEWAY, AND YOU'VE NEVER LAID A SINGLE STONE, I WOULDN'T RECOMMEND THIS AS A DIY PROJECT.

Successfully installing a patio is about using the right materials and following the right steps. If you don't have a deep enough base layer, or you use the wrong kind of gravel, your patio won't drain properly, and you could run into problems when the ground freezes and thaws. If you jump the gun and put in a patio in a new subdivision, those stones will probably sink and heave over the next winter or two. A patio can last 20 or 30 years if it's done right. If you take shortcuts, it will look terrible, and the sight of it every day will drive you crazy.

"Hardscaping" is really like any other renovation. If you're planning on redoing your entire backyard and you're prepared to spend $30,000 on walkways and patios, get a professional to do it. If you're just looking to put down a small flagstone walkway to your shed, try it out. Start small, take baby steps and learn as you go. But if you're a first-timer, ask yourself how you're going to feel if you do all that work and then the patio looks like garbage in a year. Remember that when you decide to put in a patio, you're fighting Mother Nature, and she's a force to be reckoned with. Working with stone and pavers is time-consuming and back-breaking: carrying two skids of patio stones from the driveway to the backyard might not be for you. Like tiling, it's not something you can rush, so be honest about your skill level and how much you will enjoy it.

PATIO AND WALKWAY BASICS

DIFFICULTY: 8 OUT OF 10

Patios and walkways can be made from an almost limitless variety of natural stone and man-made pavers. Linear designs are easiest for DIYers to work with. The more curves and angles, the greater the likelihood you'll have some awkwardly cut stones to fill in. These jobs require a lot of planning, and, of course, experience makes everything easier. If you don't want to rent a concrete saw, which is dirty and noisy, keep it simple and forget the rosettes. Even for the pros, laying down a complicated design is a big investment of time and energy.

The most important step is taking the time to properly lay a solid base layer of gravel for drainage, topped with another layer of finer gravel that can be firmly tamped down to create a level surface for the paving stones.

CHOOSING PATIO AND WALKWAY STONES

• **Flagstone** is a general name for sedimentary rock that is quarried in flat, thin pieces. It may be limestone, sandstone, slate or other similar type of rock.

• **Pavers** are man-made stones, typically cast in regular shapes so they fit together in interlocking patterns. They come in an almost infinite number of varieties.

TOOLS AND MATERIALS YOU'LL NEED

- measuring tape
- landscape paint (for marking out your plan)
- shovel
- long pipes for grading
- level
- screed (a straight-edged board for smoothing out gravel or screenings)
- compacter (best to rent one)
- rubber mallet
- knee pads
- gloves
- concrete saw

MISTAKE #181:
INSTALLING A PATIO AROUND A BRAND NEW HOME

Some people move into newly built subdivisions, and they want to get to work improving the yard. I know it's tempting to roll up your sleeves and start adding patios and paths right away, but there are good reasons not to rush in. A big mistake is installing a patio on backfill that hasn't had time to settle. (Backfill is the soil used to loosely fill out the landscape after excavating the foundation for a new house.)

The excavation process unsettles tons of dirt that will naturally grade itself toward your house as that soil resettles. If you're lucky, the builder will have compacted the soil after backfilling the area, but that's not the case in many neighbourhoods. A patio built on disturbed soil can wind up sloping toward your house as the soil settles, which will pull the flow of rainwater and snow melt right down against your foundation.

I suggest you wait at least a year or two before building a patio (or a deck or fence, for that matter), which is how long it typically takes for soil to sink and settle after excavation. Wait until lots of water has been through the ground since water naturally helps the process of compaction. Running a sprinkler frequently in the summer can help speed up the process. As the ground naturally compacts and sinks toward the house, be sure to add fill and grade the soil away from your house to avoid unnecessary pressure on your foundation, which could result in water in the basement.

MISTAKE #182:
BUYING NEW STONES INSTEAD OF FIXING A BUMPY PATIO

Let's say you've inherited a problematic patio or walkway. I've seen a lot of people pull them up, get rid of the stones and order new ones. What a waste! The problem isn't the stones: either the base wasn't laid properly, or it was laid too early in an area where the backfill hadn't settled.

The benefit of paving stones is that you can reuse them anywhere. If they weren't installed properly, the solution isn't to throw them out; it's to lift them out and redo the job properly. If the previous owner just put the stones on an inch of sand, you can remove the stones, excavate another several inches and lay a proper base. (See Mistake #187, page 291, to learn about laying the right base for a path or patio and Mistake #186, page 289, for the steps for installing a patio.) Then re-lay all the patio stones where they were.

If the patio failed because the previous owner laid it on loose backfill, but the soil has since had a chance to become naturally compacted, it's the same fix: pull those stones out, add the right base, compact it again, and put the stones back on top. Yes, you'll invest your time and elbow grease in getting it right, but you'll save a lot of money on stone, and you'll prevent a whole lot of perfectly good material from going to waste.

MISTAKE #183:
MAKING A PATIO TOO SMALL

When planning a backyard patio, you usually start by making a drawing. Maybe you sketch out a rough idea on paper and add or change things until the drawing looks like the patio you want. Well, here's a tip: as you sketch the layout, scale the drawing just like designers and landscape architects do. All the items in the drawing—patio, furniture, planters—need to be measured in proportion to everything else. You might use a 1:36 scale, where 1 inch on paper equals 3 feet in reality, or whatever makes sense for your particular backyard.

What happens if you don't pay attention to those details? Let's say you're happy with the drawing, so you go ahead and install the patio. Then you pick out a table and chairs and a barbecue, and suddenly you realize the patio that looked so big in your drawing is actually too small for these items.

When my crew is redoing a backyard, we use spray cans of lawn paint to physically see the layout before we even lift a shovel (don't worry—this paint is water-based, so it's safe for plants and washes away with a garden hose or a few rainfalls). Set up your table and chairs on the grass, and mark out where you think your patio will go so you can walk around, sit down, move your chair and so on. You can even plot out walkways, garden beds and other elements.

As you walk through the space, you might realize that if you get up and push a chair back from the table, you're going to fall off the patio! That's why I recommend this step—because it allows you to fix those potential problems before you start digging. You can determine how your furniture and patio are going to work together right there in real space. I can't say it enough: planning is key.

MISTAKE #184:
BUILDING TOO CLOSE TO TREE ROOTS

I'm guilty of this one myself. There's a path that leads up to my parents' cottage. It's a stone pathway that goes through the forest, and certain sections are made of wood. We poured these transition parts in concrete back in 1998. At the time, I remember, there was a tiny root, and I chipped away most of it thinking, No big deal, I'll pour over this. Now that root is 3 inches thick, and the concrete's broken. And everyone knows who's

responsible because etched in the concrete, right beside the broken part, is "BB '98."

What I didn't realize at the time—what I'm sure most people don't—is how powerful roots are, and that they typically extend as far out as the tree's canopy. So if you're building a walkway or patio around trees, I suggest you draw a circle around the tree to where the farthest branch reaches. If that tree is five years old now, imagine how big it might be in another 10 years. A huge, mature tree is probably not going to grow much bigger, but don't underestimate a sapling—its roots might be pushing up your patio one day.

If you do encounter a tree root while excavating for a patio, you can't just start hacking away at the roots. Believe it or not, municipalities have protection laws in place for trees. Sometimes when we come up against tree roots while we're excavating, we have to call in an arborist—a tree doctor who knows how to cut branches and roots in a way that won't damage the tree.

MISTAKE #185:
CHOOSING THE WRONG PATIO STONES

There are two main categories of material to choose from when you're thinking about patios: man-made or natural. Concrete products such as interlocking pavers are popular because, at about $3 to $10+ per square foot, they're more budget-friendly than natural stone, and they're available in standard sizes. The options are just about unlimited as far as size and design and colour are concerned. They're also available just about everywhere—stone yards, big-box stores—so they're easy to buy.

As for natural stone, there are tons of options, too. The most common is flagstone, a term that includes many different varieties of sedimentary rock. Now they even make patios from granite: they cut it into slabs

There's a huge array of choices, but patio stones fall into one of two categories: precast pavers (*left column*) and natural stone (*right column*).

and fire the face with a cutting torch to give the stone a raised texture, almost like non-slip finish. (It's durable—up to four times stronger than concrete—and it looks great, but it's expensive!)

On the lower end of the stone spectrum are crushed stone with pea gravel as filler, or even pea gravel on its own. Pea gravel brings a Zen look and sound to gardens and pathways—some people like the way it crunches underfoot, though it's not the easiest to walk on if you like to wear high heels. It's also sometimes used to cover roots and hold back weeds at the base of a tree.

Some people just want a path of stepping stones. If you're going with flagstone, you should know it gets delivered on a skid with random sizes and shapes. There's some cutting involved. Families on the show often tell us they want flagstone, and then they take one look at the delivery and ask, "Where do I put this?" You need to sort through the stones and roughly plan how they'll fit together. The stones aren't flat, linear or the same shape or size—they aren't going to line up perfectly, and that's part of the look. There's also more leeway in laying them. It's a little more artistic.

On the other hand, concrete paving stones, which are precisely cut and mechanically formed, aren't meant to be installed haphazardly. They're a good choice for a simple linear patio, since the stones fit together in nice, neat rows. I don't know if I'd say one kind is more difficult than the other to install, but pavers are certainly more mathematical, and flagstone is a little more creative. Both have their challenges.

Once you decide between stone and pavers, you have to select a material to go between them. Pavers require loose filling such as sand or screenings. The fill pretty much disappears between the cracks—you don't really see it.

But the cracks between flagstones are larger, and your choice of jointing material affects the finished look. You can fill them with polymeric sand, which hardens like concrete when it gets wet. Or you can use pea gravel, mortar or screenings—it all depends on your desired look and functionality. Loose fillings like screenings (¼-inch bits of limestone) or pea gravel have a more casual appearance, and they move around (though the flagstones won't). Mortar is like cement, so it will dry to create solid joints between stones. Mortar is the most durable (and most expensive) option for installing a rigid patio or walkway from flagstone or cobblestones.

You've got two main options for mortar between patio joints: resin-based or cement-based. Both have their pros and cons. Type M or Type S cement mortars are best for patios because they are better than lower grades of mortar for resisting pooling water and salt. Resin-based mortars tend to be more durable. A wet, slurry mortar (where the mortar is mixed on site and applied while wet) tends to be stronger than a dry, brush-in mortar, which is easiest to install: just sweep it into joints with a broom.

Some people might add clay bricks to the list of man-made walkway materials. The problem is that brick absorbs a lot of water and breaks down quickly from the freeze–thaw cycle. Before you know it, you'll have a red-dust walkway. I wouldn't recommend bricks as a long-term solution. If you like that look, you can find pavers that have the appearance of brick but are a lot more durable.

MISTAKE #186:
NOT FOLLOWING THE RIGHT INSTALLATION STEPS

If you skimp on the base layers for a patio—either by rushing, not including enough material or skipping essential steps—be prepared for your patio to sink or

The base layer of gravel is the most important step in the process. If you rush through it, you'll end up with a patio that sinks, heaves or slides.

buckle sooner than later. You might be surprised to hear that I recommend a 6- to 8-inch gravel base under a standard patio. That's a lot of sod and soil to excavate from your backyard, but the base layer is essential for drainage, and the thickness of the base depends on how resilient you want your patio to be. How much traffic and weight does it need to handle? Those are the two factors landscapers use to gauge the base: the greater the abuse, the thicker the base needs to be. A driveway would need even more excavation, since you have to set it up to handle the weight of a car or two. For a driveway, a 12-inch base is typical.

Base layer: Laying a base is the most important part of the process. If you do the base right (see Mistake #187, next), it's a lot easier to install the stones. You can't rush this step. I've watched guys spend hours getting the base perfectly smooth and level—it's worth taking the time to do it right so you don't end up with a patio that sinks in a few years.

Grading and screenings: Once the base layer is in, calculate the depth for the screenings—the layer

sandwiched between the base and the patio stones or pavers. To get the depth, you have to subtract the thickness of the stone, and another 5 millimetres because you want your combined base and screenings to end up above ground level to allow for settling.

It's hard to eyeball the grade when you're installing screenings, but there's a good pro trick. Take a narrow pole or pipe that will be long enough to span the width of your patio, and lay it out perpendicular to the house. Add additional poles every 4 to 6 feet, parallel to the first one. Next, press the poles into the base, sloping them away from the house on your desired grade (at least 2%) so that water won't pool on your patio or drain next to the house's foundation. Make sure that each of the poles is level with the others right beside the house, about halfway down and then at the far edge of the patio.

Fill in the area between those pipes with a layer of limestone screenings or granular A gravel (¾-inch gravel is too big for the surface layer). Then use something with a straight edge—an aluminum bar or a box beam—to screed between those bars and level off the gravel. *Screeding* is the term for using a long, straight board to remove excess screenings to even up a surface. If you use a 2 × 4, make sure it isn't warped, or you won't be getting that level surface you need. Place the board across the surface of the poles and slide it along the tops of the bars holding the screenings in place—the screenings sitting above the surface of the pipes will be moved to areas that weren't sufficiently filled; excess screenings will be removed, and you'll be left with an even surface of screenings.

Compacting: Next, pull out those pipes or bars, and run a compactor over everything so that the surface is perfectly smooth, flat, compacted and set to the right height before you add your stone. Landscapers use a power compactor, or tamper, which vibrates the ground and helps everything settle. (You don't want settling to happen later, or that will mess up your patio, so that's why you do it now.) You can compact the surface by hand using a hand tamper, which is a heavy tool with a tubular handle and a steel plate that you raise and drop on the gravel. I recommend power tampers because they're more effective and they do the job a lot faster. When you're finished tamping, your surface will be surprisingly hard, almost like concrete.

Laying patio stones: Now it's time to put down the stones or pavers. If you've done your base prep right, the stones can go in fairly quickly. Keep a pile of extra screenings nearby. As you lay your stones, a little bit of screenings may be needed to bring a stone up to the level of the others. Use a rubber mallet to beat the stone in and make sure it's flat and in plane with all the ones around it.

Compacting and adding sand: Sweep sand over everything and bring in a compactor again. (To minimize chipping and cracking of clay or textured pavers, attach a rubber mat to the compactor plate.) If any stones were installed at a higher level than the others, they'll be pushed in line, and the sand actually locks the pavers together and holds them in place. Trust me: you'll appreciate a smooth surface in winter when it's time to shovel.

Some people use polymeric sand at this stage. This fine sand comes premixed with additives that form a binding agent when the joints are sprayed with water, so it hardens almost like concrete. An advantage is it helps keep weeds at bay. The downside is that it doesn't completely fill the joint, and it breaks down during the freeze–thaw cycle.

MISTAKE #187: INCORRECTLY LAYING THE BASE LAYER

Digging down and installing a well-packed base is the most critical step with a patio or walkway. Patios heave typically because the layers underneath weren't prepped properly, not because the stones went in looking sloppy. The base wasn't set up to handle the freezing and thawing that Canadian patios must endure.

Laying a patio with stone or pavers is like tiling: preparing the surface below—called the substrate—is more important than what you lay on top. If the substrate is smooth and you've used the right materials, the installation is easy. Sure, you can install patio stones on an uneven surface, but you have to put a lot more stone down to make that surface level.

You need 6 to 8 inches of ¾-inch clear crushed gravel to form a sturdy foundation that also allows surface water to drain. "Clear gravel" is good for patios and pathways leading to the entrance of your house, because it holds less moisture—water drains right through it. The gravel pieces are an average of ¾ inch, so no matter what you run overtop—a bulldozer even—this layer will never compress to the point where it's going to hold water. (In a minute, I'll explain why that's so important.) Clear gravel isn't mixed with sand, so it's also less likely to cling to shoes and boots and get tracked into the house. If you install a good weed barrier below the clear gravel, there's less chance of plants sprouting in your pathway—or popping up from below the patio, anyway. Most weeds that grow in patios sprout from seeds that have blown into the cracks between stones.

Above your base, you need a few inches of granular A gravel—a mix of ¾-inch crushed gravel with sand—or limestone screenings. Both are like topcoats.

Use a screed (a bar or piece of straight lumber) to smooth out your screenings. Lay the stones one by one, using a rubber mallet to tamp down and slide each one into place. Check frequently to make sure your rows remain level.

They contain some finer bits that allow the material to be packed tightly. When you tamp them down, you get a surface that's practically solid. The key is these materials are coarse enough that they're not going to fill up the spaces in your base layer. If you use something like sand, it's fine enough that it will work its way down to the base layer over time, which can cause problems with drainage.

Don't be tempted to take the shortcut of just throwing a few inches of gravel on the ground and laying the patio on top. It might look fine for a little while, but the soil underneath the gravel is full of moisture that freezes and expands in the winter. That heaves your patio. When the soil thaws, the patio comes down again, but the weight of those stones on that thawed earth will actually squeeze water out of it and compress the land. This heaving process goes on and on until the patio eventually sinks.

MISTAKE #188:
MESSING UP ON GRADING

Grading protects the land around your home from water by giving a slight slope so as to redirect moisture away from the foundation. Sloppy grading is a big mistake that could cost you a lot of headaches and money down the line. Putting in a patio beside or behind your home—especially one that you're planning to grout or mortar in place—creates a hard surface that won't drain water like grass does. The patio will basically function as a giant catch basin for everything that lands on it, and if it ends up sloped toward your house, that's where it's going to direct rainwater. In other words, you're going to be throwing a ton of moisture at your foundation. After you put in a nice patio, you may discover you've got a new problem—a leaky basement.

Municipalities set their own guidelines for grading, so make sure you check with your building office before excavating. The general rule is to grade at a 2% slope away from the house. That means for every foot you dig down, slope the surface about ⅛ inch.

Make sure your grade won't interfere with your neighbour's yard or drainage: you can't make changes in your yard that result in water getting dumped on your neighbour's property. If your landscaping changes mess up someone else's drainage, you'll be on the hook to fix the problem. That might involve ripping everything out and starting over. The placement and proper grading of a patio can be challenging—at the very least, I recommend you check with the local building and planning department to determine if permits are required and to ensure your plan adheres to municipal bylaws. When all else fails, hire a professional to give you guidance or to take over.

Of course, if your patio sits 30 feet from the house, you don't need to worry as much. Grading depends on the location and size of the patio. The bigger the surface, and the closer it is to the house or other building, the greater the need for it to drain safely away from the foundation (including the foundation of a shed). Standing water on a patio causes other problems, too. If the stones remain soaking wet, they might freeze all the way through when winter arrives.

MISTAKE #189:
AIMING FOR AN EXACT MEASUREMENT ON A PATIO OR PATH

You can't really say "I want a walkway that's exactly 36 inches wide" and expect the stones will work out perfectly to that dimension. For one thing, there's always a stone that's a bit bigger than the rest. Don't worry: it's easy to adapt, because a small change in design won't make a huge difference. The nice thing about working outdoors is that you've got more space to work with in landscaping than you do with interiors. When you're tiling a room, you end up cutting tiles to fit the dimensions of your space, but if you're flexible, you don't necessarily have to cut patio stones. And really, does it matter if the path measures 36 inches or 38 inches?

Let's say you're installing a walkway along the side of a garage to your front door. It makes sense to start with a full stone at the garage and build out from there because you probably have a decent width of space available. You can add a brick, take out a brick—whatever looks right. Outside, you're usually not going to have to work around a fixed obstacle like a wall, unless you're building a path between two houses that are placed close together. That's a whole other kind of fun.

Once the stones are laid out, if it looks like you're going to end up with a gap at the side or end, increase the spacing between the stones using more filling, like pea gravel, in between them. Setting stones with thicker joint lines for gravel can accomplish two things. First, it creates a surface that allows better water drainage. Second, since you're spreading out the stones, you can cover more space with them: it's cost-effective.

If you don't want to do all the math required to space things out, you can look for special pavers that take away some of the guesswork. Permacon's Modulo line is especially good for do-it-yourselfers. Each paver is a large stone with false joints to make it look like a collection of smaller stones, and you just add your screenings or pea gravel in between. (They remind me of those tiny 1-inch tiles you see on backsplashes or in showers: they're laid out in a grid pattern pre-glued to a mesh backing, so when you install one piece of mesh, it looks like you've put up over 100 tiles.) Some of these modular pavers are designed to look random, which is a surprisingly hard thing to do if you're laying the stones one by one.

MISTAKE #190:
UNDERESTIMATING THE DIFFICULTY OF CUTTING STONES

If you plan your walkway or patio carefully, you can get away without making a single cut. That's what I'd recommend if you're someone who doesn't typically play with saws. Cutting stones and pavers is loud, potentially dangerous and messy. Everyone on the block knows when masons are working down the street—you can't miss the screaming saw and the giant cloud of dust. (Stone saws often have an attachment that feeds water over the blade to keep the dust down.) That's why I recommend avoiding cutting if you can. If you must cut stone or pavers, you're going to need proper eye and ear protection. Be sure to get a copy of the manual to learn about the proper use of the stone saw. Get well acquainted with your saw so you don't get well acquainted with your local paramedics.

There are some less noisy options than stone saws. You can find mechanical guillotines for splitting stone: you load a stone or a paver, tighten some knobs to secure it in place, then crank down on the spring-loaded handle like you're using a paper cutter. I don't see a lot of pros using these. Masons probably enjoy the noise and dust—it looks more impressive! And in skilled hands, the cuts are more accurate and versatile.

MISTAKE #191:
OVERLOOKING THE EDGES

You may notice that some patios and walkways are finished with a strip of edging. Using some kind of edging helps contain the surface so everything looks more polished. Edging also provides structure as you're doing the installation—it can help stop the stones from moving around as you get the pattern going.

Put in the edging on one side of your project and start building out from there. You can dig out a trench and use PT lumber, or you can install manufactured edging made of plastic or metal. Install heavy-duty plastic edging after excavation and before you put down landscape fabric (a dark woven material used to control weed growth by limiting exposure to sunlight) and your base layer of ¾-inch gravel. Same with metal edging: the stones sit on top of the angled brackets, which are held in place with stakes. Some edging, though, can go in after the fact. The product often has spikes built into it so you can install the strips in sections to clean up the lines where the patio or walkway meets the grass.

Foot traffic and weather will cause your patio stones to slide. Use edging to keep them in place.

ACKNOWLEDGEMENTS

I never thought I'd write a book, but here it is! I assure you, I'm as surprised as you are. From my perspective, this was a DIY project of epic proportions, but as is always the case, doing it yourself doesn't mean you have to go it alone. I certainly wasn't alone in the concept, creation and composition of this book.

My deepest thanks go to my beautiful wife, Sarah. I could never have made my way through this process without your love and support. Our household, my schedule and our four energetic children are a challenge when we're both on duty, but you always manage to gracefully hold down the fort on your own when my attention is elsewhere.

Thanks to those four energetic children: Quintyn, Charlotte, Lincoln and Josephine. From the holes in our roof to the bruises on your knees—Daddy fix. I love you!

To my mom, Colleen, and my dad, Werner: Thank you for everything. I literally wouldn't be here without you! You provided me with so much opportunity and gave me the heart, skills and work ethic to surpass even my own perceived limitations. To my two brothers, Paul and Mike, thanks for mostly pointing me in the right direction in the early years, and for the occasional course correction since.

From day one, I've been amazed by the energy and literary genius of Kate Cassaday and the entire HarperCollins team, especially Alan Jones and Kelly Hope. Without your collective knowledge, assistance, support and more than occasional crack of the whip, this book wouldn't exist. Thank you so much for the opportunity to work with such a talented group!

Thanks to Dan Bortolotti for endless hours of listening, questioning and suggesting, and for all of your hard work putting this together. And to Shannon Ross for making beautiful pictures and chasing me around muddy, dusty and often dangerous construction sites with your camera.

I also want to thank everyone at HGTV and Shaw Media for giving me an incredible platform to share my passion for building, and for the viewers, fans and critics who watch, read and comment on every swing of the hammer. My production partners and film crews deserve a big pat on the back not only for tolerating me, but for making the puppet dance and for putting on a great show, literally and figuratively.

My partners, Paul and Stu, and my entire staff at the Baeumler Group of Companies—you always manage to keep the ship pointed in the right direction when I'm absent from and/or asleep at the wheel, and I appreciate it every day. A special thanks to "The Guys"—Josh, Dave, Joel, James and Evan—for all of your patience, dedication and help on-site.

To my right-hand man, Adam—over the years you've absorbed so much information, acquired so many new skills and flipped so many machines. Your trustworthiness, hard work, dedication and friendship are very much appreciated.

As I am, this book is the sum of its parts. If I have seen further, it is only by standing on the shoulders of giants.

Bryan Werner Baeumler

INDEX

Page numbers in *italics* indicate illustrations.